BUILDING MODELS FOR CONSERVATION AND WILDLIFE MANAGEMENT

BIOLOGICAL RESOURCE MANAGEMENT

A Series of Primers on the Conservation and Exploitation of Natural and Cultivated Ecosystems

Wayne M. Getz, Series Editor
University of California, Berkeley

Adaptive Management of Renewable Resources, by Carl Walters
Building Models for Conservation and Wildlife Management, by A. M.
    Starfield and A. L. Bleloch
Mathematical Programming for Economic Analysis in Agriculture, by
    Peter B. R. Hazell and Roger D. Norton
Range Economics, by John P. Workman

BUILDING MODELS FOR CONSERVATION AND WILDLIFE MANAGEMENT

A. M. Starfield
University of Minnesota
University of the Witwatersrand, Johannesburg

A. L. Bleloch
St. John's College, Cambridge

Macmillan Publishing Company
NEW YORK

Collier Macmillan Publishers
LONDON

Macmillan Publishing Company
866 Third Avenue, New York, NY 10022

Collier Macmillan Canada, Inc.

Printed in the United States of America

1 2 3 4 5 6 7 8 9 10·   6 7 8 9 0 1 2 3 4 5

Library of Congress Cataloging-in-Publication Data

Starfield, A. M.
  Building models for conservation and wildlife
management.

  (Biological resource management)
  Includes bibliographies and index.
  1. Nature conservation—Mathematical models.
2. Nature conservation—Africa—Mathematical models.
3. Wildlife management—Mathematical models. 4. Wildlife
management—Africa—Mathematical models. I. Bleloch,
Andrew L. II. Title. III. Series.
QH75.S664 1986   639.9   85-19904
ISBN 0-02-948040-X

Contents

Preface

This is a book about modeling that is built around examples in wildlife management. Although it uses computers and mathematical ideas, it is not a textbook on applied ecology, computer programming, or biomathematics. There are many good books on all of these subjects, but while a growing number of people are building and using models, there are not many books on *how* to build and use them.

The models commonly used in the physical sciences are based on established principles. The theory is so well accepted that little attention is paid to the art of formulating models. In this book we will be concerned with the more amorphous problems of the nonphysical sciences —problems that are often poorly defined, where the processes and mechanisms are not well understood, and where data are often scant and perhaps difficult to obtain. The challenge is to develop a structure for a model under these circumstances.

We have chosen to use examples in conservation and wildlife management to illustrate this class of problems. The examples are, we hope, fascinating and intelligible to all readers. We believe they provide ample scope for demonstrating our pragmatic approach to modeling. In particular, by looking at the problems within the context of management, we find a focus that makes it somewhat easier to meet the challenge of developing an appropriate structure. Each chapter of the book therefore begins with a management problem and describes how a model can be constructed to address that problem. We show how the model may have to be modified in the light of the available (or, more often, unavailable) data, how the model can be exercised, and what can be learned from it. Modeling is presented as a discipline that draws (in the first instance) on the perception of the detective rather than the expertise of the mathematician. Mathematical and computational techniques are introduced as tools that amplify our ability to structure and organize our thinking. The computer is viewed as a laboratory for exploring the consequences of our models.

The first five chapters of the book can in fact be read with no more than a high-school background in mathematics. Calculus is only used in Chap. 6. Linear programming is introduced in Chap. 7 and matrices in Chap. 8, but in a way that should be accessible to nonmathematicians. Although there are cross-references, the individual chapters are more or less self-contained and can be read in isolation. For this reason we have provided a summary and ideas for further reading at the end of each chapter. Our references are not meant to be exhaustive, but have been chosen either because they offer the reader more background to our case histories, or because they develop or apply the techniques we have mentioned in useful or interesting ways. We have not included listings of computer programs or detailed specifications for the various models we describe because we do not believe there is much to be gained by exercising our models. We would, however, urge our readers to build models of their own, using our ideas and techniques in the context of more familiar problems. In the classroom we recommend that students be encouraged to work in small groups to build models and to play with them.

This is largely a book of ideas rather than facts, so it may need to be supplemented when it is used as a class text. It could be read with texts on biomathematics or ecology at hand, and there is plenty of scope for the lecturer to discuss what has been left out of our examples, either from the mathematical or ecological point of view. Our intention is to generate excitement and promote discussion, and our examples and comments provide a framework for discussion in much the same way as we believe that a model provides a framework for understanding.

One of the pleasures of model-building is the cooperation it engenders. We would like to thank all those who worked with us at various times on the models we describe. Ken Jordi and Norman Owen-Smith contributed to Chaps. 7 and 8 respectively. Sollie Joubert, Peter Goodman, and Willie Gertenbach interacted with us in the work that led to Chaps. 3, 5, and 9, and Joe Venter and his colleagues from the Natal Parks Board helped us test the ideas contained in Chap. 9. Students from the Department of Applied Mathematics at the University of the Witwatersrand helped us write programs and explore different approaches. Special thanks are due to "Butch" Smuts for his encouragement when the work that led up to this book was first started, to Julian Shiell for his early enthusiasm (and the photograph at the beginning of Chap. 8), and to both of them for their contributions to the models described in Chaps. 2 and 4.

One of the pleasures of writing a book is bouncing ideas off friends and colleagues and pestering them to read and react to numerous drafts. We would like to thank everybody for their comments, criticisms, and enthusiasm. Particular thanks are due to Michael Sears, John Field, and Sam Sharp for reading the entire manuscript. This is also our opportunity to thank Ellen van der Westhuizen for the early morning cups of coffee, Mark Hudson for his help with the photographs, Di Franz and Carol Cardoso for their cheerful efforts on the diagrams, and Keith Joubert, as much for his enthusiastic curiosity as for the cover design and the sketches in Fig. 1.2.

Last, but certainly not least, we are grateful to Wayne Getz, Sarah Greene, and Sheila Gillams for their encouragement, support, and editorial comments.

Tony Starfield
Department of Civil and Mineral Engineering
University of Minnesota
Andrew Bleloch
St. John's College
Cambridge

BUILDING MODELS FOR CONSERVATION AND WILDLIFE MANAGEMENT

1

In Which We Provide a Context

A model is any representation or abstraction of a system or process. We build models because they help us to (1) define our problems, (2) organize our thoughts, (3) understand our data, (4) communicate and test that understanding, and (5) make predictions. A model is therefore an intellectual tool.

People's perceptions about models and modeling can be very different depending on the types of problems they usually face and hence the types of tools they commonly use. There is a vast difference, for example, between trying to predict next week's weather and plotting a rocket's trajectory to the moon. These differences are reflected in the models chosen and how they are used.

Holling (1978) has a diagram (Fig. 1.1) that provides a simple and useful classification. The horizontal axis represents how well we understand the problem we are trying to solve; the vertical axis represents the quality and/or quantity of relevant data. Holling divides the quadrant between the two axes into four areas, corresponding to four classes of problems.

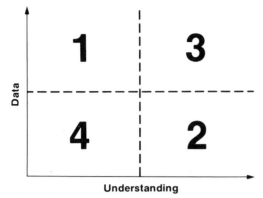

Figure 1.1 Holling's (1978) classification of modeling problems. This book is concerned mainly with regions 2 and 4.

Area 1 is the region of good data but little understanding. This is where statistical techniques are useful; they enable one to analyze the data, search for patterns or relations, construct and test hypotheses, and so on.

Area 3 is the region of good data and good understanding. Many problems in engineering and the physical sciences (for example, the problem of plotting the rocket's trajectory to the moon) belong to this class of problems. This is the area where models are used routinely and with confidence because their effectiveness has been proved repeatedly.

In area 2 there is little in the way of supporting data but there is some understanding of the structure of the problem; in area 4 even the understanding of the problem is tenuous. Many of the problems in the nonphysical sciences belong to either region 2 or 4, and these are the types of problems we will address in this book. They present us with two rather daunting challenges:

1. From the management point of view, decisions may have to be made despite the lack of data and understanding. How do we make good, scientific decisions under these circumstances?
2. How do we go about improving our understanding and collecting the data we need? (In other words, how do we progress from area 4 to area 3 of Holling's diagram?)

We will attempt to show how models help us meet both these challenges.

Some would argue that this attempt is bound to fail. They believe that the first priority is to collect as much data as possible and that model building should be postponed until the data have accumulated and been analyzed statistically. Others, noticing the routine way in which models are used in area 3 of Holling's diagram, are convinced that their problems are too ill-defined to model in that way.

The latter are correct; one does not use exactly the same tools in the same way in areas 2 and 4 as in area 3. However, they are incorrect in their assumption that the modeling toolkit is designed only for the well-defined problems in area 3. The purpose of this book is to show:

- How models can be built, very tentatively at first
- How the properties of the models can be explored
- How one can speculate, using hypothetical data
- How one can then cautiously reach some conclusions and search for evidence that supports them

Models built this way are bound to be speculative. They will never have the respectability of models built for solving problems in area 3 because it is unlikely that they will be sufficiently accurate or that they can ever be tested conclusively. They should therefore never be used unquestioningly or automatically. The whole process of building and using these models has to be that much more *thoughtful* because we do not really understand the structure of the problem and do not have (and cannot easily get) supporting data.

We therefore build models to *explore the consequences* of what we believe to be true. Those who have a lot of data and little understanding of their problem (area 1) gain understanding by "living with" their data, looking at it in different ways, and searching for patterns and relationships (Tukey, 1977). Because we have so little data in areas 2 and 4, we learn by living with our models, by exercising them, manipulating them, questioning their relevance, and comparing their behavior with what we know (or think we know) about the real world. This process often forces us to reevaluate our beliefs, and that reevaluation in turn leads to new versions of the models. The mere act of assembling the pieces and building a model (however speculative the model might be) usually improves our understanding and enables us to find or use data we had not realized were relevant. That in turn leads us to a better model.

The process is one of *boot-strapping:* If we begin with little data and understanding in the bottom left-hand corner of Holling's diagram, models help us to zigzag upwards and to the right. This is a far healthier approach than one of just collecting data because we improve our understanding as we go along. (Those who collect data without building models run the very real risk of discovering, when they eventually analyze their data, that they have collected the wrong data!)

The approach we are advocating can never be routine. It is a subtle process, which is why we need a whole book and not just an introduction to describe it.

A TRIVIAL MODEL

To introduce some of the concepts and terminology of modeling, consider a very simple process—converting U.S. dollars into German marks. We can write an equation that models this process:

$$M = kD \qquad (1.1)$$

where D and M represent the number of dollars and marks respectively and k is the conversion rate. A number of points are worth noting about even as trivial an example as this.

    1. The model has an *input* and an *output*. We feed in D, the number of dollars, and it returns M, the number of marks. We call D and M the *variables* of the model. They are what the model is all about—we want to know how M changes as we vary D.

    2. We call the exchange rate k a *parameter* of the model. It is not a variable because it is a quantity we have to estimate before we can use the model; it mediates the relationship between the variables. If exchange rates were fixed officially and did not change for years at a time, the parameter k would be a *constant* of the model.

    3. We can distinguish between results that are a consequence of the *structure* of the model and results that depend on specific *data*. The structure of the model is determined by the governing equations. In this case we have only one equation and its significant property is that it is *linear:* If we draw a graph of M versus D we get a straight line. Moreover, the line passes through the origin, so if we double the number of dollars we wish to convert, we will get exactly twice the number of marks—i.e., as we increase or decrease the input, so the output increases or decreases in the same proportion.

    Results such as this, which follow from the structure of a model, often have important practical implications. If our example were not so trivial, we might well be excited to discover that it makes no difference whether we exchange $200 in a single transaction or in two separate transactions of, say $100 each. This result is independent of the exchange rate k. On the other hand, if we want to know how many marks we will actually receive for our $200, we have to know the value of k—i.e., we need data. Results that are a consequence of the structure of the model are thus independent of the data and are general in their scope. Specific instances, or numerical examples, however, require data.

    4. If we probe into the details of currency exchange, we will discover that Eq. (1.1) is an oversimplification and that the general result of the previous paragraph is not always valid. For example, the commission charged on very small transactions is likely to be higher (as a percentage of the transaction) than that charged on large transactions. Four hundred transactions of 50 cents each would in practice yield fewer marks than a single exchange of $200. It is fortunate for our purpose that there is this discrepancy between our model and the real world because our trivial model is a little too slick. Models are an abstraction, a simplification of a process rather than a replication of the process. They never describe the real world *exactly* and often do not even attempt to do so.

People working in the physical sciences distinguish between first-order and second-order effects; the former explain much of the observed behavior of a system, while the latter can be considered as refinements. In our trivial model, Eq. (1.1) contains the first-order effect; the question of commissions is a second-order effect.

It follows from this discussion that it is always possible to find limitations to a model. As a result, we have to be wary on two counts: first, not to rely on a model when it is stretched to the limit and, second, not to undervalue a model because it has limitations. The fact that a model is only valid within certain limits or under certain conditions does not detract from its usefulness within those limits. *The quality of a model does not depend on how realistic it is, but on how well it performs in relation to the purpose for which it was built.* For most tourists Eq. (1.1) is an adequate and useful model.

5. Equation (1.1) is a *deterministic* model. Given a value for the exchange rate k, once we have converted, say, \$100 into marks, there is no point in repeating the calculation; the model is entirely predictable and contains no element of uncertainty. Suppose, however, we knew that the exchange rate fluctuated, within certain limits, from day to day. For example, our information might be that k can vary from 2.70 to 3.20 (in steps of, say, 0.02) and that on a particular day it is as likely to have any one value as any other value within that range; in other words, our data is in the form of a *statistical distribution* for k. In this case the shape of the distribution is flat or uniform (equal probability) over the range 2.70 to 3.20.

One property of a long sequence of random numbers is that the trend of the numbers is predictable even though the individual numbers in the sequence are unpredictable. Think, for example, of throwing a die. We cannot tell what number will come up next, but we know that if we throw it often enough (and if it is unbiased), all the integers from one through six should come up with equal frequency (another uniform distribution). A *stochastic* version of our dollar-to-mark conversion model is one that uses a sequence of random numbers to provide a value for k each time we need it. It follows that the stochastic model contains an element of uncertainty—if we repeat a calculation we are likely to get a somewhat different answer every time.

How do we obtain an appropriate sequence of random numbers on a computer? We use subroutines called *random number generators* that can be modified to produce a sequence with the required statistical properties. When we use stochastic models we will often want to run the model once with one sequence of random numbers, then run it again with another sequence. The "seed" of a random number generator is a number (any number) that we feed in at the beginning of a simulation; the subroutine uses it to choose a starting point in the sequence of random numbers. We can produce as many sequences as we need by changing the seed.

The choice of whether to build a deterministic or a stochastic model depends on the purpose of the model. For the average tourist there would be no point in building a stochastic model. Even if he knew that the exchange rate fluctuated he would probably be satisfied with a deterministic model that used the average value of k.

Suppose, however, that our model is going to be used by a vice-president of a large corporation who knows that he will have to convert $10 million into marks some time within the next week. He is quoted an exchange rate of 2.98 today; should he convert or should he wait in expectation of getting a better exchange rate later in the week? The deterministic model cannot answer this question, but the vice-president could use a stochastic model (in the absence of any understanding of the relevant market forces) to estimate the probabilities of losing or gaining by postponing the decision. Generally speaking we use stochastic models whenever the *variance* in the behavior of the system is important. Two examples of this will be found in Chaps. 3 and 4.

6. Complete treatises could be written on currency exchange; we have written one simple equation. Should we build a more detailed model? Should we, for instance, try to predict the value of k on the basis of other information (such as the balance of payments and prime interest rates in the two countries)? These questions relate to the *resolution* of the model, and the discussion of resolution merits a section of its own.

Before moving on to that section, note that the answers to these questions will depend, just as in points 4 and 5, on the *purpose* of the model.

Note also that points 4, 5, and 6 will crop up in various guises throughout this book. We introduce them here only to alert the reader to some of the issues involved in model building.

THE RESOLUTION OF A MODEL

We will use a number of different analogies to illustrate what we mean by resolution. We use the word in the same sense as the resolution of a microscope or telescope, where we are concerned with the extent to which the optical instrument enables us to distinguish the components of the object we are viewing. Similarly, the resolution of a model tells us which aspects of the subject being modeled are distinguishable or clear and which are hidden, ignored, submerged, or blurred.

Whenever we observe the world around us, we do so selectively; we pay attention to some features and ignore others. Think of driving along a highway. We pay particular attention to the cars immediately in front of and behind us, some attention to road signs, less attention to the rest of the traffic, and only peripheral attention to the scenery. The way in which our attention is divided depends on circumstances. If the route is strange, we will pay more attention to the road signs; if it is scenic, we will take more notice of the scenery. Moreover, the speed of the neighboring cars is their important attribute, not their color, style, or attractiveness of the occupants. If we are unobservant, or look at the wrong things, we will be bad drivers. If we notice too much as we drive, we are also likely to impair rather than improve the quality of our driving.

The same is true of modeling. If our resolution is too coarse, the model will be inadequate. If it is too fine, we will be distracted by irrelevant detail. The balance is important too. The driver who concentrates on the scenery at the expense of watching the cars closest to him is likely to have an accident. A model that is not properly balanced can be equally disastrous. There are thus two aspects to the concept of resolution: first, which components we include in our model and which we leave out, and second, how much detail or emphasis we ascribe to the components we include. By *resolution* we therefore mean a combination of *scope* and *detail*.

In Fig. 1.2 we change our analogy to illustrate how the resolution of a model determines what the model can and cannot do. In each diagram we are concerned with two antelope. In Fig. 1.2(a) we are interested in the two antelope within the context of the herd; our model enables us to make statements such as "those are the two, the ones in the middle of the herd" or "they are in a large herd" (or "a small group" or "a dense herd"). We emphasize the context at the expense of being able to say something specific about the two animals themselves; we do not even know whether they are male or female. In Fig. 1.2(b) we ignore the context—i.e., we reduce the scope of the model. The only statements we can make with this model are ones such as "the one is bending down while the other is looking up" or "they are standing close together." Figure 1.2(c) has the same scope as Fig. 1.2(b) but considerably more detail. Here we can identify the one antelope as a female kudu, the other as an oryx. We can comment on the stripe patterns on the kudu or the shape of the oryx's horns. Figure 1.2(d) illustrates a model that is unbalanced. Unless there are good reasons for concentrating on the two rear stripes on the kudu and the upper back legs of the oryx, there is something wrong with the resolution in this diagram.

Comparing Fig. 1.2(a), (b), and (c) highlights the extent to which the resolution of a model really determines what the model is all about. In each case the subject is two antelope, but the three representations of those antelope lead to three models that have very different structures, data requirements, and types of output. It is often useful, when trying to choose a suitable level of resolution for a model, to sketch something similar to these three diagrams and list for each what the model will be able to achieve and what data it will require.

There is good reason for belaboring the concept of resolution. Those

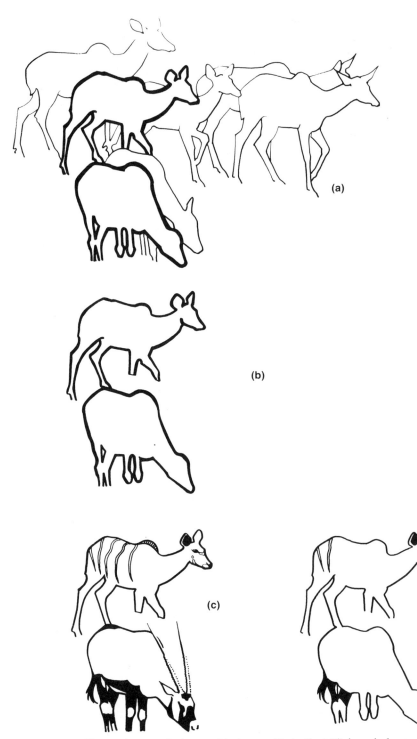

Figure 1.2   Illustrating resolution and balance. Note that (d) is unbalanced.

who build models in the physical sciences scarcely give a thought to the question of resolution. Years of experience have been transmitted from one generation to the next in such a way that a physicist or engineer automatically and almost instinctively chooses the resolution appropriate to a particular problem. This experience has *not* been developed to the same extent in the nonphysical sciences, and perhaps the most important skill to master in disciplines such as ecological modeling is choosing the appropriate level of resolution. The choice depends as much on the purpose of the model as on the structure of the system. It also depends on the *time scale* of the model. (We can ignore changes in the polar icecaps in a model with a time scale of decades, but not if we are trying to predict climatic changes over thousands of years.)

In the next section we introduce time-dependent models and show how questions of time and resolution are interlinked.

TIME-DEPENDENT MODELS

Our trivial currency exchange model is static; time does not feature explicitly in it. However, if we modified it to predict how the exchange rate might change as a function of time, it would be a *time-dependent* model. Most models are time-dependent for the simple reason that we tend to collect data, think, and plan in terms of time. Often our objective is to project into the future. We want to know what might happen if we do this instead of that.

There are different ways we can model the passage of time. Suppose, for example, that we are responsible for the control of mosquitoes in a city. We might want to monitor and model what happens to the mosquito population from one year to the next. We then have the choice of representing the population either as a *continuous* or a *discrete* function of time. If we choose the continuous representation, mathematically we can think of the population as some function P of the time t, and in practice we could choose *any* value for t and our model would give us an estimate of $P(t)$. If we plot P versus t we will get a continuous graph, although the value of P could be zero throughout the winter months and suddenly increase at the beginning of summer.

Alternatively, we might choose to look at the mosquito population only once a month or once a year. The appropriate mathematical representation would then be one in which we use subscripts—for example, P_t might represent the population at time step t, in which case the population at the next time step would be P_{t+1}. This is the discrete representation. If we use it, it is not meaningful to ask what the population is at any time other than the specific times t, $t + 1$, etc.

Thus, a continuous model is one in which time *flows,* while a discrete model is one in which time *jumps.* Which representation should we choose? The answer depends partly on the format of our data, partly on mathematical convenience, but mainly on the objectives and resolution of our model.

Suppose our objective is to predict how the mosquito population will respond to various control measures. At one level of resolution, those control measures might be described in fairly gross terms, such as "tons of insecticide used per year." In this case our model would be unbalanced if we thought of the number of mosquitoes as a continuous variable. The appropriate model is discrete with a time step of one year. P_t might then represent the total number of mosquitoes hatched during year t or the peak value of the population during the year.

However, at a different level of resolution we might want to look at how and when we actually apply the insecticide. We will then need to model changes in the mosquito population during the year. If we believe that mosquitoes hatch in an asynchronous manner, a continuous model is appropriate (although we may prefer to use a discrete model with a time step related to some characteristic time in the life cycle of a mosquito). On the other hand, if eruptions in the mosquito population are triggered by events such as rain storms, a discrete model would be mandatory. In the latter case the time step of the discrete model would not be constant; the interval between P_t and P_{t+1} could be quite different from the interval between P_{t+1} and P_{t+2}. We distinguish between *time-driven* discrete models (where time jumps regularly) and *event-driven* models (where time jumps forward only when something important occurs).

Most models are mathematical, if only in the sense that they use the language and notation of mathematics. However, in some cases we may design the model with the intention of using mathematical theorems and operations. We will call these *analytical models,* and several examples are given in Chap. 6. In other cases, the model may be designed as an *algorithm* or set of computational rules (as in a flow chart) without any attempt at formal analysis. We call these *simulation models.*

Since the mathematics of continuous functions has been studied more assiduously than that of discrete functions, it follows that if we are trying to build an analytical model, and if there is no compelling reason for choosing a discrete representation, we may prefer to make our model continuous. On the other hand, discrete models are easy to implement on a computer. So if we are building a simulation model, and if there is no compelling reason for a continuous representation, we may prefer to make our model discrete. We do, however, have to be cautious, because there are differences between a discrete and continuous representation of the same system; some of these are highlighted in Chap. 6.

PROVIDING A CONTEXT

The important issues we have raised so far relate to such questions as:

1. The purpose of the model, its expectations, and its limitations

2. How to choose the appropriate level of resolution
3. Whether the problem lends itself to simulation or an analytical approach
4. Whether to use a discrete or continuous representation of time
5. Whether to build a stochastic or deterministic model

The answers to these questions depend on the purpose of the model, so we begin to see that it is futile to talk about modeling outside a context. We cannot criticize or evaluate a model unless we know the problem the model was designed to address. It follows that a book that describes how to build and use models must rely heavily on case histories. The examples we will use all relate to the management of game parks (or game preserves; we will use the words synonymously) in African savannas.

There are several reasons for choosing this theme:

1. The most important is that the authors have the experience of building models in this context.
2. Next is that the context highlights most of the difficulties one encounters trying to build models in the nonphysical sciences.
3. Finally, it can be advantageous, when writing about models, to use examples that are somewhat removed from the experience of the reader. This enables the reader to approach the model with an open mind and to concentrate on the arguments rather than worry about some of the finer details. Most of the readers of this book will not have experienced the difficulties of making management decisions in an African game park. All will, we hope, find the context fascinating and will recognize in it themes that parallel their own experiences.

African Savanna and Game Parks

"In recent years the term 'savanna' has become synonymous with African plainslands—grasslands studded with flat-crowned acacias and carrying a profusion of wild ungulates." This is a quote from Huntley (1982). He goes on to give a wider definition, but this one, though somewhat tongue-in-cheek, will suffice for our purposes.

Our experience is based on various African game parks, some of them extensive (2×10^6 ha) and some relatively small (2×10^4 ha), some containing large predators (such as lion, Cape hunting dog, leopard, cheetah, and spotted hyena), and others not. In addition to "grassland studded with flat-crowned acacias," there is a mix of open grassland and areas of denser shrubs or woodlands, and the proportions vary from park to park. Rainfall and climate vary too. There are parks of arid savanna receiving about 200 mm of rainfall per year, and others in more moist savanna where the annual rainfall exceeds 600 mm. Topography and soil types vary too, not only from one park to another, but also within a park.

The various parks also have certain features in common. All are partly if not totally fenced in. Migrations of large herds of ungulates were once a feature of African savanna; the fences either restrict migrations or prevent them altogether. The rainfall, whether it is high or low on average, tends to be variable. There are years of relatively abundant rainfall and years of drought. In some areas there is tentative evidence of a periodicity in the rainfall, cycles with a period of about 20 years during which half the cycle is relatively dry and the other half relatively wet. Particularly in the more arid parks, the bulk of the rainfall occurs during the summer months and the ungulates can be stressed during the long dry periods, especially if summer rains are late. Fire, either natural or man-induced, is also a common feature during the dry months and can influence the regeneration of trees, the balance between bush and grass, and the grazing patterns of the ungulates. These features are all important in relation to the management of a game park.

Management Problems and Options

There is a lively and ongoing debate about the role of management in a game preserve. One can argue convincingly for as little management as possible in a game park that is very large and very far from the pressures of civilization. Unfortunately, such a park is hypothetical. African game parks have lost their innocence—either they are too small and surrounded by fences, or they are subject to increasing pressures from human population on their borders. Under these circumstances, a game park is not a pristine, natural ecosystem but a human artifice, and the decision not to manage is just one of many other management options; it also needs to be justified.

How much management, then, is necessary? From the ecological viewpoint, much depends on the size of the park (in relation to the size of the home ranges of the larger mammals) and the diversity of the vegetation. Over and above that, the perceived purpose and objectives of the game park are of paramount importance, and these tend to change with time and the pressures of human populations.

It is not our purpose to get involved in this debate. The interested reader is referred to Jewell and Holt (1981) and Owen-Smith (1983) for an introduction to some of the issues and positions. For our purposes we will accept stated management goals and use them as a foil for showing how various modeling techniques can help to refine or meet those goals. Similar techniques would still be useful if the goals were different.

The following are some of the actions that management may take or contemplate in a game park:

1. Not to intervene (as pointed out, this is as much an action as any other action).
2. To build dams or provide water artificially (to compensate for water

losses to irrigation upstream or for the fact that the animals can no longer move out of the park in search of water during a drought).
3. To crop (cull or remove) some of the animals. This may be done for a number of reasons:
   a. To prevent predators from moving out of a park.
   b. To protect a rare animal or plant species.
   c. To prevent an animal species that has been too successfully protected from damaging its environment.
   d. To limit the number of herbivores in a park where natural predators have been eliminated.
   e. To control disease.
   f. To finance the maintenance of the park.
4. To reintroduce and foster species that are either extinct or rare within the park.
5. To introduce fire-breaks and other fire control measures.
6. To deliberately burn sections of the park. Possible reasons for burning are:
   a. To compensate for natural fires that would have occurred if there had been no fire control in the park.
   b. To alter the pattern of the vegetation.
   c. To prevent bush encroachment.
   d. To produce a flush of fresh, nutritious grass for the herbivores.

The major problem management faces is that it cannot be sure these actions will actually achieve the objectives that prompted them; nor can it be sure that an action initiated to solve one problem will not generate other problems or undesirable side-effects. No two situations are ever quite the same, so it is not easy to draw on past experience or the experience of others. Assumptions have to be made; for example, are the next few years likely to be unusually dry or unusually wet? Frequently, decisions have to be made during a crisis, such as a severe drought, when there is no time to collect data or perform an experiment. Even when data are available, they may turn out to be the wrong kind or at the wrong level of resolution. Experiments can be suspect or open to more than one interpretation because it is often difficult to design a control experiment or to evaluate results in the light of environmental factors that changed during the experiment.

It is against this background that one has to evaluate whether models can be useful and, if so, what types of models to build and how to use them. It is a background that forces one to be pragmatic; if the model is not ready in time, decisions will have to be made without it, and if data are not available for the model, the model may have to be built without them.

If we look back at Holling's diagram (Fig. 1.1) we see that these considerations place the problems to be solved squarely in area 2 or 4. Our context thus illustrates the class of modeling problems we have chosen to address in this book. If these considerations add to the difficulties of building models, they also add to the interest and importance of doing so.

Apart from ecological management, there are many other fields in which there is a need to build models pragmatically.

LEARNING TO COMPROMISE

As a first step toward building pragmatic models, we must learn how to compromise. Figure 1.3 represents an ecosystem at different levels of resolution. The circles in each case represent the components of the ecosystem and the arrows indicate that one component has a direct influence on another. Double-headed arrows indicate a mutual interaction, while the thick arrows represent external influences (the "driving forces" on the model) such as sunshine, rainfall, and management actions.

We will use diagrams of this kind as a sort of logo at the beginning of each chapter to depict the contents of the chapter. In a model, the circles in the diagrams would be associated with variables (a circle might represent one variable or a group of variables) and the arrows with equations. An arrow that starts and ends on the same circle implies that the component has an influence on itself. (Examples are births within a population or density-dependent effects.)

Many people think of ecological modeling in terms of diagrams such as Fig. 1.3(a). Their preconception is that ecosystems are made up of components that interact in a complex way and that models should be built to represent that complexity. However, as we shall see in Chap. 5, it is not easy to build a model as complex as that shown in Fig. 1.3(a), and often

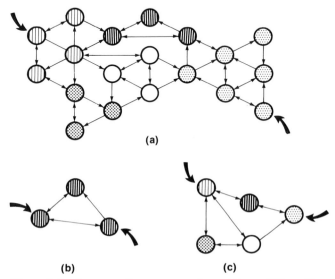

(a)

(b)   (c)

Figure 1.3   Representing an ecosystem at three different levels of resolution: (a) a detailed system model, (b) isolating a part of the system, (c) a less detailed ("lumped") system model.

the usefulness of such models, once they have been built, is disappointing. Our first compromise is therefore one of *simplification*. The way to accomplish this is to start with the management problem itself (rather than with a mental picture of the ecosystem), then to find the abstraction of the ecosystem that enables us to contribute effectively to the solution of the problem. This approach usually leads to models at a completely different level of resolution, as illustrated in Figs. 1.3(b) and (c).

In Fig. 1.3(b) we have a management problem that relates to only a part of the ecosystem (the three circles in Fig. 1.3(a) with narrow vertical lines). We therefore focus on that part and try to separate the relevant components and their interactions (the first-order effects) from the rest of the system. Obviously the context within which the chosen components interact cannot be ignored entirely. It is often useful to think of and represent the effect of the rest of the system on the subsystem as an artificial driving force (thick arrow). We will introduce various ways of doing this in Chaps. 2, 3, 4, and 8.

In Fig. 1.3(c) the management problem relates to the system as a whole, but to say something useful with our model we have represented the system at a coarser level of resolution. Here we have combined (or, to use modeling jargon, "lumped") all similarly shaded variables in Fig. 1.3(a) into grosser components and we have concentrated on only the key (or first-order) interactions in the system. We will introduce examples of this in Chaps. 5 and 6.

Obviously the appropriate level of resolution must depend on the management problem to be solved, but in choosing that level we must pay as much attention to what we are likely to achieve with the model as to how well the model represents the problem we are trying to solve. Choosing the appropriate level is thus a pragmatic compromise between the complexity of ecosystems on the one hand, and the need to solve a problem, with limited data and in a reasonable amount of time, on the other. Much of this book will be concerned with learning how to make the most of that compromise.

To quote Bernard Berenson: "Representation is a compromise with chaos."

FURTHER READING

An appealing definition of a model can be found on pages 7 and 8 of Hall and Day (1977). Approaches to modeling and management that overlap with those described in this chapter can be found in Silvert (1981), in the last chapter of Mann (1982), in a recent book by Walters (in press), and in a paper by Overton (1977). The latter contains a good discussion of resolution. Although the book by Tukey (1977) addresses problems of data analysis rather than modeling, it espouses a similar philosophy. Simon (1982) provides a philosophical and practical approach to complexity in general.

A Simple Single-Species Model

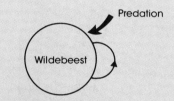

Predation

Wildebeest

The central grasslands (comprising about 5×10^5 ha) of the game park we are considering had always supported large herds of zebra (*Equus burchelli*) and wildebeest (*Connochaetes taurinus*). The decade of the sixties was unusually dry, and while zebra and wildebeest both thrived during those dry years, by 1965 there was evidence of range overutilization. This led management to initiate a cropping program. The number of zebra and wildebeest to be cropped each year was set on the basis of data from the annual aerial census of the park.

The censuses showed that by 1969 the two populations had leveled off at about 14,000 zebra and a similar number of wildebeest. Thereafter, their numbers started declining.

The drought was broken in 1971 by unusually heavy rains, and the grasslands recovered rapidly. Cropping was progressively reduced and finally discontinued after 1972. While the zebra population first remained steady (at a reduced level), and then showed a modest increase, the censuses continued to show a decline in the wildebeest population that persisted unabated even after cropping had stopped.

At first it was thought that the census figures were an undercount. The large wildebeest herds fragmented during the wet years and this, together with the higher grass, made it more difficult to count them from the air. However, by 1975 it was obvious that there were fewer than 7000 wildebeest in the central grasslands. Various explanations were proposed for the continued slide in wildebeest numbers, all of them related in some way to the changes in vegetation. The basic argument was that tall grass was not a suitable habitat for wildebeest and their numbers had been reduced to a level where they were unable to maintain patches of short grass by their own grazing pressure.

Against this background it was decided to build a model to analyze the reasons for the wildebeest population decline and to evaluate possible management actions to reverse it. These were vague at the time, but essentially implied controlling the principal predators of the wildebeest—lions and spotted hyenas.

A MODELING STRATEGY

The first stage of model design requires us to be quite clear about why we are building the model. The objectives provide a basis for arguing about what should be included in or excluded from the model, and it is vital that they be clearly stated at the outset. In the wildebeest population model the objectives were (1) to help understand the decline in the wildebeest population, and (2) to investigate how this decline might be reversed.

To do this, we must obviously produce a model that is capable of simulating wildebeest numbers. Because lions and hyenas are their dominant predators, we might argue that the model should also be capable of simulating their numbers. This would involve a two-way interaction: The predators affect wildebeest numbers, while the availability of prey must influence the predator populations. But wildebeest are not the only important prey species for lions and hyenas; this leads one to argue that the model will also have to include the population dynamics of other important prey species (e.g., zebra, giraffe, and impala). Moreover, we suspect that grass height is important and therefore should include it as a variable that moderates the predator-prey interaction. Grass height in turn will depend on rainfall and herbivore density.

In short, we can argue that, as every good ecologist knows, the park is a system of interacting components and we need to understand all the interactions before making management decisions. Our model, it could be argued, must be a system model of the entire park.

The problem with the above argument is that, unfortunately, we do *not* understand all the relevant interactions in the system. Any model that we could build of the entire park would therefore include a large number of questionable assumptions and sheer guesses. Moreover, it would take a great deal of time and effort to try to build a model of the whole park, whereas management needs to made a decision *now*.

We are therefore going to take a very different and much more pragmatic approach. We will set out to build a model that concentrates on and is defined by the immediate problem management faces, in this case a declining wildebeest population. We will start with the wildebeest as our *only* variable and will introduce other factors only when they are significant and where they affect the wildebeest population *directly* (i.e., we will include first-order effects only). Even then we will only introduce these other factors as simply as we can. If we imagine the park system as a large painting, our model will show the wildebeest in some detail, but grow very fuzzy and abstract as we move away from the wildebeest into the rest of the system.

By doing this we deliberately ignore the argument that the wildebeest are a component of the entire, complex ecosystem. Instead, we begin with the fact that we have a decision to make, almost certainly with insufficient data and understanding to make it properly, so we force ourselves to build a model that is focused on that decision. By recognizing our ignorance and the lack of data, we prevent the model from becoming too complex. If this model helps us to understand our problem and to marshall the information we *do* have, it will have served its purpose.

Our modeling strategy is thus to use the objectives of the model to isolate the essential variables.

BUILDING THE MODEL

To build a model of wildebeest numbers, we need to ask the following questions:

1. What are the mechanisms that cause wildebeest numbers to change?
2. How often do we need to calculate these changes—i.e., what is a suitable time step for our model?
3. What level of detail do we need to describe the wildebeest population—e.g., do we need to differentiate between sexes in the model? Do we need to differentiate between various age classes?

Some ways of answering these questions are useful and others are not. We are only interested in what is essential for fleshing out the spartan structure we have in mind for the model. It is no coincidence that the very first question relates to *mechanisms*. It does not suffice to hypothesize vaguely about what caused the population decline; we have to build a model that actually *makes* the population change.

The answer to the first question is obvious—wildebeest are born and wildebeest die. In fact, the central theme of our management problem is that wildebeest are dying faster than they are being born, and we want to understand why and what we can do about it. Asking how wildebeest are born extracts the following information: Females first produce calves when they are two years old, but the fertility of that age class is considerably lower than the older females, who will nearly all produce one calf a year until they die. There is no evidence to suggest that fertility is reduced by poor grazing conditions. Calf births are synchronized—i.e., the calves are all dropped within a period of one or two weeks during the summer.

Asking how wildebeest die extracts a picture that is both simple and confusing at the same time. The simplicity lies in the answer that they nearly all die violently: Lions are responsible for most of the adult deaths and very few adults reach a ripe old age and die a natural death. (While in some parts of Africa the ratio of wildebeest to lions is more than 100 to 1, in this particular park the ratio is closer to 10 to 1.)

The confusion arises in the question of calf mortality. If grazing conditions are extremely poor, the cows are likely to be weak and many calves may starve within a week or two of birth from a lack of sufficient high-quality milk. In any case, the first week or two of a calf's life is a nightmare of predation by a whole spectrum of predators. Only when the calves are some months older will lions become their principle predator.

In the answers to our first question we can find a clue to the answer to our second question—namely, how often do we need to calculate population changes? The fact that births are confined to a very short period during the year suggests that it should be sufficient to calculate the population changes only once a year. Clearly we cannot have a larger time step or we might miss differences in calf mortality from one year to the next. From the biological point of view there is no point in having a smaller time step, because apart from the calving period, what happens to the wildebeest during one time of the year is very similar to what happens at any other time. The only other reason we might have for using a smaller time step would be if field data needed to be interpreted more frequently than once a year or if management decisions were, for example, reevaluated every quarter. In practice, we find that decisions are taken and evaluated once a year, so we shall settle on a time step of one year for our model.

The third question asks whether we need to differentiate between the sexes or between different age classes in our model. The field biologists have information about sex ratios: While at birth there are almost equal numbers of male and female calves, at maturity (i.e., two years or older) females comprise approximately 70 percent of the population. There is no evidence in the field data to suggest that this percentage changes significantly from one year to the next. This last piece of information leads us to conclude that we do not need to differentiate between the sexes.

We already know from answers to the previous questions that calf mortality is more complicated than adult mortality, that calves and yearlings do not breed, and that the fertility of two-year-olds is not the same as adult fertility. Clearly, we do need to differentiate between the age classes. However, all wildebeest over the age of two breed and die in much the same way. (Remember that very few wildebeest actually die of old age. Nearly all adults are killed by lions, and we speculate that an older wildebeest has much the same chance of being caught as a younger one. What it lacks in speed is compensated for by experience!) We only need, therefore, to keep track of age classes up to the age of three—i.e., we can lump all wildebeest aged three and over into a single class we will call "adult."

We are now ready to introduce a convenient notation. Suppose we look at the wildebeest population a few weeks after the end of the calving season in year number t. Let c_t denote the number of calves at that time. Similarly, let y_t denote the number of yearlings (the calves that have survived from the previous year), w_t the number of two-year-olds, and a_t the number of adult wildebeest (three or more years of age), all at year t.

Our model must enable us to predict population changes from one year to the next. Given c_t, y_t, w_t, and a_t, we must therefore develop equations that enable us to calculate c_{t+1}, y_{t+1}, w_{t+1}, and a_{t+1}. We begin by writing these equations in words:

c_{t+1} = the number of calves born to those two-year-old and adult females alive at the beginning of the calving season in year $t + 1$

$y_{t+1} = c_t$ minus those calves that died during the year

$w_{t+1} = y_t$ minus those yearlings that died during the year

and

$a_{t+1} = w_t + a_t$ minus those two-year-olds and adults that died during the year

Figure 2.1 shows schematically the changes that take place in the population from year t to year $t + 1$.

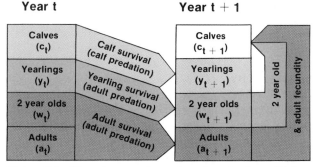

Figure 2.1   The changes that take place in the wildebeest population from one year to the next.

The next step is to replace these words with mathematics. If we begin with the equation for c_{t+1}, we need to know how many two-year-old and adult females there are at the beginning of the calving season in year $t + 1$. We know that there were w_t two-year-olds and a_t adults a week or two after the last calving season, but this is not very helpful because a significant proportion of them might have died before the current calving season. A closer estimate of two-year-old and adult wildebeest at the time of the calving season in year $t + 1$ would be w_{t+1} and a_{t+1}. If we let p represent the proportion of the adult population that is female, we can expect that there will be very nearly $p \times w_{t+1}$ two-year-old and $p \times a_{t+1}$ adult cows at the time of calving. If we now let b represent the fecundity of adult females and β the lower fecundity of two-year-old females, then pa_{t+1} adult cows will produce bpa_{t+1} calves and pw_{t+1} two-year-old cows will produce βpw_{t+1} calves. So we can write,

$$c_{t+1} = \beta pw_{t+1} + bpa_{t+1}$$

Note that at this stage of the calculation we do not know w_{t+1} and a_{t+1}. So, although we have written this equation first, we will not be able to use it until we have calculated both w_{t+1} and a_{t+1}.

The equation for y_{t+1} is potentially the most difficult to derive; so many factors affect the number of calves that die during a year. So many, in fact, that we could not possibly model them all with any degree of confidence. Instead of trying to cope with all of them, our strategy will be to cut through the problem by introducing a factor q_t, which we will call the calf survival rate during year t. We will deal with how to estimate and interpret it later. The point we are stressing in our notation (by writing q with a subscript) is that calf survival is likely to change from one year to the next. With this concept, if we started with c_t calves at the beginning of year t, only $q_t \times c_t$ will be left at the end of year t, so our equation for the yearlings becomes,

$$y_{t+1} = q_t c_t$$

The only complication in the equations for two-year-olds and adults is, again, the number of yearlings, two-year-olds, and adults that die during the year. But here we have introduced a reasonable simplifying assumption—namely, that they are all killed by lions. The only questions that remain to be answered are how many lions are there, how many wildebeest will a lion kill each year, and do lions have a preference for yearlings, two-year-olds, or adults?

These questions, if taken to experts in predator-prey interaction, could lead to a number of different theories, and each theory in turn would lead to a different model. Since we have no evidence to support one theory over another, and since we want to avoid questions relating to other prey species (which will inevitably arise in trying to model prey selection), we again take a very simple approach and postulate that during year t there are l_t lions, that each of them eats, on average, s_t wildebeest, and they do not differentiate between yearlings, adults, and two-year-olds. By manipulating l_t and s_t we can then make use of any data we are able to find about the lions and their kill-rate, or we can simulate a particular theory of predator-prey interaction if we wish to do so.

On this basis, the total number of yearlings, two-year-old, and adult wildebeest at the beginning of year t will be $y_t + w_t + a_t$, and a total of $l_t \times s_t$ of them will be killed, indiscriminately, by lions during the year. If we assign the numbers killed in each age class on a proportional basis, then $(l_t s_t y_t)/(y_t + w_t + a_t)$ yearlings and $l_t s_t (w_t + a_t)/(y_t + w_t + a_t)$ two-year-olds and adults will be killed during the year. Our final two equations can thus be written,

$$w_{t+1} = y_t - \frac{l_t s_t y_t}{y_t + w_t + a_t}$$

and

$$a_{t+1} = a_t + w_t - \frac{l_t s_t (w_t + a_t)}{y_t + w_t + a_t}$$

To implement these equations we need an initial population structure at year 1, estimates of the parameters b, β, and p, and estimates of q_t, l_t, and s_t for year 1 and all subsequent years. Note that we never really need to estimate l_t and s_t separately. Only their product is important to our model, but it helps to *think* of the number of lions and how much each lion eats as two separate entities. In the next section we discuss how we estimate the parameters in our model and try to fit the model to the available data.

FITTING THE MODEL TO FIELD DATA

Our concern thus far has been with the abstract relationships leading to the equations that describe our population model. To use and test the model we need numbers rather than symbols. Some of the numbers will be available immediately. For others we may only have very rough estimates. While yet others will have to be inferred indirectly from whatever field data are at our disposal. The process of fitting the model to the field data is thus rather like detective work: We have facts, clues, and hypotheses, and from these we must attempt to construct a convincing case.

From information gleaned in the previous section, we already have an estimate of p, the proportion of adults that are female—namely, 0.7. We also know that the adult fecundity b is close to 1.0, while β is approximately 0.3. These are our only firm estimates. On less firm grounds, rangers and field biologists tell us they suspect there are 400 to 600 lions in the park and that each lion will, on average, eat between two and four wildebeest a year. Apart from emphasizing that the calf survival rate can fluctuate from one year to the next, the field biologists can only guess very roughly that its value might vary between, say, 0.1 and 0.6.

Indirect evidence is available from the annual aerial censuses of the park. Specifically, there are estimates of the total wildebeest population for most of seven years, though for various reasons some of these estimates are thought to be more accurate than others. Finally, a rough idea of the proportion of calves and yearlings in the population is available from road counts.

Given this information, our strategy will be to take successive guesses at the calf survival rate and see whether, using values for the number of lions and the lion kill-rate that are reasonable, we can relate results from the model to the aerial census and road-count data. Specifically, we will try to reproduce six years of field data using the model. (We use the census data for the first year as the starting point of our computation.)

There are, however, two additional complications:

1. Wildebeest were cropped during four of the six years, and obviously we must take account of this in our model. Accurate records were kept of the total number, let us call it g_t, cropped during year t, and we know that the actual cropping process consisted of removing small groups of wildebeest entirely. We suspect, therefore, that the effect of cropping on the various age classes was very similar to the assumptions we made about the effect of predation on the age classes. If this is so, we can model the cropping process merely by replacing the product $l_t s_t$ wherever it appears in our equations with the expression $l_t s_t + g_t$.

2. The census data were not taken immediately after the calving season. This is a problem because calf mortality is particularly high during and shortly after the calving season. As an estimate, we will assume that 30 percent of the calves that die during a year will have died by the time of the census.

Figure 2.2(a) represents one attempt to fit the model to the census data. In this case we have chosen the fecundity rates β and b to be 0.30 and 0.92 respectively and we have kept the number of lions fixed at 500 for all six years of the simulation. We have assumed an initial population of 14,000 (from the 1969 census) and distributed it among the various age classes in proportions that seem sensible to the field biologists. We have then varied the calf survival rate q_t and the number of wildebeest killed by each lion in a year, s_t, to obtain a reasonable fit to the field data. We have also used the available data on the number of wildebeest cropped. The full details are given in Table 2.1.

Figure 2.2(b) shows two other attempts to fit the model to the data. Both are identical to our first attempt except that we have manipulated the

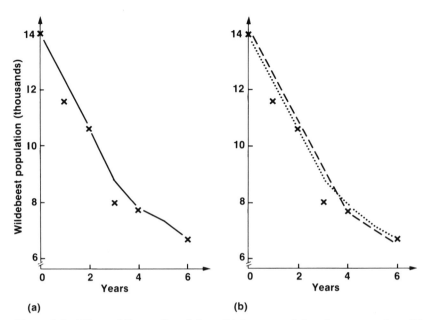

Figure 2.2   Three different fits of the wildebeest model to the census data (X). (a) Case 1: the first attempt. (b) Case 2 (dashed line): higher calf survival and higher kill-rate, and case 3 (dotted line): lower calf survival and lower kill-rate.

calf survival rate and lion kill-rate in different ways. In one case (case 2) we have assumed a higher calf survival and a higher kill-rate and in the other (case 3) a lower calf survival and a lower kill-rate.

It should be noted that we have not tried to reproduce the census data exactly. First, they are not sufficiently reliable to make such an attempt worthwhile (in particular the census figure for year 3 was almost certainly an undercount). Second, the model itself is not sufficiently accurate to warrant the effort. Our fits, therefore, are meant only to show similar trends to the field data.

How to choose between the three fits? All three reproduce the census data with equal accuracy and use assumptions and parameters that are plausible too. All show a pattern that suggests that once wildebeest numbers had dropped significantly, calf survival increased and the lion kill-rate decreased; this, too, makes a great deal of sense.

The only information we have not used is the fact that field biologists can distinguish calves and yearlings from the rest of the population and have some data on what proportion of the population they constitute. We are wary of using data on calves because, as we have noted, they depend strongly on when exactly they were collected. Figure 2.3 therefore shows the percentage of yearlings in the total population (excluding calves) for all three of our test cases. Field data suggest that this should be about 20 percent, so our first fit is likely to be better than

TABLE 2.1 DETAILED INPUT AND OUTPUT FOR THE WILDEBEEST MODEL, CASE 1

	Input parameters				Computer results					
Year (t)	Lions (l_t)	Kill rate (s_t)	No. cropped (g_t)	Calf survival rate (q_t)	Calves (c_{t+1})	Yearlings (y_{t+1})	Two-year-olds (w_{t+1})	Adults (a_{t+1})	Total	Census total
0	500	4.5	572	0.35	3640	2240	1680	6440	14,000	14,000
1	500	4.5	550	0.35	2903	1820	1630	5908	12,261	11,800
2	500	4.5	302	0.35	2569	1451	1275	5283	10,578	10,600
3	500	3.8	78	0.42	2160	1285	989	4468	8,902	8,000
4	500	3.3	0	0.48	1872	1296	908	3856	7,932	7,700
5	500	3.3	0	0.48	1702	1284	943	3467	7,396	—
6					1546	1167	912	3132	6,757	6,700

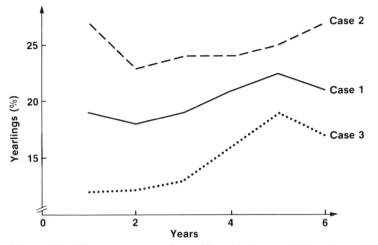

Figure 2.3 The percentage of yearlings in the population for each of the three cases in Fig. 2.2.

the other two. The evidence, however, is not so clear cut that we can afford to discredit the other two fits entirely, and we must remember this when we try to make deductions from the model.

EXERCISING THE MODEL

Now that we have in some sense "tuned" our model, we can try to use it to gain a better understanding of what has happened to the wildebeest population. We do this by modeling different scenarios. For example, we could ask what might have happened if there had been no cropping of the wildebeest during years 1 through 4. Figure 2.4(a) shows what we obtain from the model by using exactly the same input data, except for the number cropped, as in case 1. The result is provocative. It suggests that the continuing decline in the population in years 5 and 6 was in fact precipitated by the cropping. The picture that emerges is that the field biologists failed to realize that with increased rainfall the wildebeest were subject to increased predation, so they continued to crop when they should have desisted. In fact, their cropping tipped the balance in such a way that predators subsequently were able to remove more animals in a year than the wildebeest could replace, hence the continued sharp decline.

This is too dramatic an interpretation to rest on the evidence of case 1 only. Figure 2.4(a) also shows what the model produces if we ignore cropping but otherwise use the same parameters as in the two cases we tentatively discarded. The picture that emerges remains intact!

The response of the field biologists to this suggestion is, however, as

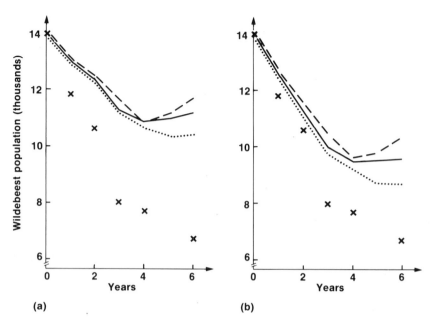

Figure 2.4   What the wildebeest model predicts might have happened if (a) no wildebeest had been cropped and (b) predators were cropped as well as wildebeest. [The three cases are shown as solid, dashed, and dotted lines respectively, and the crosses (X) are the original census data.]

follows: "We had to crop the wildebeest during those years, otherwise they would have had a deleterious effect on the vegetation." Let us accept this explanation but ask what they could have done if they had understood the consequences of increased predation plus cropping. One suggestion might be that they should have cropped lions as well as wildebeest to maintain some sort of balance.

Figure 2.4(b) shows the results obtained from all three cases if we reintroduce cropping of the wildebeest, but assume that for all six years the lion population was controlled in such a way that the average annual population was reduced by 10 percent—i.e., we use a figure of 450 instead of 500 for the number of lions in our model. All three cases show that this would have been a sensible approach, although in the third case, where calf survival is more of a bottleneck, the result of reducing the number of lions without increasing calf survival is less effective. In contrast, if we take our original three cases and ask what lion population in year 6 would have halted the decline in the wildebeest population (assuming all other things to be equal), the answers would have been 335, 390, and 350 respectively. This means we would have to remove about 30 percent of the lions!

Up to now we have only been using the model to try to understand what happened during the six years of wildebeest decline. The last calculation in the preceding paragraph is our first attempt to suggest what should be done to halt and reverse the decline. Our model implies that there are really only two controls on the population—calf survival and the product of lions and kill-rate (i.e., the number of wildebeest, other than calves, taken by the lions in a year). The question we asked at the end of the last paragraph can be generalized into "What combination of controls would stabilize the population?" A fair amount of experimentation with the model on the computer leads to the set of graphs shown in Fig.2.5. Here we summarize how different combinations of calf survival and numbers killed by lions will lead to a sustained population at different constant levels.

It would be prudent at this stage to remember that we built our model with very little data or understanding; could the structure we have produced or our interpretation of the results be spurious? What is the weakest link in our logic? There are only two important processes in the model—births and deaths. There is supporting evidence for the way in which we have modeled births; our major assumption is that deaths are due to predation. If the wildebeest would have died in any case (perhaps of disease or starvation), our interpretation collapses.

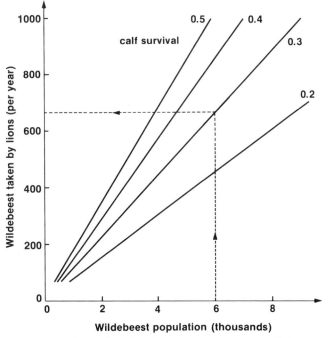

Figure 2.5 Predation thresholds. (For example, if the wildebeest population is 6000 and the calf survival is 0.3, the population will remain constant if the lions kill 666 wildebeest per year but will decline if predation is any higher.)

There is no information to suggest that adults were ill or likely to die of starvation, but there is a real possibility that calves would have died even if there had been no predators in the park. Fortunately, the way in which we have modeled calf mortality is so general that we can interpret it as we please. We could, for example, link the calf survival rate to grass height or nutrition without detracting from the rest of our argument. Figure 2.5, in general terms, shows what level of predation the wildebeest can sustain depending on *new recruitment*. We begin to see that a compelling reason for building simple models when we have insufficient information is that their very simplicity permits a variety of interpretations.

Figure 2.5 is therefore a useful guide to managers. It is important to note however, that it only tells them the magnitude of their problem, without really telling them *how*, in practical terms, to resolve it. And that is something our model *cannot* do; it is the price we have to pay for the approach we took in constructing the model and the simplifying assumptions we made along the way.

COMPARISONS BETWEEN WILDEBEEST AND ZEBRA

Once a small model such as this has been built and used in the context of its original objectives, it is often useful to stand back and ask whether the model itself, or perhaps a modified version of it, could have any useful novel applications. Wildebeest and zebra are often seen together. During the period we have simulated using the wildebeest model, field data collected on zebra told a tale that was both similar to and yet intriguingly different from the wildebeest saga. The obvious next step was to see whether the wildebeest model could be modified and used to explain both the similarities and the differences.

At the beginning of the period, there were approximately 14,000 zebra in the park—i.e., there were similar numbers of wildebeest and zebra. Zebra were cropped more heavily than wildebeest and for a longer period. In fact, while a total of about 1500 wildebeest were cropped during the first *four* years, more than 3100 zebra were cropped during the first *six* years of the drought. Like the wildebeest population, zebra numbers declined during the years of cropping; when cropping was halted there were only 6000 zebra left. Unlike the wildebeest, however, the zebra population did not continue to decline once cropping was halted; on the contrary, it showed a modest but significant increase.

The biologists concerned were not surprised at this difference. Zebra, they claimed, are able to utilize taller grass more effectively than wildebeest. One would thus expect them to go into the areas of taller grass (resulting from the years of abundant rainfall after the drought) that wildebeest were unwilling to use. By grazing in these areas, the zebra reduce the grass height, opening the areas up for subsequent utilization by the wildebeest. If conditions were such as to favor a herbivore population recovery, they argued, one would expect the zebra to lead the recovery. In other words, zebra are "higher in the natural succession" than wildebeest.

The important parameters in the wildebeest model are calf survival, the number of lions, and the lion kill-rate; grass height never appears explicitly in the model. Would a similar model, one wonders, without direct reference to grass height or the "natural succession," explain the zebra data?

Zebra mares mature one year later than wildebeest cows. The only structural modifications that needed to be made to the wildebeest model to convert it into a zebra model were to introduce a three-year-old age class, to adjust the equations so that two-year-olds did not breed, and to allow three-year-olds to reproduce at a lower rate than adults (where adults are now understood to be four or more years old). The basic assumptions of the model remained unchanged—i.e., it was assumed that zebra foals were subjected to all sorts of predation, lumped together in the concept of a foal survival rate, while all other zebra were killed by lions who did not discriminate between the various age classes.

The actual numbers used in the zebra model were of course different from those used in the wildebeest model, except for the number of lions, since the same lion population was preying on the two herbivores in much the same parts of the park at the same time. Field data for zebra led to values of 0.12 and about 0.44 respectively for the three-year-old birthrate times the proportion of three-year-olds that were female and for the adult birthrate times the proportion of adults that were female. This lower fertility than the wildebeest was compensated for by the fact that lions killed zebra at a reduced rate—there is that much more meat on a zebra—of between one and two kills per lion per year.

Using these figures and a foal survival rate that increased from 0.20 to 0.35 during seven years of simulation (there was an extra year of census data for zebra), a plausible fit of the model to the census data for zebra was obtained, as can be seen in Fig.2.6(a). In particular, the simulation showed the same slight increase in population as the census once cropping was terminated.

Figure 2.6(a) also shows an extrapolation of the zebra simulation for a further four years, assuming no further change in either calf survival or lion kill-rate. The extrapolation has been made assuming, first, that the lion population is controlled and kept fixed at 400, then repeated for lion populations of 300 and 200. All three simulations show a healthy recovery in zebra numbers. The same exercise was then conducted on the wildebeest model using the first of the three data fits, and Fig.2.6(b) shows the extrapolations in this case. It can be seen that the wildebeest population continues to decline with a lion population of 400 and increases only modestly if there are 300 lions.

Comparing the two models thus shows that the zebra population is indeed more resilient than the wildebeest. It either shows an increased rate of recovery or, under similar conditions, recovers when the wil-

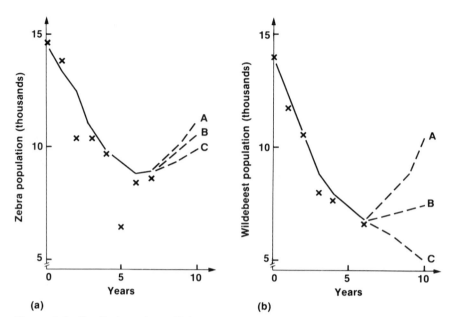

Figure 2.6   Predicting what will happen (a) to the zebra population and (b) to the wildebeest population, if the number of lions is reduced after year 6 to 200 (A), 300 (B), and 400 (C) respectively. The crosses (X) are the census data.

debeest population only shows a slower rate of decline. What is intriguing, however, is the fact that neither of our models relates to the question of succession in any way. This suggests that while succession may indeed play a part, one can explain the resilience of the zebra population purely in terms of the structure of that population, its fertility characteristics, and predation pressure!

THE MODEL IN RETROSPECT

In this section we will review briefly what was learned from this and subsequent models of the wildebeest population.

   Perhaps the most important contribution of the modeling exercise was the fact that it focused attention on wildebeest births and wildebeest deaths. The field biologists knew that they had a declining wildebeest population, but their explanations for it were varied and vague. Building a model forced them to establish a mechanism, and that mechanism turned out to be predation. Exercising the model and comparing it with census data provided a plausible explanation for the decline, one that could be interpreted in a way that was consistent with both the available data and peripheral field observations.

   The following picture emerged. While in theory a reduction in the wildebeest population should have led to a reduction in the number of wildebeest killed by lions, in practice the high grass conditions and the fact that the large wildebeest herds had broken up into smaller, scattered groups made it possible for the lions to maintain a high wildebeest kill-rate. This situation was aggravated by the cropping which, at a critical time, further reduced the wildebeest population to the point where it was unable to replace the wildebeest falling prey to lions.

This explanation enabled the managers to look back on their past actions in a critical but constructive way. The fact that they had continued to crop wildebeest when the population was already evidently in a decline was, with hindsight, attributed in part to a lack of confidence in the census data. Because the large wildebeest herds had fragmented into smaller, scattered groups, they were much more difficult to count, and so the lower census counts were at first interpreted as an undercount rather than a population decline. Recognizing the dangers of misinterpretation of census data led the biologists to think about supporting data that could usefully be used to reinforce the annual census. This in turn led them to take samples from road counts of sex ratios, calf-to-cow ratios, and yearling percentages, on a regular basis during the year.

Ironically, collection of this new data highlighted the inadequacies of the model that had been built. For instance, it was discovered that the adult sex ratio was not as constant as had been thought, and it was suspected that increased predation on yearling males was an important reason for this. This led to the construction of a more complex model that (1) introduced sex as well as age classes, (2) allowed for different predation rates between different sexes and for different predation rates from one age class to another, and (3) simulated the population at intervals of three months to facilitate comparisons with seasonal sampling data.

In turn, exercising the new, extended model showed how easy it was to misinterpret the new data that were being collected. This illustrates an important point. It is very seldom indeed that one has *all* the information at the start of a modeling exercise to build a model that can be used, unchanged, forever. Usually one is groping in a situation where data are scarce or fuzzy, where understanding of mechanisms is hazy, and even understanding of objectives is poor. The interplay between modeling and data collection then becomes crucial.

This interplay consists of an iterative process or bootstrap operation as suggested in Chap. 1. The first version of the model is defined in scope by management objectives, while its detailed structure is often constrained by those data that are available from monitoring programs. The model in turn can often refocus management's perception of the problem and lead to a new interpretation of the data or highlight the need for different or additional data to be collected. This in turn leads to a new version of the model, which again changes data requirements or even redefines management objectives, and so on.

The process described in the previous paragraph is very different from the clear-cut recipe of first building a model, then validating it, and finally using it. Validation in this example consisted of comparing the model with census data and discovering that one could fit the data in a number of different ways. There was some evidence (in percentage yearlings) to help define one fit as being better than another, but this evidence was not compelling. The modeling exercise was "saved" by the fact that the model was robust—all fits led to the same general interpretation and conclusions. Validation in a formal sense is often impossible; it is replaced by an iterative process, such as that described in the last paragraph, during which one slowly gains confidence in the model.

The fact that one model is subsequently replaced by another does not necessarily mean that the first model is outmoded. Despite the fact that it was subsequently extended, the original wildebeest model served the valuable purpose of defining conditions, in terms of calf survival rate and the number of adult wildebeest killed per year, under which the decline in the population would be halted or reversed.

The extended model did not significantly alter these guidelines. In fact, by the time additional data had been collected and used to redesign the model, the original model had already led to specific management actions. Faced with the enormous task of possibly having to remove 30 percent of the lion population (as suggested by efforts to stabilize the model population), the biologists exercised their imaginations and ultimately embarked on the clever strategy of reducing predator (lion and hyena) numbers even more drastically, but only in those localized areas where wildebeest traditionally congregated during the calving season. At the same time, to encourage the wildebeest to congregate in those areas, management implemented a policy of burning the grass at a suitable time of the year. In due course the wildebeest population recovered.

SOME COMMENTS ON THE MODELING APPROACH

Field biologists often stress the importance of thinking holistically and are very aware of the fact that they are dealing with a system of complex interactions. This awareness is often lost at the decision-making level, where attention is focused on a "problem." The process of *building* a model highlights the aspects of the system that are crucial at the decision-making level.

The practical results of a modeling exercise can often *appear* trivial or disappointing. The suggestion, in this example, that lions *should* have been cropped while the wildebeest were being cropped was, in retrospect, obvious. That it was neither trivial nor a waste of time is evident from the fact that the lions had *not*, in practice, been cropped.

In Chap. 1 we pointed out that at each level of resolution there are appropriate questions to ask of a model. The way in which we use Fig.2.5 illustrates this. It shows what combination of calf survival and number of adult wildebeest killed by lions per year will stabilize the wildebeest population, but it does not *and cannot* suggest specific ways of engineering these conditions. It has neither the data nor the structure to produce remedies. Figure 2.5 does, however, encourage management to think usefully about remedies, and asking, for example, *how* to double the calf survival rate eventually leads to practical solutions.

Note how the construction of a zebra model, similar in design to the wildebeest model, extended the data base for this exercise and enabled us to make useful comparisons. It is interesting to note that many modelers would have been tempted to build a model that encompassed wildebeest, zebra, lion, and their interactions, including a mechanism for prey selection as prey numbers changed. There were in fact no data to support such a model and no compelling reasons for building it. (If zebra and wildebeest had been the *only* important prey species for lion, that might have been a reason for building a more complex model despite the lack of data.)

Unless there are good reasons for doing so, the temptation to build more complex models in ecology can often usefully be resisted and transformed into the building of a few simple, parallel models that can be interpreted in combination. The purpose of building models is not to *mimic* nature, but to enable one to *think usefully* about a problem.

It should also be noted that we have succeeded in extracting part of a system and modeling it, just as we suggested in Chap. 1. The secret of doing this lies in the way in which we *manipulate* the lion numbers, killrate, and calf survival to account for the rest of the complex system. If we did not manipulate these parameters, the model would be too simple; if we tried to *predict* the way in which the parameters change, the model would be too complex in relation to our level of understanding.

Finally, it is important to note how we have used numbers in this modeling exercise. To begin with, numbers are very important. Our model reflects the way in which an accountant would audit the wildebeest population, and the crucial feature of the audit is whether or not the wildebeest population is showing an annual profit or loss. However, we know that some of the numbers we have used are nothing more than reasonable guesses, so we have to be wary of trusting the numbers produced by the computer model. The approach we have taken is to treat these numbers *qualitatively*. We have argued that this is the sort of thing that happens if we assume certain numbers, then we have shown that the qualitative argument is robust if we assume different numbers. This approach of interpreting numbers qualitatively and searching for robust conclusions is the nub of good and effective modeling.

A model is *not*, ultimately, concerned with numbers. The numbers are only a vehicle for the logic.

FURTHER READING

Background information on wildebeest and zebra can be found in Estes (1976), Talbot and Talbot (1963), and Smuts (1976a). The management problem addressed in this chapter is discussed by Smuts (1978a). The response of predators to prey availability (which we deliberately did not include in the model) is analyzed in Holling (1965). The original paper on the wildebeest model is Starfield et al. (1976) and the use of the model under different circumstances is described in Berry (1981).

Walters and Gross (1972) describe single-species models that are similar in approach to the wildebeest model and show how they can be used by management. Pojar (1981) reviews a number of simple single-species models and discusses the reasons for their success or failure from a management point of view. Euler and Morris (1984) describe a model of white-tailed deer where man is the predator, while the model on caribou dynamics by Walters et al.(1975) was built to identify the important factors inhibiting the growth of the population. Connolly (1978) reviews various models of birth and death processes used to evaluate control measures on coyote. A somewhat different wildebeest model is described by Sinclair and Hilborn (1979).

The concept of using numerical models to think in a qualitative way is illustrated most effectively in Ludwig et al. (1978).

An Exploratory Stochastic Model

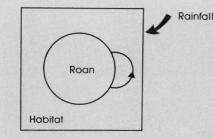

The roan (*Hippotragus equinus*) is a magnificent antelope that inhabits tall open grasslands. It is a fussy feeder, prefering the inflorescent tips of mature grasses, and for this reason is seldom found in high densities. There are areas of Africa where populations of roan antelope thrive, albeit still at low densities. The park we are considering, however, lies at the edge of the geographical range for roan in Africa and has a small population of some 300 animals. Management's concern is how to protect (if necessary) and maintain this population.

Roan are to be found in small breeding herds of up to about 15 animals. They breed at any time during the year, and a mature cow can produce six calves in a period of five years. Consequently, they have a high breeding potential. For the first six weeks of its life, a calf is left concealed in tall grass and is only visited and suckled by its mother early each morning. These six weeks are the most vulnerable of a roan's life, and mortality during this period can be as high as 80 percent when there is insufficient cover to conceal the

calf effectively from predators. This, together with their grazing per-
ferences, determines the mix of habitat that roan require. The availability
and distribution of habitat is thus believed to be an important influence on
roan population dynamics.

Each roan herd is in the care of a single mature bull. He largely determines the herd size and the area utilized by the herd. He will evict
young bulls and sometimes even heifers when they reach sexual maturity
(at about $2\frac{1}{2}$ years). The evicted young males form bachelor groups in
which there is an established hierarchy. The dominant bull in this group
will eventually challenge a herd bull and secure a herd of his own.

Each herd utilizes a large area of about 6 to 10 thousand ha. This so-
called activity zone contains both prime and marginal habitat. The herd
bull does not actively defend the entire activity zone, but in a sense
"sweeps" it clear as the herd wanders through and utilizes different areas.
In this way the size of the activity zone is really determined by the bull
and not directly by water and food (which will always be there in excess in
such a large area). However, the impetus to maintain large activity zones,
and hence low densities, probably evolved from the roan's special habitat
needs.

Calves join the herd when they are six weeks old. There they tend to
associate with animals of a similar age. This association develops into a
strong bond that is still apparent when they are adults, and like-aged units
form identifiable subgroups within a herd. Subgroups are sometimes also
based on cow-calf bonds.

Within a herd there is also a strict hierarchy among the cows. This
can lead to friction between the dominant cow and the next cow in line,
who may then try to avoid the dominant cow and gradually drift away
from the main herd with her subgroup. In due course this splinter group
may be picked up by an adult bull and form a new breeding herd with an
activity zone that probably overlaps the zone of the original herd to a certain extent. Since the new herd is likely to be subordinate to the main
herd, it will utilize less suitable habitat most of the time.

Despite roan's high breeding potential, roan densities are always
low. It follows that the low densities must be related to habitat
requirements and must be maintained, as we have seen, by social behavior. When densities are low and rainfall fluctuates, there is always the possibility that actual numbers will become, in the words of the manager,
dangerously low, especially when the habitat in a park is not ideal for
roan. The management problems we therefore face are: Do roan need
special care in a park of this kind? If so, what are appropriate management actions?

BUILDING THE MODEL

In Chap. 2 we stressed how important the management objectives are in
helping us design an appropriate model. Our approach there was to design

the model from the top (i.e., the management objectives) down instead of from the bottom (i.e., the system components) up. We will use the same approach here.

The management objectives for roan are broadly similar to those for the wildebeest in Chap. 2. Management wants to know what, if anything, can be done to help promote the population. In the case of the wildebeest, however, this question was asked during a crisis and was clearly focused on the problem of a rapidly declining population. Here the question is more subtle; it stems from the fact that the park is at the edge of the normal geographic range for roan. Consequently, there are only a few areas in the park that provide the kind of habitat roan need, so the total population is small. This in itself is not a major concern. The problem is that the population also fluctuates, and in so doing generates concern for the roan whenever it is close to the low point of a cycle. Management wants to know what can be done about this. Answering that question requires an understanding of the internal mechanisms and external influences that contribute to changes in the roan population, and of how they interact. This is where building a model can be useful.

Our strategy, therefore, is to identify the most important influences on the roan population, to put them together in a model, then to explore their interactions. In this way we hope to gain some insight into the manager's dilemma.

The Important Influences on Roan Dynamics

From the description of roan in the introduction we can identify the following important factors:

Suitable habitat: We know that roan occur in low densities and require a large activity zone. We also know that they have specific requirements (for calving and feeding) within that activity zone.

Rainfall: In a suitable habitat, the amount of rainfall determines the quality of that habitat from year to year. Roan depend on mature grass stands for both food and cover for their calves.

Predation: Since roan occur in low densities, they can never be an important component in a predator's diet, but they will be taken opportunistically, and young calves will be especially vulnerable if there is insufficient cover.

Competition with other grazers: Large herds of zebra, wildebeest, or buffalo could keep the grass low and unsuitable for roan. Their presence could also attract predators and increase opportunistic predation on roan.

Reproductive potential: We know that a mature cow can produce up to six calves in five years.

Social influences: We suspect that the ejection of the occasional heifer from the herd and the formation of subgroups that split off from the herd and perhaps form new herds are important both as dispersal mechanisms and in their effect on the dynamics of the population.

A Preliminary Design

This chapter and Chap. 2 started out with similar management questions, but because the context in which those questions are asked is different in the two cases, and because roan and wildebeest behave in very different ways, the model we are about to build for roan should be completely different from the wildebeest model. It is useful to define the differences:

1. With wildebeest we were dealing with large numbers (several thousands), while with roan we are trying to model a population of a few hundred.
2. We hypothesized that predation was a crucial factor in wildebeest population dynamics, whereas predation would appear to be only one of a number of factors affecting roan population dynamics.
3. The social behavior of wildebeest was never an important issue. While we saw that large herds tended to fragment into smaller groups when the grass was high, we had no need to ask how this happened or to model the smaller groups independently. We suspect that social behavior may be an important factor in the roan model.
4. Wildebeest (except for lone bulls) are not territorial animals, but the use of territory, in the sense of activity zones, is important to roan.

Chance effects are more noticeable and important in the dynamics of a small population than in a large one. Point 1 therefore tells us that while a deterministic model is suitable for the wildebeest, we will almost certainly have to build a stochastic model for roan. We may in fact have to simulate the life history of each individual roan.

Points 2 and 3 remind us that the roan model will have to be more complex and detailed than the wildebeest model. We will address this later.

Point 4 tells us that we will have to model the spatial aspects of roan behavior—the model must somehow represent the activity zones utilized by each breeding herd. This is a good starting point for our preliminary design.

We need to represent both prime and marginal activity zones and the way in which they overlap or border on each other. A simple way of doing this is to imagine a set of squares, as in Fig. 3.1, where each square represents a prime habitat for a single herd. Interspersed between and around these squares are circles representing the marginal habitats. These could

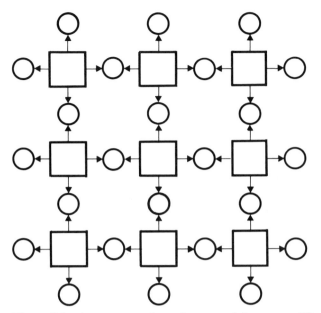

Figure 3.1 A representation of roan activity zones. The squares denote prime habitat and the circles marginal habitat.

be utilized by splinter groups that leave the herd and eventually attract (or are attracted by) a bull to form a new breeding herd.

Since the splinter groups are likely to remain close to and perhaps partly in the activity zone of the herd they have left, we can specify which marginal habitats are associated with which prime habitats by drawing arrows as in Fig. 3.1. We assume that some marginal habitats will be accessible from more than one prime habitat. There will be many more marginal habitats than prime habitats.

Recognizing the importance of habitat and representing activity zones in this way is an important step toward defining the type of model we are going to build. Think of Fig. 3.1 as a board, rather like a chessboard, on which we are going to design a game that simulates the dynamics of the roan population in the area of the park the board represents. The pawns in this game will be individual roan antelope and each roan will be associated with a particular activity zone. The rules of the game must allow roan to produce calves, to split off on occasion to form a splinter group, and to die or survive from one time step to the next depending on rainfall, predation, interspecific competition, and whether the roan has the use of a prime or marginal activity zone.

This game includes all the important influences we listed earlier and reflects the complexity we decided would distinguish the roan model from the wildebeest model. It provides a framework within which we will be able to keep track of each roan as an individual. To do this, the following information will have to be computed and stored for every roan on the board: (1) sex; (2) age; (3) if the roan is female, when it last produced a calf; (4) which activity zone it occupies; and (5) its associates and position in the male or female hierarchy.

There are approximately 300 roan in the entire park. The population in an isolated area represented by our model is therefore unlikely to exceed about 200. From the computational point of view there is no difficulty in storing this level of detail for each animal. The only task that might require some imagination is the design of an algorithm to represent association (subgroups within the herd) and position in the hierarchy.

The model is beginning to take shape. The next question is deciding on a suitable time step. We want to compute the population at least once a year; are there any compelling reasons for computing it more often? The answer is no, unless we take cognizance of the information that on average a mature cow will produce six calves in five years.

There are two ways we can model this: Choose a time step of 10 months and postulate that every mature cow produces one calf during each time step, or choose a time step of a year and allow cows on occasion (in fact with a probability of 0.2) to produce twins. The disadvantage of the first method is that a time step of 10 months is clumsy to work with. It is difficult to relate the output to annual censuses and also difficult to convert data such as mean seasonal rainfall to intervals of 10 months. We therefore choose the second method.

We have already decided that our model should be stochastic. What does this mean? Suppose we know that the survival rate for roan calves is 0.6. In a deterministic model we assume that 60 percent of the calves will survive. In a stochastic model we interpret the survival rate as a survival *probability*—i.e., the probability that a calf will still be alive after one year is 0.6. We then compute whether or not each calf survives as follows. For each animal we generate a random number from a flat distribution between 0 and 1. (A flat distribution implies that all numbers between 0 and 1 have an equal chance of coming up.) If the random number lies between 0 and the calf's probability of survival (in this case 0.6), the calf survives; if not, it dies.

On average, for a large number of calves, this algorithm will ensure that only 60 percent survive, but in any one year, if there are only a few calves, almost anything can happen. This approach ties in well with our chosen method for modeling births. We can use the same random number generator to decide (with probability 0.2) whether or not each mature cow will produce two calves during the year.

At this stage, the algorithm for our model is as follows:

1. Set up a chessboard of prime and marginal habitats.
2. Define an initial population, specifying the age, sex, activity zone, position in the hierarchy, and associates of each animal.
3. To update the model from one year to the next:
   a. Choose an appropriate survival probability for each roan.

b. Determine stochastically whether each roan survives. If it does, note the fact that it is one year older.

c. Allow all mature cows to produce one calf and possibly two.

d. Model social interactions such as expulsion of young males, changes in hierarchy, formation of subgroups, and splintering and formation of new herds.

Steps 3a and 3d are the most difficult to implement. We begin by thinking about the *minimum* information we need to define the survival probabilities in step 3a. First, we have to account for differences in age and sex. As a minimum we can assume one set of survival probabilities for calves, irrespective of sex, and another two sets (one for males and one for females) for all roan over the age of one year. Next, each set will have to be modified, depending on the mean annual rainfall (which will affect calves and adults in different ways) and also whether the roan occupies a prime or marginal activity zone. Finally, the survival probabilities will have to be modified yet again to reflect predation and competition with other grazers. This entails a lot of information, most of which will be sheer guesswork on our part!

At this stage we get the feeling that our model is running away from us. A logical approach is leading us toward a model that requires a great deal of data we do not have. Moreover, if we look back at our objectives, this is going to be an exploratory model, which means we want to see what happens when we change our data. The more data we have, particularly when it comes from guesswork, the harder it will be to see what happens. The approach we are following could be very fruitful if we had access to good, detailed data for roan, but for our purposes it is likely to be confusing rather than enlightening. We need to find a way of simplifying our design without sacrificing any of its vital components.

A Simplified Design

The habitat aspect of our preliminary model is essential. If we are to simplify the model in any way, it will have to be in our representation of the roan themselves. A useful question to ask, whenever one models a population, is whether the males can be ignored. The answer in this case is yes: It is reasonable to assume that a breeding herd or splinter group will always find or be found by a mature bull. We can then concentrate in our model on the breeding herds, or more specifically the females in the breeding herds.

This suggests a further simplification. Suppose we model each herd as an entity instead of trying to model every individual cow. The major disadvantage of doing this will be a loss of resolution. We will no longer, for example, be able to distinguish between calves and mature cows. The major advantage will be in having a model that is easy to manipulate and understand. This is an advantage we will come to appreciate in what follows.

The revised algorithm for our simplified model is then:

1. Set up a chessboard of prime and marginal activity zones (as before).
2. Define an initial population (i.e., specify the number of females in each herd in each activity zone).
3. To update the model from one year to the next:
   a. Depending on the annual rainfall, predation, and interspecific competition, choose two rates of increase (or decrease), one for herds in prime habitat, and one for herds in marginal habitat.
   b. Apply the appropriate rate of increase to each herd.
   c. If a herd drops below a specified level (let us call it H_{min}), assume it is no longer viable and dies out.
   d. If the herd exceeds a certain size (let us call it H_{up}), assume it may split with a probability P.
   e. If the herd does split, assume a fraction f will break away while the rest remain behind.
   f. Move the splinter group at random to any vacant adjacent activity zone.
   g. If all the adjacent activity zones are occupied, assume that the splinter group dies out.

This structure is in fact almost a complete set of rules for "playing the game" on the activity-zone chessboard. It considerably reduces both the detail and the amount of input data. For example, it is far easier to guess a rate of increase for the female segment of a herd than to specify survival probabilities for the different age and sex classes in it. At the same time it allows for a simulation that takes into account all the important influences on the roan population. In the following sections we will fill in further details of this simplified model, guess at the input data, and explore its behavior.

IMPLEMENTING THE SIMPLIFIED MODEL

We begin by looking at some of the details involved in updating this model from one year to the next. The first step is to define precisely what we mean by the rate of increase of a herd, then to choose appropriate rates of increase for herds in prime and marginal habitat. If $herd_t$ is the number of females in a herd in year t and $herd_{t+1}$ is the number of females in the same herd in year $t + 1$, the equation for updating the herd from one year to the next is,

$$herd_{t+1} = herd_t + k \, herd_t \qquad (3.1)$$

We call k the rate of increase if it is positive and the rate of decrease if it is negative. The factors that will affect k are predation, interspecific competition, and rainfall (via its effect on the vegetation). Of these, rainfall is likely to be the most important.

We have no data at all on the effect of rainfall on the roan (contrast this situation with that of the kudu model in Chap. 8), so there is no point in trying to specify rainfall too precisely. On the other hand, we want to explore how variations in rainfall are likely to influence the roan. A good compromise is to treat the rainfall qualitatively. We could do this by introducing four classes of rainfall, numbering them from 1 to 4, where 1 represents a very dry year and 4 a very wet year. We could then argue (again, because we have no real data) how the rate of increase k might be influenced by each of the rainfall classes. For example, in a very dry year (class 1) but in prime habitat, we might expect to lose all new-born calves and possibly also an older cow. If we guess that one cow in ten is really old, this suggests a rate of decrease for the herd of about 0.1—i.e., $k = -0.1$. In a marginal territory, more adults are likely to die, suggesting a rate of decrease closer to 0.2.

On the other hand, in a very wet year (class 4) in prime habitat, probably six out of ten cows will be mature and are likely to produce about seven calves in a year, so three to four female calves could be added to the herd. If only one of these dies and all adult cows survive, we could have a herd increase rate of about 0.25. In a very wet year the differences between prime and marginal habitats are likely to be less marked, so the rate of increase in a marginal habitat would probably be close to 0.20. Table 3.1 summarizes plausible values for k for all combinations of rainfall and habitat types. We will use these values in what we will call our standard set of input data.

TABLE 3.1 THE STANDARD DATA SET FOR THE ROAN MODEL

Annual growth rates k				
	Rainfall			
	1	2	3	4
k in prime zones	−0.08	+0.02	+0.12	+0.22
k in marginal zones	−0.15	−0.05	+0.05	+0.15

Herd parameters
Smallest viable herd, $H_{\min} = 3$
Proportion that split off, $f = 0.33$
Smallest herd that can split, $H_{\mathrm{up}} = 8$
Probability of splitting, $P = 0.5$

Standard 12-year rainfall cycle
2 2 1 1 2 2 3 3 4 4 3 3

We now have an idea of how we can put numbers into a model even when we have no data. Similarly, we can modify the numbers to simulate the effects of predation and interspecific competition. For example, we could ignore interspecific competition in a year of good rainfall, but further reduce the rate of increase of the herd in a dry year if we know there are large herds of competing grazers in the area. Conversely, an increase in predation will have little effect in a dry year (we have in any case assumed that all calves die) but will reduce the rate of increase in a wet year.

Referring back to the structure of the simplified model, we next need to specify the size of the smallest herd that is likely to survive (H_{min}); this would probably be two or three. (We will choose three for our standard data set.) Then we need a value for H_{up}, the herd size when splitting could first occur. This must lie somewhere between five and ten; we will use eight in our standard data set. The probability that the herd will split should increase as the herd grows, but since we have no data to support this, we will assume a simple step function: The probability is 0 for all herds below H_{up}, has a value P (at a guess $P = 0.5$) for all herd sizes between H_{up} and twice H_{up}, and is 1.0 thereafter—i.e., any herd that grows to twice H_{up} will definitely split at the next opportunity. The fraction f that breaks away when a herd does split will probably lie between 0.2 and 0.5; we will choose a value of 0.33.

What happens if we have a herd of 10 and the model decides it is about to split with the fraction f equal to 0.33? Obviously we cannot remove 3.3 animals. What we do in this case (and other similar cases) is generate a random number from a flat distribution between 0 and 1. If the random number is less than 0.3, we form a splinter group of four and leave behind a herd of six, otherwise the splinter group is three and the herd seven. Why? Exactly the same technique is used to determine the herd size whenever herd$_{t+1}$ as calculated from Eq. (3.1) is not an integer. Our simplified model is thus still a stochastic model: One set of results can be quite different from another even if we do not change any of the input data other than the seed for the random number generator. However, it is not as stochastic in detail as the design for our preliminary model.

We now have enough of a feel for the input data our model requires to set up a trial run. What should we try to simulate? Trial runs should always be chosen in such a way that they exercise the model as extensively as possible. In our case we want to model a situation that leads to large changes in the roan population. One way of doing this is to start with a small population and see how it grows and disperses. This is in itself an interesting exercise. Management may want to consider introducing or reintroducing roan into areas that might be suitable for them. It will also test out the mechanisms we have introduced for herd splitting and the algorithm, summarized next, for movement of a herd from one activity zone to another.

The chessboard depicted in Fig. 3.1 does not at all imply that roan activity zones, viewed from above, would look like a chessboard. On the contrary, an activity zone is a loose concept and Fig. 3.1 is merely a convenient way of depicting the association between marginal and prime activity zones. The figure does not show how marginal zones may overlap, but this is made clear in the following algorithm:

1. If the herd in a prime activity zone splits, the splinter groups can move into any marginal zone that overlaps with that prime zone.
2. If a prime activity zone is vacant, the largest (and therefore most dominant) herd in the overlapping marginal zones will move into it.
3. If a herd in a marginal zone splits, the splinter group can move into any other marginal zone that shares the same prime zone. (If a marginal zone is associated with two prime zones, the herd can search for a vacant place in any of the seven other marginal zones that overlap with one or other of the two prime zones.)

GROWTH AND DISPERSION: INITIAL RESULTS

Figure 3.1 depicts an area that contains 9 prime activity zones and 24 marginal activity zones. Suppose that it represents an area that initially contains no roan and that we introduce two herds, each containing ten females, into the first two prime activity zones. What subsequently happens to those roan will depend to a large extent on how the rainfall varies from one year to the next. To facilitate direct comparisons between different simulations we need to standardize the rainfall pattern that drives the model. We will assume that the rainfall is the same over the entire area and will use a rainfall cycle of 12 years that is repeated indefinitely. The first six years of a cycle are low rainfall years, the rest high rainfall years, as described in Table 3.1. We introduce the two herds at a time that corresponds to the fifth year of a cycle (i.e., just after the two driest years).

Since our model is stochastic rather than deterministic, we cannot compute a single simulation, then present just one graph to show what would happen to the roan population under the above circumstances. Each time we change the seed of our random number generator, we are likely to get a different result.

Figure 3.2(a), however, is typical of the kind of result the model produces if we use the standard data set described in Table 3.1. It is a plausible result. It shows the population increasing during the wet portion of the rainfall cycle and declining during the dry portion, but in such a way that there is a net upward trend. A more detailed look at the computer output shows that herds in prime activity zones provide the main reservoir for growth and dispersion during the wet years. Losses during the dry years are particularly high for newly established herds in marginal zones; they all suffer a reduction in size and some are eliminated entirely.

Figure 3.2(a) suggests that our standard data set represents a fairly

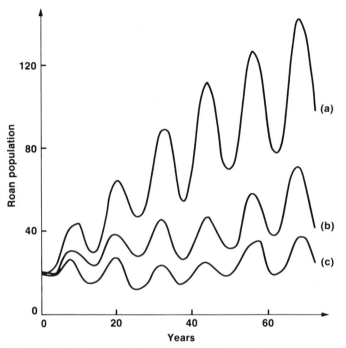

Figure 3.2 The growth of a roan population from an initial population of two herds. The rainfall cycle repeats itself every 12 years. (a) shows a typical result using the standard data set; (b) and (c) are examples of results obtained if the conditions in the prime activity zones are less favorable for roan.

healthy roan population. In view of roan's high reproductive potential, one could imagine roan growing and dispersing at a faster rate under ideal conditions, but perhaps not all that much faster if the rainfall fluctuates in the way we have specified (with 2 really bad years out of 12).

What happens if we try to model a roan population in less favorable circumstances? Suppose that the prime activity zones are only slightly better than the marginal zones. We could model this by subtracting, say, 0.04 from all the herd growth rates that apply to prime habitat in Table 3.1. Two typical results are shown in Fig. 3.2(b) and (c). Both results suggest that the roan are struggling to establish themselves, more so in Fig. 3.2(c) than in Fig. 3.2(b).

There are several interesting points to be made if we stop and look in some detail at the results from these (and similar) simulations.

We built the model in the hope of gaining some insight into what differentiated a healthy roan population from one under stress. Figure 3.2 shows that by manipulating the input data we can get output from our model that can indeed be interpreted as "healthy" or "struggling."

The difference between the two examples is brought home by looking at how the populations dispersed in each case. After four rainfall cycles (48 years), all nine prime activity zones in the simulation corresponding to Fig. 3.2(a) were occupied, and at various times there were up to 14 herds in marginal zones. After the same period there were only five and three herds in prime zones in the simulations corresponding to Fig. 3.2(b) and (c) respectively, and at no time were there more than four herds in marginal zones.

This suggests a *qualitative* difference between the results depicted in the two figures, one that can be confirmed by performing more simulations with similar input data (but different random seeds). All simulations using input data for Fig. 3.2(a) tell the same story, that of a population that realizes its high reproductive potential during the wet years and expands and sends out splinter groups. Some of these groups die out during the dry years, but some survive and in turn grow and disperse during the wet years. The population always has a strong upward trend, and although one simulation may differ from another in detail, all can be represented in essentials by the graph shown in Fig. 3.2(a).

On the other hand, the simulations using the input data for Figs. 3.2(b) and (c) are more variable. Some, such as Fig. 3.2(b), suggest a very slow but fairly steady net increase in the population, while others show a population that can barely maintain itself, as in Fig. 3.2(c). Here, conditions in the prime activity zones prevent the roan from fully exploiting their high reproductive potential. The herds do indeed grow during the wet years, but more slowly, so they tend to split less frequently. When they do split, the splinter groups tend to be smaller. As a result, very few survive the dry years, so the process of splitting often weakens the herds in the prime zones without contributing to dispersion of the population.

Under these circumstances, chance plays an important role. If a herd delays splitting for a year, or if a small splinter herd happens to survive the dry years or manages to find a vacant zone of prime habitat sooner rather than later, this can have a marked effect on the total population. Figures 3.2(b) and (c) illustrate this effect. The basic story behind these two figures is similar, and the obvious differences between them (differences that would be very important to a manager) are in fact purely a matter of chance!

It is fascinating to note that even at this preliminary stage of exercising the model we have produced results that are exciting to interpret. These results are of course implicit in the way in which we have constructed the model—we have made them happen, but they come as a surprise. They lead us to two hypotheses we would probably never have thought of if we had not built the model.

The first is that there are two basically different types of dynamics a roan population can exhibit. One type is what we will call the *acceleration mode*—the population is like an engine that starts up and accelerates without any difficulty. This is illustrated by Fig. 3.2(a). In the second type the engine is always on the verge of stalling and one is never quite sure if and when it will finally accelerate. We will call this the *stalling mode* and it is illustrated by Figs. 3.2(b) and (c).

The second hypothesis is that the stalling mode leads to results that are far less predictable (i.e., far more variable) than the acceleration mode. Trying to prove or disprove these hypotheses give us a definite direction to take when we explore the properties of our model more fully.

GROWTH AND DISPERSION: FURTHER RESULTS

Now that we have some confidence in the way our model operates and have tentative hypotheses to test, the time has come to explore the behavior of the model in a systematic way. In the previous section we showed the results of just a few simulations. To draw robust conclusions from a stochastic model one has to do more than this. Each simulation has to be repeated a number of times, each time using a different seed for the random number generator. It is as though we were performing an experiment in the field. Repeating the calculation with a different seed is like adding one more replicate to the experiment. Conclusions can only be drawn by looking for common trends in the replicates (i.e., calculating means) and evaluating the reproducibility of those trends (i.e., calculating variances).

Thus, to compare the two cases illustrated in Fig. 3.2 in a statistically meaningful way, we would first simulate, say, 20 replicates using the standard data set in Table 3.1, then compute another 20 replicates using the modified data set with lower growth rates for the prime activity zones. We would then have to compare two sets of 20 graphs each, an impossible task unless we can identify specific features that can be extracted and compared systematically.

For example, since we are trying in our computer experiments to see how fast an initial population of 20 females will grow and disperse, we might want to record when the population first reaches 40, when it first reaches 60, and so on. These times will vary from one replicate to another, but we can easily adjust our computer program to record them, then calculate average values and variances for the 20 replicates.

Some results obtained in this way are shown in Figs. 3.3. and 3.4. They contain just a few results from computer experiments aimed at exploring how growth and dispersion were affected by changes in the various parameters of the model. The figures should be looked at carefully because, together with the data they were based on and data from similar computer experiments, they lead to interesting conclusions.

In Fig. 3.3 we have varied H_{min}, the size of the smallest herd that can survive as an entity. Increasing H_{min} from 2 to 3 has only a small effect, but increasing it from 3 to 4 severely retards the growth of the population. What has occurred (and this is supported by the detailed computer output) is a switch from one mode of behavior (the accelerating mode) to another (the stalling mode). When H_{min} is equal to 4, very few of the splinter herds manage to survive. The figure supports our first hypothesis.

Comparing Fig. 3.3(a) with Fig. 3.3(b) we see that the effect of one

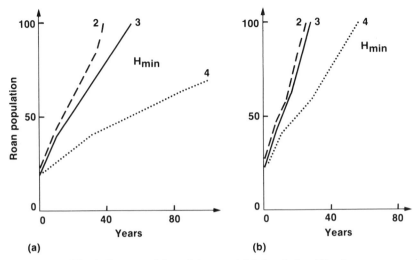

Figure 3.3 The influence of the minimum viable herd size (H_{min}) on an expanding roan population: (a) using standard herd growth rates and (b) increasing herd growth rates in both prime and marginal zones by 0.025. (*Note:* These graphs are the average of 20 replicates.)

parameter on the model can be modified by the effect of another. Both figures show a significant change in behavior when H_{min} is increased from 3 to 4, but the effect is less noticeable at higher growth rates. This has implications for management. Certain actions or events might have effects that are barely noticeable in suitable habitat. The same actions or events could, however, have a major impact in areas that are less suitable for roan.

In Fig. 3.4 we have altered the growth rates, first in marginal zones, then in good zones. The figure again supports our first hypothesis: The effect of reducing growth rates is at first relatively small (we are still in the accelerating mode of behavior), but at some stage there is a switch from the accelerating mode to the stalling mode, evidenced by a sudden and major retardation in population growth. Again, by comparing Fig. 3.4(a) and (b), we see that this effect can be mediated by changes in other parameters of the model.

Figure 3.4 also shows that the model is far more sensitive to a reduction in the growth rates in prime habitats than to a corresponding reduction in growth rates in marginal habitats. This is of direct consequence to management. It suggests that one can more effectively help roan to colonize a new area by improving conditions for them (e.g., by controlling predators or discouraging competing herbivores) in the choice habitat rather than in the more marginal habitat portions of that area.

So far, we have only been looking at average values for the time it takes the population to reach specific target values. We also need to look

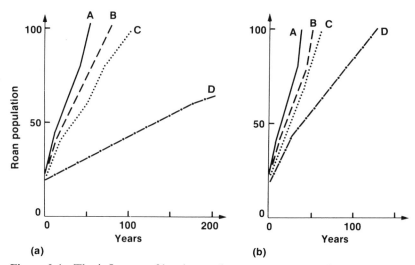

Figure 3.4   The influence of herd growth rates on an expanding roan population: (a) $H_{min} = 3$, and (b) $H_{min} = 2$. The cases considered are: A—standard growth rates; B—growth rates in all marginal zones reduced by 0.04; C—growth rates in all prime zones reduced by 0.02; D—growth rates in all prime zones reduced by 0.04. (*Note:* These graphs are the average of 20 replicates.)

at the variance, which is a measure of how the actual values deviate from the mean. Suppose, we wish to compare the variance in the time taken to reach a target of 60 roan in the standard run with the corresponding variance when we reduce the growth rates in good zones by 0.04. From Fig. 3.4(a) we can see that the average times taken to reach the target population are 26 and 177 years respectively. Because one time is so much larger than the other, we would expect the variance in the latter case to be correspondingly larger, even if the behavior of the system in the second case were intrinsically no more variable than its behavior in the standard case.

We can get around this difficulty by scaling the variance—i.e., we calculate the *coefficient of variation,* defined as the square root of the variance divided by the mean. If we find that the coefficient of variation in one case is larger than in the other, we can safely conclude that the behavior of the population is inherently more variable in the case with the larger coefficient.

Table 3.2 shows the coefficient of variation as computed for some of the cases graphed in Figs. 3.3 and 3.4. It shows a striking increase in the coefficient of variation for those cases we have identified as the stalling mode of behavior. This is evidence in support of our second hypothesis—that the population growth in the stalling mode is inherently more variable (and therefore more unpredictable) than in the acceleration mode.

This has unfortunate implications for management. It implies that the roan populations that are most likely to need management action are also the population where the outcome of any management action is least predictable.

An example of the unpredictability of management action follows. Suppose that management decides to introduce not 20 but 40 roan (4 herds of 10) into the area represented by our standard data set. If we simulate this, we discover that *on average* this is beneficial. The population reaches the specified targets in a shorter time. However, the last entry in Table 3.2 shows that the coefficient of variation in this case is extraordinarily high. Sometimes the 40 roan are lucky in the first few years of the simulation. The population grows and disperses quickly (and so the management action is justified). At other times the roan are unlucky in the first few years of the simulation, their population dwindles, and it takes as long to recover as it would have taken if fewer roan had been introduced in the first place.

The innate variability in the population dynamics in the stalling mode has yet another unfortunate consequence for management. It implies that one cannot draw definite conclusions from limited field data or from the results of previous management actions. For example, if an attempt to improve conditions for roan in an area fails, that does not necessarily imply unsound management; under slightly different circumstances that same attempt might well have succeeded.

There are many other ways we could explore how the parameters of our model influence the growth and dispersion of a small roan population. We cannot, however, make an exhaustive study here. Our examples suffice to give a flavor of what one can learn about growth and dispersion by exploring the properties of a stochastic model.

TABLE 3.2 THE COEFFICIENT OF VARIATION IN SIX SETS OF SIMULATIONS STARTING WITH TWO HERDS OF TEN ROAN EACH

| | Coefficient of variation | |
Description of the simulation	in the time taken to reach 60 roan	in the time taken to reach 80 roan
The standard data set	0.27	0.23
Putting $H_{min} = 2$	0.20	0.27
Putting $H_{min} = 4$	0.73	0.43
Growth rates in all marginal zones reduced by 0.04	0.33	0.20
Growth rates in all prime zones reduced by 0.04	0.60	0.63
Similar to previous run, but starting with four herds of 10 roan each	1.50	1.00

EXPLORING THE BEHAVIOR OF AN ESTABLISHED ROAN POPULATION

So far we have only used our model to explore how roan might establish themselves in a new area. Our original management problem was concerned more with a roan population that was already established but whose numbers were fluctuating in response to changes in rainfall. In this section we will use the model to look at how an established roan population might respond to changes in rainfall from one year to the next.

Imagine a population spread more or less uniformly over the area represented by the chessboard of Fig. 3.1, and suppose that the rainfall varies in time but not in space—i.e., rainfall is also uniform across the board. If we then look at any one prime activity zone together with its overlapping marginal zones in isolation, we can argue that on average the immigration of roan into that area from the rest of the board should balance emigration from that area to the rest of the board. This suggests a further simplification to our model: If we are looking at an established roan population we should be able to get a very good idea of how it behaves just by modeling one prime activity zone with its adjacent marginal zones.

We can also justify this simplification from another point of view. When we were modeling dispersion, movements from marginal to prime habitat occured and played an important part in the simulation. In an established population, however, all prime activity zones are likely to be occupied, and since a herd in prime habitat is unlikely to die out while there is still a viable herd in the overlapping marginal habitats, movement is likely to occur from prime zones to marginal zones but not vice versa. This enables us to concentrate on one prime zone. In the following examples we will in fact model one prime activity zone with four overlapping marginal zones.

This additional simplification is welcome because we want to simulate the population dynamics for very long time periods. To explore the effect of rainfall on the roan systematically, we need to specify a number of different rainfall cycles, then simulate the population's response when each cycle is repeated many times. In this way we can again evaluate trends statistically. The important characteristics of a rainfall cycle are its period (the number of years before the cycle repeats itself) and the mix it contains of wet and dry years. We want to see what happens when we change each of these.

Acceleration Mode and Stalling Mode

When we modeled dispersion we identified two modes of roan dynamics—the acceleration mode that occurred when conditions for roan were favorable and the stalling mode that was induced by less favorable conditions. It would be interesting to know whether the same two modes can be found in an established population and, if so, whether a switch from one mode to the other can be brought about by a change in the rainfall. This suggests a computer experiment in two parts. First, we subject an established population to a long sequence of very favorable rainfall cycles, then we repeat the experiment with a long sequence of much dryer cycles.

Before performing a computer experiment it is always useful to ask two questions: Which numbers in the output should we look at? What do we anticipate they will show?

If we use a 12-year rainfall cycle for both parts of our experiment, we would expect the population to decline during the relatively dry years of the cycle and to recover during the wetter years. To iron out these fluctuations within cycles, we could calculate the average population for each 12-year cycle and see how those averages varied from one cycle to the next. Since the populations in both parts of the experiment are well established, we would expect the average population per cycle to be more or less constant, but at a different level for the two parts of the experiment. If we have thoroughly absorbed what we have learned from our simulations of a dispersing roan population, we might also anticipate more variation between cycles for the experiment with the less favorable (dryer) rainfall.

Figure 3.5 shows a typical pair of results, using the standard data set of Table 3.1 with two different 12-year rainfall cycles. (For the very favorable cycle the two 1's in the standard cycle were replaced by 3's, while for the dryer cycle two 3's were replaced by two 2's.) The average population

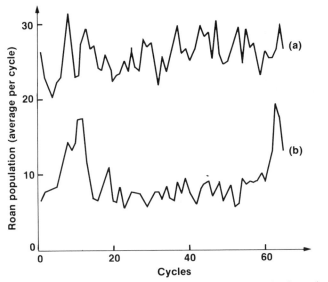

Figure 3.5   The average number of roan (per cycle) in a single prime habitat and its associated marginal habitats: (a) for a cycle of rainfall wetter than the standard (b) for a dryer cycle than the standard.

per cycle is less constant than we anticipated in the previous paragraph. Reasons for this are easy to find: The population will change as herds split, find vacant activity zones, or die out. These variations remind us that our model is stochastic. In fact in Fig. 3.5(a), corresponding to the favorable rainfall cycle, the average number of roan per cycle varies about a mean value of 27 in the random sort of way one would expect from any stochastic model. In Fig. 3.5(b), however, there is more structure to the variations. For the most part the population is low, but every now and then it breaks out to higher values that cannot be sustained. This is precisely the sort of behavior we would expect in our stalling mode.

Looking at the two graphs we also see that the average population per cycle in Fig. 3.5(b) varies between wider limits than in Fig. 3.5(a). This can be substantiated by computing the coefficients of variation—0.38 and 0.08 respecitvely. As in our results for a dispersing populations, we find the stalling mode associated with a greater degree of variability and hence unpredictability.

An interesting feature of the results for dispersing populations was the rather dramatic switch they showed from one mode of behavior to the other. Further computations show that this does not occur in an established population. Instead, as we alter the rainfall cycle, we find a fairly gradual change from the behavior we associate with the acceleration mode to the distinctive dynamics of the stalling mode. (The acceleration mode is in any case a misnomer for an established population.) It is nevertheless useful to think of the two modes of behavior as the two ends of a spectrum, where the acceleration mode is characterized by larger average populations, healthy herds in the marginal activity zones, a low variability, and a resilience to chance events, while the stalling mode is associated with smaller populations, ephemeral herds in marginal zones, and a high degree of variability, hence a vulnerability to chance events.

Several differences between the two modes are important for management. First, it is a population in the stalling mode that requires attention. (In some replicates using the input data for Fig. 3.5(b) the population actually died out.) It would therefore help if one could diagnose, from field observations, whether or not the dynamics of a specific roan population could be classified in the stalling mode. It is far easier to distinguish between the two modes on the computer than in the field, but the model does suggest that the resilience of the splinter groups in marginal habitat is indicative of the health of the population as a whole.

The fact that populations in the stalling mode are so vulnerable to chance events implies that some management actions will have short-lived results. Looking at Fig. 3.5(b), for example, we can surmise that it would not make much difference if management tried to boost the population by introducing a new herd in a marginal zone. The new herd might prosper for a short time, but in the long run it will almost certainly die out.

We can therefore distinguish between management actions that are likely to be ephemeral in their effect (those that do not lead to a switch from the stalling mode to the acceleration mode) and those that could be beneficial in the long run. It is the latter that are significant.

While it is interesting to see what happens if we change the rainfall cycles, from the management point of view we have to learn to live with the rainfall as it is. If the prevailing pattern of rainfall leads to the stalling mode of dynamics, we have to ask what other parameters of the model might have the effect of pushing the system away from the stalling mode toward the acceleration mode. Rainfall, after all, is not the only parameter that determines the dynamics of the population. If we can identify those parameters, we can ask how management actions might alter them, and so identify actions that are potentially significant in the long run. In the next section we will explore the sensitivity of an established roan population to the various parameters of our model.

SENSITIVITY ANALYSIS

In a sensitivity analysis, one systematically and comprehensively tests to see how changes in the parameters of the model affect the model's output. Usually one starts with a typical set of parameter values (such as our standard data set in Table 3.1), then alters parameters one at a time. For a linear model (i.e., one in which all the equations and relationships can be represented by straight lines) this is often sufficient. If the linear model is also deterministic, a great deal of information can be obtained by performing as many simulations as there are independent parameters. An example of sensitivity calculations for a linear model can be found in Table 8.1 of Chap. 8.

Our model is neither linear nor deterministic. This complicates the sensitivity analysis in a number of ways:

1. Because the model is stochastic, each time we alter a parameter we have to perform a set of replicate simulations (each with a different seed for the random number generator) to determine the mean values of our output.
2. Because the model is nonlinear, the consequences of a large change in a parameter cannot be deduced from the sensitivity to a small change.
3. We have already seen in Figs. 3.3 and 3.4 how changing the value of one parameter can mediate the effect of changing another. We therefore have to change parameters individually, in pairs, and, if we are to be thorough, in all possible combinations.
4. Because the model is nonlinear, its sensitivity to different parameters will also depend, in ways that are not obvious, on where we start our sensitivity analysis. We therefore need to repeat the whole analysis using a number of different sets of starting values.

A complete sensitivity analysis of a nonlinear stochastic model can thus be a major computational operation, and anything that reduces the amount of work to be done (and helps us comprehend what we are doing) is welcome. A number of steps can be taken to get the most out of the analysis without pursuing it exhaustively.

We have already taken the first and most important step. In the design of our model we have taken every opportunity to simplify the structure of the model and to limit the amount of input data the model requires. This is where it really pays to have a "lean" model.

We can often reduce the number of independent parameters by combining them in different ways. For example, in the wildebeest model of the previous chapter, our results depended only on the product of the number of lions and the number of wildebeest killed per lion per year. There was therefore no need to investigate these two parameters separately.

A standard way of combining parameters is to group them in dimensionless expressions. For example, both H_{min} and H_{up} are measured in units of "herbivores," so the ratio $H_{min}:H_{up}$ is dimensionless. This is a particularly simple example of a *dimensionless parameter*. The parameters of a model can usually be grouped together in dimensionless expressions in a number of different ways. However, every model has a fixed number of independent dimensionless parameters, and no matter how they are grouped, they are fundamental to the structure of the model. If H_{min}/H_{up} were an independent dimensionless parameter of the roan model, it would be unnecessary to investigate the effect of changing H_{min} and H_{up} separately. Increasing H_{min} would have the same effect as decreasing H_{up}.

A few computations confirm this. For example, we noticed a switch in Fig. 3.3 from the acceleration to the stalling mode as we increased H_{min}. We see the same switch if we decrease H_{up}. It follows that we can also express herd sizes as a fraction of H_{up} instead of in herbivores, in which case we have a *dimensionless variable*. We can think of H_{up} as a natural unit in which to measure herbivores.

We can use the objectives of our model, our intuition, and our experience with the model to concentrate on sensitivity calculations that are likely to be fruitful.

The last point implies a less clinical and more thoughtful approach to the sensitivity analysis—one in which we explore, slowly and step-by-step, what happens as we change the parameter values. In this way we try to understand and absorb what we discover at each step, using that to decide what to alter next. Taking this approach and applying it to the model for an established roan population led to the following conclusions:

1. The dispersion model showed a switch from the acceleration mode to the stalling mode of dynamics as the ratio $H_{min}:H_{up}$ was increased. This provided a good starting point for the sensitivity analysis, which showed that the established population was also sensitive to this ratio. In the dispersal model, a higher value of $H_{min}:H_{up}$ reduced the chances of survival of splinter groups in marginal zones and inhibited dispersal of the population. An increase in the ratio has a similar effect here. Splinter groups are unable to establish temselves in marginal habitat, particularly if they break away during a time of low rainfall. The sensitivity analysis also showed that higher $H_{min}:H_{up}$ ratios made the population more sensitive to all the other parameters of the model. Parameter changes that were insignificant at lower ratios (e.g., changing the fraction f of a herd that split off) had a large effect at higher ratios.

    2. The dispersal model was also sensitive to the herd growth rates in the prime activity zones. An established population is insensitive to growth rates in the prime zones unless they are reduced to the point where, with fluctuations in rainfall, the herd in a prime zone is unlikely to grow to H_{up}.

    3. The dispersal model was not sensitive to herd growth rates in the marginal activity zones. An established roan population is extremely sensitive to these growth rates, which, more than any other parameters, determine the size of the established population and, in particular, how low the population drops during dry periods. For example, using the standard data set of Table 3.1, we find that during 44 percent of all rainfall cycles the total population in the one prime and four marginal activity zones drops below 10 roan. If we reduce the growth rates in the marginal zones by 0.02 for every category of rainfall, the population drops below 10 in 90 percent of all cycles. If instead, we increase the growth rates in the marginal zones by the same amount, the total population never drops below 10.

    4. The established population is sensitive to the length (period) of a rainfall cycle. Longer periods lead to a higher variance between cycles and lower populations during the dry years.

    Points 2 and 3 are illuminating for management. They imply that when a roan population is dispersing in a new area, the herds in the prime habitats are the ones that should be nurtured (e.g., by predator control). In an established roan population, management should concentrate on improving the quality of the marginal habitat areas. In particular, this is the most useful action that can be taken to prevent roan numbers from becoming dangerously low during dry periods.

DISCUSSION

Some interesting ideas arise out of our experiences with the roan model.

    The model was built with certain management concerns and objectives in mind. The impetus for building models often comes from scientific curiosity rather than management needs. For instance, we might have asked, without any reference to management, what determines the geographical range of the roan antelope. If we had done so, we would have established the need to understand the interaction between rainfall, habitat, and the social behavior of roan, and built a model to explore that interaction. The objectives of the model would thus have been so similar to our management objectives that we might well have designed much the same model.

In fact, we can attempt to answer the scientific question on the basis of what we have learned from our model. We can hypothesize that toward the edge of the geographical range the quality of the habitat deteriorates. This will have a detrimental impact on the roan population, particularly if the marginal zones deteriorate. In poorer habitats there might be more social friction or competition within the herd, so herds might tend to split sooner (i.e., H_{up} is lower). Also, very small herds would be less likely to survive (H_{min} increases), so that the net effect is an increase in the ratio $H_{min}:H_{up}$. We have seen that this eventually induces a switch from the acceleration mode to the stalling mode of dynamics, resulting in smaller and more variable populations that are particularly vulnerable to chance events.

In summary, we can hypothesize that social behavior that is normally optimal for the dispersal and growth of a roan population actually becomes counterproductive at the edge of the geographical range. Rainfall could also have a large effect, especially if rainfall cycles are longer toward the edge of the range. Our model thus leads to a number of stimulating hypotheses that could then be tested against data from different parts of Africa or, if those data were not available, suggest what data should be collected.

The reader should note that the advice we are able to give to management on the basis of our model is very general. We can say that some actions are likely to be useful, while others are unlikely to have more than a short-term effect. At no stage do we give specific advice. This is not surprising because we have built a model with virtually no pertinent data. The advice that comes out of the model is purely a consequence of the structure of the model. If that structure bears a strong similarity to the way in which roan behave, the advice will be good; if the structure is spurious, so is the advice.

What is surprising is that we learned so much about our problem when we had so little to start with. This happens so frequently when one builds models that there must be a good reason for it. A model *forces* us to think constructively, to synthesize whatever information we have, then allows us to *explore* the consequences.

The reader should also note the extent to which the model enables us to *think* about the dynamics of the roan population. The most important outcome of the model is a concept—that of different modes of roan dynamics. From that concept we are able to argue about the likely efficacy of management actions. Again, because we have not used real data, the concept comes out of the structure of the model, but it does help us think about what data we would like to obtain.

Whenever we build a model there is a trade-off between the

complexity of the model and our ability to interpret and understand the results it produces. Every detail added to the model, every attempt to make it more realistic, comes at a price—measured not in the cost of the computation, but in the loss of our intellectual grip on the model. This cost is especially high in a stochastic model, where there is in any case no clear thread between the input data and the model output. For this reason we have stressed the need to simplify the model wherever possible. If we had pursued our initial design for the model, we would have added considerably to the data requirements and expanded the number of parameters in the model. This in turn would have made it that much more difficult to explore the properties of the model, particularly when exploring its sensitivity to the input parameters.

A good model is one that is properly balanced between simplicity (not so simple that it misses important aspects of the system being modeled) and complexity (not so complex that it loses its edge as an intellectual tool).

We cannot guarantee that in the process of simplification we will not miss something of significance, but the effort required to obtain that guarantee is disproportionate. What we can do is first make the simplifications, then thoroughly explore and understand the simplified model, and only then try to build a more complex model. For example, we have managed to get a great deal of useful information about an established roan population because it has been so easy to manipulate the simplified version of the chessboard—i.e., the model with only one prime activity zone. It would be prudent to go back to the full chessboard model and test to see whether the major conclusions still hold. We leave it to the reader to think about where differences between the two versions are likely to occur.

RECAPITULATION

We began this chapter with a management concern (that a small roan population at the edge of its geographical range was vulnerable to adverse conditions) and a management objective (to understand the dynamics of the roan population and to determine what could be done to nurture it).

This objective was used together with what was known about the social behavior and habitat requirements of roan to design a stochastic model. The basic unit for that model was neither individual roan (as is usually the case in stochastic models of small populations), nor the number of animals in different age classes (as in the wildebeest model of the previous chapter). It was the number of females in each herd.

Choosing this unit was an important factor in reaching a compromise between the lack of data about roan and the need to model the population dynamics in some detail. Although we did not compute the number of male roan at any time, their effect on the social behavior of the herds was implicit in the model.

Another important factor in the design of the model was the idea of representing the activity zones of the different herds as a kind of chessboard on which the "roan population game" could be played.

In the absence of real data for the model, a standard set of parameters was postulated (on the basis of plausible but subjective arguments) and was used to test the model. As a demanding test case, we tried to predict the subsequent growth and dispersal of two herds introduced into an area suitable for roan. The model produced plausible results. By altering the values of the standard set of parameters it was possible to test how sensitive the model was to the assumed input data.

In the process of doing this we noticed two distinct patterns in the behavior of a dispersing population—the acceleration and stalling modes. The concept of these two modes proved to be extremely useful in characterizing the dynamics of the roan population. We also noticed, and subsequently confirmed, that the population was far more variable and unpredictable in the stalling mode of dynamics, and this had important consequences for management.

We went on to exercise our model in the case of an established population that fluctuated in response to changes in rainfall. We were able to argue in this case that the chessboard could, for all practical purposes, be reduced to a single prime-activity zone with adjacent marginal zones. This simplification enabled us to explore and understand the behavior of the model under a wide range of conditions. We again found the concept of two modes of dynamics to be useful, and argued that the important management actions were those that had the potential to shift the dynamics of the population away from the stalling mode. We identified the improvement of conditions in the marginal zones as the most effective way in which this could be achieved.

This model introduced us to some of the practical difficulties inherent in exercising and understanding the behavior of stochastic models—the need to compute replicates of every simulation, the care that must be taken in deciding what output to produce and how to present it, and the caution that must be exercised when interpreting that output, looking at both the averages and the variance. We developed an approach that is epitomized by the use of the word "exploratory" in the title of this chapter.

First, we played with our model and looked at some preliminary results, not in a rigorous way with the appropriate number of replicates, but interactively on a microcomputer, running an example, looking at the output on the computer screen, and responding to it with remarks such as, "That looks interesting. I wonder what will happen if I try this?"

This phase eventually led to hypotheses that were than tested more rigorously in carefully planned computer runs. Each case was simulated many times (anywhere from 20 to 100 times depending on the extent to which the replicates varied) and the program extracted information from each replicate, stored it, and combined all the output to compute means and variances.

Once hypotheses were established, we investigated their sensitivity to the parameters of the model. Here too the investigation was exploratory. We did not attempt any formal or comprehensive sensitivity analysis; instead, we changed parameters in a way that depends on what we had learned en route.

The success of this exploratory approach depended on maintaining an intellectual grasp of the model; all output had to be explained in a satisfactory manner. To maintain that grasp it was essential to keep the model as simple as possible and to minimize the number of parameters. Recognizing dimensionless parameters (such as the ratio $H_{min}:H_{up}$) helped to reduce the number of computations. The success also depended on the interaction between the user and the model, an interaction enhanced by using a microcomputer.

The results we eventually obtained from the model highlighted how essential it was in this case to build a stochastic model. The calculation of coefficients of variation provided the key to understanding the different modes of dynamics and hence the potential impact of management actions.

Our approach in this chapter was largely dictated by the fact that we had some information about roan but no real data. In Chap. 1 we suggested a bootstrap operation—first build a speculative model, then explore its consequences, then decide what to measure, in order to improve the model. The reader can see here how that operation might actually work.

FURTHER READING

Our description of roan behavior is based on the paper by Joubert (1974). Hilborn (1975) describes a model containing dispersion cells similar in concept to the activity zones in the roan model. Walters et al. (1981) develop a model that includes an algorithm for the splitting of wolf packs that is akin to the algorithm in the roan model for the splitting of herds.

A number of interesting stochastic models have management implications. Lett and Benjaminsen (1977) develop a stochastic model of the northwestern Atlantic harpseal and a stochastic model of how it is harvested. De Angelis et al. (1984) use a stochastic model to reinterpret field data, and Walters (1975) investigates how the mean and variances in the catch are related in a fishery. Wu and Botkin (1980) describe a stochastic model of long-lived species, with implications for the management of elephants, for example, and Shugart and West (1977) develop a stochastic model of succession in a deciduous forest. They use the average of 100 different runs to assess the impact of chestnut blight.

A book by Tomovic (1963) and papers by Miller (1974) and O'Neill et al. (1980) deal with the question of sensitivity analysis. Gardner et al. (1980) look at how errors in parameters propagate in six different models, and Reed et al. (1984) show how one can design a sensitivity analysis for a large model in much the same way as one might design replicates for a field experiment. Mohn (1979) is a good example of a problem-oriented sensitivity analysis. The concept of dimensionless parameters and an introduction to dimensional analysis can be found in the book by Legendre and Legendre (1983).

A mathematical treatment of stochastic population models can be found in the book by Bartlett (1960), while a mathematical exposition of more general stochastic processes can be found in Karlin and Taylor (1975). The book by Goel and Richter-Dyn (1974) contains a chapter on the stochastic growth and extinction of populations.

A Complex
Single-Species Model

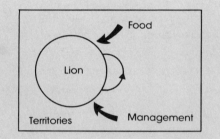

In Chap. 2 we suggested that two or three simple models of different aspects of a problem are sometimes more useful than one large interacting model. The problem of a declining wildebeest population was reduced essentially to an interaction between wildebeest and lions. However, while the lions have a very important effect on the wildebeest, the wildebeest are only one component in the diet of a lion. This is therefore an example where it makes more sense to model the two populations separately.

In this chapter we will develop a lion population model without any direct reference to the wildebeest, although the reason for building the lion model in the first place arose directly out of the wildebeest problem.

The reader will recall that the wildebeest population had declined dramatically, and predators, notably lion, were removing more animals each year than the wildebeest could replace. The wildebeest model indicated that lions would have to be cropped dramatically if this decline were to be reversed. The park biologists argued that if grass could be burned in such a way as to encourage wildebeest to congregate in certain areas during their breeding season, and if lions and spotted hyenas could be very nearly eliminated from those areas, this would have the same effect as cropping more lions throughout the park.

The question thus arose as to how one could create areas of very low lion density in an otherwise healthy lion community. This led, on the one hand, to carefully monitored field experiments, and on the other, to the construction of the lion model that will be developed in this chapter.

A PRIDE OF LIONS

The important socio-biological unit in a lion population is the *pride*. The life of a male centers on gaining control of a pride, and females outside established prides seldom breed successfully. Prides are spatially distinct; the pride males will mark and defend a territory that "belongs" to that pride. Research has indicated that although the males defend the territory, the females characterize the pride because they provide the continuity through generations. So we shall begin by describing, briefly, the life history of a lioness.

The Life History of a Lioness

For the first few weeks of her life, a young lioness is kept with her siblings out of sight of the rest of the pride under the care and protection of her mother. Thereafter, the young cubs join the pride. Often two or more of the lionesses in the pride have produced cubs at much the same time, so the young lioness is likely to join a nursery of cubs, all cared for and indiscriminately suckled by those lionesses in milk. Life may become more precarious in the ensuing months as the cubs are taken to kills to feed themselves. Depending on the size of kill and general availability of food, the cubs may find that if they are not adventurous they do not get enough to eat, and if they are adventurous they run the risk of being reprimanded, perhaps fatally, by an adult.

Mortality during the first two years of the lioness' life (the period during which we will think of her as a cub) will thus be high. If she survives, she may, depending on food conditions, be permitted to join the adult lionesses of the pride on a more equal and permanent basis. She will not, however, reach sexual maturity until about four years of age, at which stage she will mate with one of the current pride males (who, after four years, is unlikely to be her father) and will, on average, produce three cubs every two years. However, should she lose all her cubs, she is likely to mate and produce another litter before the two years have passed. After the age of about 10 she will begin to lose her teeth. Consequently her physical condition will deteriorate and she will probably die (or be killed by hyenas) during the next few years.

If the sub-adult lioness is not retained as a member of the pride, some time between the ages of two and four she will be ejected from it, probably in a group of like-aged sub-adults. Initially this group will only be polarized from the pride at kills and in other competitive situations, but as new cubs are born, tolerance for the group will decrease. Eventually the group will move out of the territory of its birth and lead a nomadic existence.

Life in a nomadic group of sub-adults will be stressful. The animals will all, at first, be relatively inexperienced in hunting, and they will not be welcome in the territories where they hunt. They will therefore try to avoid contact with the resident pride lions, and in so doing will frequently move (or else be chased) from one territory to another. Only in the absence of other lions will they all be able to settle down together and form a nucleus of a new pride, although cases have been observed of resident pride males attracting nomadic females and establishing them as a "subpride" within their territory. However, in such cases, all young males associated with the nomadic females are expelled.

One seldom finds an old nomadic lioness. If she is not recruited by a pride, she will probably succumb to the rigors of the nomadic lifestyle.

The Life History of a Lion

Male cubs will lead a similar life to their sisters for the first two years of their existence. However, while sub-adult lionesses may join the pride they were born in, sub-adult males will, with very rare exceptions, always be ejected. There are thus likely to be more males than females in a nomadic group, and this will become more pronounced if females are sometimes recruited by the resident pride males in established territories.

The young males in a nomadic group have a particularly high mortality. In interactions with established prides, the nomadic males are more likely to sustain serious injuries than the females. They will normally be forced to move out of a territory by pressure from the resident pride males, but if in these interactions the nomadic males perceive themselves to be sufficiently strong, the tussle may escalate into a fight that may be won by the young males. The young males then remain in control of the territory and the pride lionesses until they in turn are ousted. When new males take over a pride, they often kill the young cubs. The explanation usually given is that this is likely to ensure a more rapid propagation of their own genes. The average tenure of a pride male is about three years.

A nomadic male group is unlikely to split up. In fact, two groups sometimes merge; in particular, solitary male nomads are likely to join forces. Ousted pride males will occasionally join up with nomadic males or find a new territory, but for the most part they will either be killed during the take-over fight or become permanent nomads that no longer interact with the rest of the population.

DESIGNING A LION POPULATION MODEL

With this background, we are now in a position to think about the structure of a lion population model. As always, we must begin with the problem we are trying to solve and establish the objectives of the model. In this case, our problem is with the wildebeest and the fact that we need to reduce predation drastically in certain areas of the park. The objective of the model is thus to establish and compare different cropping strategies for creating lion-free "islands," or areas where the lion density is greatly reduced, within the park.

Often, management action has to be taken before a model can be built, and this case is no exception. The model thus has a second and perhaps equally important objective—to help interpret data collected during carefully controlled and monitored cropping operations.

Given these objectives, it is obvious that there is a spatial aspect to our problem (we will be cropping in some areas of the park and not in others); hence the territorial behavior of the lions will be important. So too will be the fact that some lions are permanent residents of fixed territories, while others are nomadic and move from one part of the park to another. Our model must therefore distinguish between nomadic and territorial lions. This implies that the model must include much of the social behavior of the lions, for it is the social behavior that determines the relative proportions of nomadic and territorial lions within the population.

Finally, we will be concerned with changes in lion numbers over a period of at least a few years. The cropping experiments were a three-year exercise, and from management's perspective we may be interested in maintaining areas of low lion density for even longer periods. So our model must reflect the natural birth and death processes occurring in the lion population. These processes, too, will depend on the social structure of the lion population.

This suggests a model with the following features:

1. The park should be divided into a set of discrete territories.
2. Within each territory there will be an established pride, and the model will simulate birth and natural death processes within the pride.
3. Sub-adults will be ejected from the pride to form nomadic bands, and the model must allow these bands to move from one territory to another and also simulate their survival.

4. The model must allow for recruitment of sub-adult females into
   the pride.
5. The model must allow for challenges between sub-adult males
   and pride males for control of the pride.

We will now consider each of these features in more detail.

The Territories

From our point of view, the important features of the territories are the
connections between them (so we can model how nomadic groups move
from one territory to another) and their size (not in absolute terms but in
terms of the size of pride that each territory can support).

We can model interconnections by first giving each territory an identifying number, specifying how many contiguous neighbors it has, and finally by giving the identifying numbers of all of those neighbors.

It has been found that while the total size of a pride (including cubs)
will fluctuate from one year to the next, the number of females in it (adults
plus recently recruited sub-adults) is very nearly constant. This is not
surprising, since these lionesses form the hunting core of the pride. We
will therefore represent the size of a territory by specifying the number of
lionesses that will normally be found in the resident pride, and we will call
this number the *pride strength* for the territory.

Figure 4.1 shows a representation of 31 territories in the park. The
circles represent the territories and the spokes between the circles indicate that those territories are neighbors—i.e., there is easy, direct
access between them.

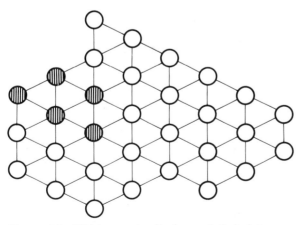

Figure 4.1 Thirty-one territories and their interconnections. The shaded territories are those in which lions were cropped.

The Pride: Composition, Deaths, and Births

We have not yet chosen a time step for our model. Lionesses normally breed every two years, which provides an upper limit to our step size, but consideration of other factors, such as cub survival and the fact that lionesses can breed more frequently if they lose their cubs, suggests that a time step of one year would be more appropriate. On the other hand, there is no compelling reason to choose a shorter time interval, since field data is reviewed once a year, as are management decisions. We will therefore simulate our lion population once a year.

In Chap. 2 we saw that wildebeest have a very short, definite calving season, which gave us a reason for choosing one time of the year rather than another for making our calculations. Lions will produce cubs at virtually any time of the year, although they are more likely to give birth in spring or summer, so our only specification is that the model should simulate the lion population at about the same time each year.

Once we have chosen a time step of one year, it is fairly obvious that the sex and age composition of the pride in the model should be:

1. Small cubs (aged 0 to 1 year)
2. Large cubs (aged 1 to 2 years)
3. Sub-adult females (aged 2 to 3 years)
4. Sub-adult females (aged 3 to 4 years)
5. Adult females
6. Adult pride males

By omitting sub-adult males we are in effect assuming that they are expelled from the pride sometime between the ages of 2 and 3. There is evidence to support this assumption.

With this structure we can see that modeling survival in the pride will consist of promoting the lions or lionesses in one age class to the next age class, allowing for natural deaths in the intervening year. Thus, small cubs will become large cubs the following year, large cubs will become sub-adults (aged 2 to 3), sub-adults aged 2 to 3 will become sub-adults aged 3 to 4, sub-adults aged 3 to 4 will become adults, and adult lions and lionesses will grow 1 year older. In each case we must allow for mortality during the year. Before discussing mortality, a number of points should be noted.

We have not differentiated between the sexes of the cubs, for the simple reason that there is no need for it. Field evidence suggests that cubs are born with an equal probability of being male or female and that their survival during the first two years is not sex-linked. When large cubs are promoted to sub-adulthood, however, we will have to assign sexes to them. We can do this on a stochastic or a deterministic basis. For want of a reason to do otherwise, we will choose the simpler deterministic approach. Thus, half of the surviving large cubs in each pride will become sub-adult males and the other half sub-adult females.

Large cubs that have been newly promoted and assigned sexes will all form part of a new nomadic band, except for those females recruited into the pride.

We have not divided adult males and females into age classes, again because there is no good reason for doing so. It will, however, be necessary to keep track of their ages. This will be easy to do for the pride males, since they are usually all of the same age, but for the pride females we will have to estimate an average age and modify it from one year to the next depending on the number of adult females that have died and the number of sub-adult females from the previous year that have entered the adult population.

Once we have determined survival rates for the various age classes, we again have the option of applying them deterministically or stochastically. Since we will be modeling a total of 31 prides, comprising over 600 lions, the numbers we are dealing with are not small and we would expect a deterministic model to be adequate.

However, in assigning sexes and calculating the number of lions that have survived deterministically, we run into a problem with "fractions of a lion." We solve this problem by using a random number generator in exactly the same way as we used it to determine the size of a roan herd in Chap. 3.

We now have to decide how we are going to determine survival rates for each of the sex and age classes in the pride. Obviously these will depend on the availability of food, and it is at this stage in building the model that we meet the inevitable difficulty that one part of an ecosystem is always linked to the other parts of the system. Are we going to have to model each of the major prey species to be able to determine whether or not the lions will have enough to eat? If we do, we will have to model the vegetation as well, to determine how the prey populations will change with time. Soon, we will be building a whole system model.

At some stage in the process of building a model we always meet a line of argument that leads inexorably to a system model. Unless one has set out for management purposes to deliberately build a system model in the first place, this line of argument must be circumvented at all costs!

Often the way around this dilemma is to approach the problem from a viewpoint inside the part of the system we are trying to model, looking outward, instead of the usual viewpoint of an observer looking at the system from above. In this example, this approach leads us to ask the question, "How do the lions see availability of food?" The simplest answer is a qualitative one that says food conditions for the year (or at the most difficult time of the year, if conditions are seasonal) are good, medium, or poor. We will therefore *tell* the model every year whether the food condition in each of the territories is good, medium, or poor, and specify survival rates that depend on that food condition. Table 4.1 shows survival rates specified in this way.

There are a number of points to note about this approach:

TABLE 4.1   LION SURVIVAL RATES AS A FUNCTION OF
FOOD CONDITIONS

	Food condition		
	Poor	Medium	Good
Adult pride males	0.95	0.97	0.97
Adult and subadult pride females	0.90	0.95	0.97
Cubs aged 1 to 2 years	0.50	0.70	0.75
Cubs aged 0 to 1 year	0.20	0.60	0.75
All nomadic lions	0.50	0.70	0.75

It is very similar in concept to the approach we took when faced with the dilemma of how to model survival of young calves in the wildebeest model. There, we cut through the Gordian knot by introducing a calf survival rate. Here, we have introduced the concept of three qualitative food classes.

Once we have introduced the idea of food classes as a modeling construct, it is important to try to relate the classes to the real world in some way. How, for instance, could we determine from field observation whether food conditions for the lions were good, medium, or poor in any particular year? We might argue that lions will not guard or hide a carcass when conditions are good (they can easily kill again), that under medium conditions they will take pains to keep scavengers away from the carcass, and under poor conditions they will, in addition, be unusually aggressive while eating. In this way, qualitative concepts introduced to simplify the model can be interpreted and, to a certain extent, calibrated in the field.

The survival rates in Table 4.1 are all estimates. While the actual numbers used might be inaccurate, there is a logic behind their *relative* values. In fact, Table 4.1 has built into it, implicitly, a lot of accurate information about the social behavior of lions. For example, it can be seen that the pride males are barely affected by poor food conditions—they are dominant at the kill and will always eat well. Adult lionesses fare less well, but it is the cubs (and very young cubs in particular) that feel the full effects of any shortage in food. The low survival of cubs under even medium food conditions reflects the fact that once they have eaten their fill, the adults will seldom kill again for the sake of their cubs.

Finally, we have to model births. We know that on average a lioness will produce three cubs every two years, so the simplest approach would be to calculate the number of new young cubs each year as 1.5 times the number of adult lionesses in the pride. However, we have to allow for the fact that lionesses that lose their cubs will breed again within a year. This would be easy to simulate in a stochastic model, where we could keep track of each lioness' cubs. In a deterministic model we can estimate cub mortality by looking at the number of large cubs in the pride. If this is proportionately low, we can increase the number of births accordingly.

Sub-Adult Survival and Movement

The nomadic bands, when they are first ejected from the pride, are likely to stay close to the pride and may be able to scavenge from it as well as make their own kills. Later, they will wander from one territory to another, acting rather like poachers and very often being chased off their kills by the resident pride. They will thus be sensitive to food conditions and will suffer high mortality when food is poor. Table 4.1 reflects this.

It is unnecessary to model the movement of a nomadic band during the first year of its existence; we will assume that it stays in the territory of its origin. The simplest way to model movement thereafter is to assume that the nomadic bands wander at random. We know which territories border on a given territory, so we can use a random number generator to choose where a band will move to next. We will arbitrarily allow each band to move up to six times a year.

This algorithm for movement may not seem very satisfactory. One might, for instance, ask whether a nomadic band would not try to stay in a territory while food conditions there are good, or whether movement would not depend on how many other bands there are in a territory or how formidable the resident pride males are. No field evidence answers any of these questions. There is, however, evidence that nomadic bands can move around considerably. They could quite easily hunt in two or three different territories in one night. One wonders, then, if it is really adequate to allow them to move only six times a year.

The answer to these questions is that we are only interested in movements to the extent that they lead to *important* interactions with other lions. Our definition of an important interaction is one that affects the population dynamics of the lions. Our algorithm, as it stands, is an attempt to model the important interactions that might occur during one year. Later on we will have to modify it, but not for any of the reasons stated.

Recruitment

We have already specified the strength of a pride in terms of the normal number of adult and sub-adult females in it. We suspect, however, that the strength of the pride could fluctuate with food conditions. We can model this as follows. If food conditions are good, one extra female (over and above the normal strength of the pride) can be recruited, whereas if food conditions are poor, the first vacancy occurring in the pride will not be filled. Once recruited, no lioness is ever ejected, even if food conditions deteriorate.

If a pride is below strength, the model allows it to recruit additional lionesses as follows. First, it tries to recruit from among its own sub-adult females—i.e., if the pride is about to eject sub-adult females, the model allows an appropriate number of them to stay and join the pride permanently. However, if there are insufficient recruits from within the pride, the model also allows for recruitment from passing nomadic bands. The biological justification for this is not strong (perhaps the algorithm should have allowed recruitment from passing bands only if there were no large cubs in the pride), but it does perhaps reflect something similar that has been observed: The pride males may establish a new group of "mistresses" recruited from a passing band in a remote corner of their territory.

The Challenge

Nomadic males, as they mature, are constantly on the lookout for an opportunity to control a territory of their own. The model allows the whole band (males and females) to establish itself as the resident pride should it wander into a vacant territory. The model also allows the males in the band to desert the females and take control of a territory containing a resident pride that for some reason has no adult males. In addition, we have to simulate the possibility that the nomadic males may, successfully or unsuccessfully, challenge the resident pride males whenever they enter a new territory.

Male lions do not look for a fight unless they have a reasonable chance of winning; discretion is the better part of valor. We therefore need some mechanism in our model for determining the odds—i.e., a definition of the relative strength of the males in a nomadic band and the resident pride males. The factors that determine this are the number of lions in each group, their ages, and the tremendous psychological advantage of the resident males.

To get some idea of how these factors interact, the modelers in this particular exercise started asking people with field experience questions such as, "If three nomads aged 4 challenged two pride males aged 6, who would win?" The answer would usually be definite—i.e., they would have no difficulty in choosing the winner—but occasionally they would reply, "It would be difficult to choose."

It was eventually realized that those examples where it was difficult to choose the winner were in fact crucial. They represented situations where the nomads and pride males were pretty evenly matched. This led to the following approach. If, for example, three nomads aged 4 are an even match for two pride males aged 6, we can then divide 2 into 3 and say that the pride males have an advantage of 1.5 because of age, experience, and fighting on their home ground. If a situation then arises in the model where five nomads aged 4 meet three pride males aged 6, we can divide 3 into 5 (to get 1.66) and, comparing it with 1.5, deduce that the nomads will win the fight. On the other hand, if there are four pride males, 4 into 5 gives 1.25, and the nomads will either avoid a fight or, if they do fight, lose.

Table 4.2 shows the advantage of pride males over nomads as a

TABLE 4.2 THE ADVANTAGE OF PRIDE MALES OVER CHALLENGING NOMADS

Age of pride males (years)	Age of challenging nomads (years)			
	5	6	7	8
5	1.50	1.00	0.90	1.00
6	2.00	1.40	1.50	1.80
7	2.00	1.40	1.50	1.80
8	1.30	1.20	1.25	1.40
9	1.25	1.00	1.05	1.35
10	0.90	0.40	0.40	1.00

function of the ages of each group. The numbers in it were obtained by interviewing a number of people with field experience. Their answers, incidentally, were remarkably consistent. The table reflects the inexperience of young nomads and the eventual weakness of old pride males.

The challenge algorithm is evoked whenever a nomadic band enters a new territory. It compares the relative numbers of nomadic and pride males with the appropriate entry in Table 4.2. If the nomads are obviously weaker than the pride males, the algorithm assumes that a fight is avoided. If they are weaker, but nearly evenly matched, a fight takes place, the nomads lose, and a relatively small proportion of the nomads are killed. If the nomads are stronger, the pride males are all killed and the nomadic males take control of the territory. The nomadic lionesses move on.

Finally, whenever nomadic males take control of a territory, either through conquest or because the pride has no adult males, it is assumed that they kill a proportion of the young cubs in the pride. The proportion depends on how many nomadic males have taken control.

The challenge will eventually emerge as a crucial component of this model. Meanwhile, it is interesting to note how one's method for collecting information to use in a model (in this case, questioning people with field experience) can eventually influence the design of the model. Asking oneself how to collect the relevant information is often a good start toward tackling the question of how to model.

BUILDING AND TESTING THE MODEL

In the previous section we opted for a deterministic rather than a stochastic model. In fact, the first version of the model to be built was entirely stochastic. As in the preliminary design for our roan model, the computer kept track of each lion and lioness, recording its status as a member of a pride or a nomadic group, its age, and, in the case of a pride lioness, how many of her cubs still survived. The program used a random number generator to decide for each lion, one by one, whether or not it survived another year. It computed the number of cubs produced by each adult pride lioness and again used a random number generator to determine the sex of every cub. The result of a challenge was also determined stochastically. Instead of a clear-cut decision based on the relative strengths of the pride males and the nomadic males, a probability of success (equal to 0.5 when strengths were evenly matched) was introduced.

The stochastic model worked reasonably well. This statement is not particularly scientific, but it underscores again the difficulty of validating a model. It is essential at the testing stage of the exercise to have a knowledgeable field biologist sitting at the computer console to comment on each result. Inevitably, in the process of building a model, some field experience goes untapped, either because it is taken for granted, or because nobody thought to ask the appropriate questions. This information can be invaluable at the testing stage.

The field biologist, while looking at the computed results, will test them against his entire store of information. In this particular example, for instance, he will have some idea of sex ratios. These have not been specifically built into the structure of the model. The biologist also knows that the tenure of pride males is typically between two and four years, and that pride males in their prime are about six years old. These are facts that have also not been used in the building of the model. If, therefore, the model produces results that coincide with this extraneous (to the model structure) information, we are justified in saying that the model works reasonably well.

There was only one discrepancy in the first stochastic model: Pride lionesses were surviving for 20 or more years, whereas in practice they seldom live longer than 12 or 13 years in the wild. This pointed to the obvious fact that the model made no allowance for higher mortality in very old lionesses (or lions) than in younger adults. This seems, in retrospect, like a stupid oversight, and the reader may wonder why we did not choose to gloss over this embarrassing slip. The reason is that stupid oversights, in retrospect, are the rule rather than the exception, and it is as well for the reader to know this and to watch out for them while testing models. It is perhaps illuminating that this oversight only affected pride lionesses. Mortality in nomadic lions and lionesses was so high that they never reached old age, while pride lions were always ousted and killed before they attained unheard of seniority. The oversight was only "stupid" because it mattered.

The problem was resolved by introducing a very high mortality factor for all lions and lionesses over the age of 12 years.

The stochastic model, however, suffered from one major and debilitating defect that had nothing to do with its biological accuracy. Because the model was stochastic, no two runs were ever identical, so there was no simple way to compare results. Suppose, for example, we wished to test whether or not mortality of nomadic lions during fights was a significant factor. If we ran the model once with this kind of mortality included and once without it, we would be unable to say whether any differences between the two outputs reflected the effect of mortality during fights, or whether they were only the sort of differences one might expect to find in two runs that used different sequences of random numbers but were otherwise identical.

The only way to test for the effect of mortality in a stochastic model as complex as this is to first perform at least 20 simulations with the mortality factor included, another 20 without mortality, then compare *average* results. This is what we did with our roan model, but it was not nearly as complex as the stochastic lion model.

As we saw in the previous chapter, it is essential that we should *easily* be able to interact with a model and explore its sensitivity. It was not easy to do this with the stochastic lion model. We lost patience waiting for the computer to perform the replicates of each simulation, and there was no spontaneity in the interaction. This highlights our credo that a model is an intellectual tool. It is there to interact with and provide support for human reasoning. If that interaction is too slow, or is inhibited for whatever reason, the model can fail even though its structure and biological realism are beyond reproach.

The obvious next step was to rebuild the model, this time making it almost entirely deterministic. The random number generator was used only in the movement algorithm (to choose a neighboring territory for a nomadic band to move into) and to resolve the problem of fractions of a lion. The results in this case were easy to comprehend and unambiguous—they were unambiguously *wrong*.

The problem was one of tenure of pride males. Instead of being ousted after about three years, pride males remained in control of a territory for seven or eight years or virtually until they died of extreme old age. This suggested that some of the numbers being used in the model were inaccurate. Could the table used for adjudicating challenges be weighted too heavily against the nomadic challengers, or were survival rates for cubs and/or nomadic lions too low?

These numbers were therefore changed individually and in combinations, but while the deterministic model made it easy to see the effects of the changes, none of the changes resolved the problem. If they did manage to reduce the tenure of pride males, they produced equally unacceptable side effects in some other part of the model.

To test a model, one often has to emulate Sherlock Holmes. At this stage of our investigation we have a clumsy stochastic model that seems to work, and a streamlined deterministic model that does not work satisfactorily. An experienced detective would first suspect a bug in the program. In this case, none could be found.

The obvious deduction is that one or more of the stochastic algorithms in the model must be *essential* to the workings of the model. A little thought will find the culprit. In the stochastic model, each sub-adult is assigned a sex on the basis of a random number generator, while in the deterministic model half of the new sub-adults in a pride are designated male, the other half female. Both these algorithms will, *on average,* lead to equal numbers of male and female sub-adults in newly formed nomadic groups. But while in the deterministic case the nomadic bands will all have sex ratios very close to one, in the stochastic case the possibility always exists that some nomadic bands will be predominantly male and others predominantly female.

The occasional group of male nomads will have a very much larger chance of deposing pride males, and this is where the deterministic model breaks down. Merely altering that one component of the deterministic model (i.e., making the sex assignment stochastic) led to results that reduced pride male tenure from an unacceptable seven or eight years to a reasonable three or four.

The result of this exercise was to produce a model that was very nearly deterministic; it was stochastic only in those sections where the variance was important. This meant that successive computer runs were very nearly identical, and in almost all cases three runs of the same scenario were sufficiently similar to give one confidence in their mean. The hybrid model was thus sufficiently repeatable to have the practical advantages and ease of use of a deterministic model, but was sufficiently stochastic to be realistic.

By this stage, results were available from some of the field trials in which a number of lions had been removed from a specific area of the park and the recolonization of that area carefully monitored. There is no better test of a model than comparisons with good data collected during deliberate manipulation of the system. The model failed this test. It was obvious that recolonization in the model occurred much too slowly. Why?

A careful look at the computed results showed that nomadic groups often moved from one occupied territory to another, ignoring vacant areas. Since our algorithm for their movement is purely random, this is not surprising. The field trials show that nomadic groups do not move at random. The nomadic lions will know, from territorial marking and roaring, which neighboring territories are vacant or lack pride males, and they will deliberately choose to move into those territories. Once we have recognized this obvious fact (again, in retrospect), it is easy to rectify the movement algorithm. Having done so we find that the model and field results agree remarkably well.

The reader would be justified in questioning at this stage whether the lion model can really be used as a predictive management tool. Suppose no field trials had been conducted and management decisions had been taken on the evidence of the original model? Clearly these decisions would have been faulty. The model was inadequate in a section that was crucial to the management actions under consideration.

This is a problem that one has to learn to live with. Perhaps the most important lesson is that the magnitude of the problem should not be underestimated. Very often, the only reason for building a model is the fact that some proposed action is likely to alter conditions in a way never previously experienced. The model, however, can only be built on the basis of what has been experienced, and even a thoroughly satisfying validation of the model in terms of available data will provide no guarantee that the model will perform well under altered conditions.

Remember, a model is an intellectual tool, not a fail-safe predictor. We use it, in the absence of anything better, to feel our way carefully from the known to the unknown, and we have to be cautious every step of the way. It would be comforting, but not necessarily realistic, to hope that if there had been no field experiments, more thought would have been given to the model and whether it was capable of simulating localized cropping. Perhaps the importance of the movement algorithm would then have been recognized and its potential defects thoroughly explored. If nothing else, imaginative playing with the model might have underscored the need for more data on how nomadic groups actually move.

A Summary of the Model

Since we have described a number of different versions of the lion model, it is appropriate to summarize the model in its final form before presenting some of its results. The following steps are repeated every year.

A. Specify food conditions in all of the territories.
B. For each pride:
   1. Compute the number in each age class that survive from the previous year (using the survival rates in Table 4.1).
   2. Assign sexes (stochastically) to the new sub-adults.
   3. Recruit females from the new sub-adults if the pride lionesses are below strength.
   4. Expel the rest of the new sub-adults; they will form a nomadic group in the following year.
   5. Compute the number of new-born cubs (depending on the number of surviving cubs per lioness).
C. For each nomadic group:
   1. Compute the numbers that survive from the previous year (using Table 4.1).
   2. Move the group (up to six times):
     a. To a vacant neighboring territory, if there is one. They then establish a new pride there.
     b. To a neighboring pride with no pride males, if there is one. The nomadic males become the pride males and kill some of the cubs; the female nomads move on.
     c. To a random neighboring territory where:
       i. Female nomads are recuited into the pride if it is below strength.
       ii. Male nomads challenge the pride males.

USING THE MODEL

We should remind ourselves that the objective in building the lion model was to determine whether it was possible to create and maintain areas of low lion density in sensitive areas of the park (from the point of view of the lion's prey). As mentioned earlier, field trials of localized lion cropping were in fact started while the model was still being built and tested. The model was therefore used against a background of information from these trials. The salient features of the field trials are described next.

In two independent experiments, lions were removed from two entirely separate areas of the park. Each of these areas corresponded in size to about 5 of the 31 territories in the computer model. The removal of the lions took place over a period of one to two years, and recolonization of the target areas was then carefully monitored over the next one to two years. In one target area it so happened that the lions cropped were largely from prides; in the other, largely nomadic lions were removed.

These experiments suggested that:

1. In both cases the number of lions in the target area was similar to what it had been before cropping within a year after cropping was stopped.
2. There was an upsurge in the number of young cubs in the target areas soon after cropping stopped. This upsurge was particularly dramatic in the area where nomadic lions had been cropped.
3. The lions in the recently recolonized areas were noticeably younger than those that had been removed, with a shift in the sex ratio toward more males.

It was concluded that cropping of lions in a small part of their overall population range was of questionable value.

These experiments were both simulated using the lion model. Those performing the experiments on the computer, however, had several advantages over those struggling to collect data in the field.

1. They knew precisely the social status of the lions they were removing.
2. They could easily repeat their experiments.
3. The field workers had no way of knowing what might have happened in the target areas if no lions had been cropped (i.e., they had no control experiment). The computer results could be compared against simulations that were identical except for the cropping.
4. The field workers were able to monitor lions only in the target areas. It was easy, in the computer model, to monitor the entire lion population.

5. It was also easy, in the computer model, to prolong the experiments.

Table 4.3 shows results obtained on the computer for a series of short-term cropping experiments. Apart from the control simulation of no cropping, three strategies were employed: First, the whole pride was cropped in each of the target areas; second, only nomadic lions were removed from the target areas; third, only the territorial pride males were cropped. In all cases, the lions were removed shortly before year 2 of the computation and the population was simulated for an additional two years.

The first thing to note about the results in Table 4.3 is the importance of having a control experiment. The population in a small area of a park will fluctuate as cubs are born and reared and nomadic lions move in and out of the area. In the example in Table 4.3 these effects led to a significant natural decrease in the population during the period of the experiment that could easily have confused a field experiment under similar conditions. Bearing this in mind, and comparing the results after cropping against the no-cropping control, it will be seen that the data in Table 4.3 lead to much the same conclusions as those drawn from the field data. Only in the case of strategy 3 (cropping pride males) was there a significant reduction in the local population in years 3 and 4. This is presumably

TABLE 4.3 SHORT-TERM CROPPING
SIMULATIONS
Showing lion numbers in the five
target territories

	Year			
Explanation	1	2	3	4
No cropping				
Adults and sub-adults	62	67	52	53
Cubs	44	37	40	50
Strategy 1: crop entire pride				
Adults and sub-adults	71	35	44	58
Cubs	37	0	33	30
Number of lions cropped	76	0	0	0
Strategy 2: crop all nomads				
Adults and sub-adults	66	58	63	63
Cubs	42	47	64	50
Number of lions cropped	25	0	0	0
Strategy 3: crop pride males				
Adults and sub-adults	75	52	44	43
Cubs	39	4	51	50
Number of lions cropped	13	0	0	0

due to the social chaos induced by removing the pride males, and suggests that this strategy might be more effective than other cropping strategies.

These results prompted a more extensive set of computer experiments in which each of the three cropping strategies was applied over a period of six years and the lion population was monitored for a further five years after cropping was stopped. The results of this set of experiments are shown in Table 4.4 and in Figs. 4.2 and 4.3.

The table and figures suggest a number of interesting and thought-provoking ideas:

1. Cropping nomadic lions in the target areas is not a viable control measure. This was also indicated in the field trials and short-term computer experiments.
2. The other two strategies are far more effective in the long term than short-term experiments would indicate. In particular, note how the number of lions that need to be cropped falls off quite dramatically after the first year of the experiment.
3. Removing lions locally, even when (as in the case of removing nomads) it has no lasting impact on the local lion density, does indeed have an effect on the total lion population in the park. This explains why long-term cropping is more effective than short-term cropping—the pool of "free" lions in the surrounding population eventually dries up.

TABLE 4.4 LONG-TERM CROPPING SIMULATIONS
Showing lion numbers in the five target territories

	Year										
Explanation	1	2	3	4	5	6	7	8	9	10	11
No cropping											
Adult and sub-adults	62	67	52	53	61	62	51	64	61	47	57
Cubs	44	37	40	50	47	44	40	34	47	49	47
Strategy 1: crop entire pride											
Adults and sub-adults	62	41	24	17	32	2	15	24	33	26	32
Cubs	44	0	0	0	0	0	0	3	15	27	42
Number of lions cropped	83	28	19	14	20	20	0	0	0	0	0
Strategy 2: crop all nomads											
Adults and sub-adults	62	50	60	52	47	61	49	43	50	52	52
Cubs	44	38	55	47	51	30	44	32	44	40	45
Number of lions cropped	23	12	25	19	15	23	0	0	0	0	0
Strategy 3: crop pride males											
Adults and sub-adults	62	56	55	39	42	43	38	37	42	47	46
Cubs	44	7	0	0	0	0	0	59	43	53	37
Number of lions cropped	11	6	8	6	6	8	0	0	0	0	0

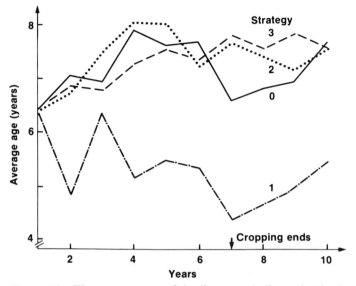

Figure 4.2 The average age of the lions (excluding cubs) in the five target territories under different cropping strategies. (Strategy 0 is the control—i.e., no cropping.)

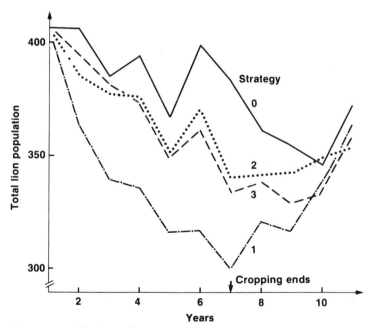

Figure 4.3 The total lion population (excluding cubs) in all 31 territories while different cropping strategies are tested in five of the territories. (Strategy 0 is the control.)

These ideas, even if tentative, add considerably to the conclusions drawn from the field experiments.

DISCUSSION

A number of points arise out of the process of building, testing, and using the lion model.

In this chapter, as in the previous two, we have constructed a model of only one animal species. The lion model, however, is much more detailed than either the wildebeest or roan models. There are three reasons for this:

1. The wildebeest population is regulated by external influences (predation), while the lion population is largely self-regulated. The details are included in the lion model because they are crucial to the population dynamics. We were, for example, able to ignore roan bulls, but we cannot ignore male lions because their actions have a direct bearing on the survival of cubs.
2. The questions we are asking of the lion model demand a high level of detail.
3. Lions have been studied assiduously throughout Africa. Enough is known about their behavior to support this level of detail.

The success (or failure) of a model depends as much on how readily it can be used as on its inherent qualities. The compromise between a stochastic and a deterministic model in this case was a particularly happy one. The model would have been meaningless if it had been more deterministic, and it is doubtful whether it would have been as useful if it had been more stochastic.

Experience with the model again highlights the impossibility of formally validating a model of this kind. What is required instead is detective work to track down anomalies in the model, then careful comparison with available data to identify gaps in the model.

It has been stressed that a model is always suspect when used to make predictions outside the range of experience used as background for the design of the model. There is no easy way to get around this; all one can do is use the model cautiously and thoughtfully.

However, the comparisons between field cropping trials and the computer simulation of those trials has highlighted the fact that *experimental data can be equally suspect*. Field biologists are often suitably suspicious of computer models but have unlimited faith in what they have measured. In an ecological system, measurements of only a small part of the system for a short period of time can potentially be as misleading as a poorly constructed model.

The computer simulation in this example highlighted how fragile the field measurements really were. First, it showed how essential it was to have a control experiment. (From the practical point of view it was not really feasible to have a control experiment in this case, but the model showed how one might well be misled without one.) Second, it highlighted the inherent variance in the data (Fig. 4.2 shows how, for example, the average age of pride lions can fluctuate even when no cropping takes place) and cautioned one to be wary of drawing conclusions from the limited field observations. Third, it showed up the dangers of not being able to measure everything in the field (how much more informative the field trials would have been if it had been possible to monitor the total lion population). It also showed the even greater danger of allowing an experiment to run for too short a time.

It is perhaps the debate over the interpretation of the field trials and the model simulations that is most exciting. Each approach has weaknesses, but our understanding of the problem is that much better when we use both approaches.

FURTHER READING

Lions have been studied continuously for nearly two decades in the Serengeti National Park. Some of the results of those studies can be found in papers by Bertram (1973 and 1975), Hanby and Bygott (1979), and Packer and Pusey (1982, 1983a, 1983b), and in books by Schaller (1972) and Bertram (1978). Studies elsewhere in Africa are described in papers by Schenkel (1966), Rudnai (1973a), Smuts (1976b), Smuts et al. (1978) and Anderson (1980), and also in a book by Rudnai (1973b).

Details of the field experiments mentioned in this chapter can be found in Smuts (1978b), and a popular account of those experiments is given in the book by Smuts (1982). The construction of the lion model is described in Starfield et al. (1981a) and some of its applications in Starfield et al. (1981b) and Starfield and Bleloch (1983a).

There are not many models in the literature that are similar in concept to the lion model—i.e., that include territorial and social behavior and have a management perspective. Preston (1973) describes a model that includes disperson of foxes. A paper by Walters et al. (1981) describes a wolf-ungulate model that contains some aspects of wolf pack behavior, while George and Grant (1983) describe a stochastic model of brown shrimps with a structure that is in many ways similar to that of the lion model. George and Grant also used their model to evaluate the effects of various management alternatives.

A System Model

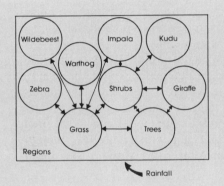

All our models so far have been single-species models. Other animals have sometimes affected the species being modeled (either as predators, prey, or competitors), but we have always found a way to represent this without actually modeling the mutual interaction. The essence of a system model is that many of the interactions are modeled explicitly.

This chapter is concerned with a relatively small park (about 25,000 ha) that contains a spectrum of herbivores but no significant predators. The principal grazers are warthog (*Phacochoerus aethiopicus*), wildebeest (*Connochaetes taurinus*), zebra (*Equus burchelli*), and the white rhinoceros (*Ceratotherium simum*). The principal browsers are giraffe (*Giraffa camelopardalis*), kudu (*Tragelaphus strepsiceros*), and the black rhinoceros (*Diceros bicornis*). Impala (*Aepyceros melampus*) and nyala (*Tragelaphus angasi*) are the two important mixed feeders. Most of the herbivores are sedentary, but wildebeest, zebra, and white rhinoceros wander in search of grazing over large areas of the park.

The herbivore distribution is strongly influenced by vegetation. One reason for this is that drinking water is either naturally available or artificially supplied throughout the park in such a way that no animal is ever far from water. The vegetation, in turn, is influenced by the soil type and rainfall. There are five distinct regions in the park (based on soil type)—the hills, a region of Cretaceous deposits, a belt of old dunes, a second region of Cretaceous deposits, and the riverine areas. The hills, for example, have a rocky substrate that supports stands of tall grass and wooded grassland, while the riverine areas consist of alluvial soils with tall trees, patches of thicket, and tall palatable grass. Mean annual rainfall in the park is 628 mm. A problem from the management point of view is that the rainfall can vary considerably from year to year.

Regular burning of some areas of the park (to prevent bush encroachment) is a standard management practice. In addition, because the park is small and because there are no significant predators, management believes it necessary to crop some of the herbivores. However, the cropping of one species will have an influence on the vegetation which, in turn, will have an impact not only on the species that has been cropped but also on the other herbivores. The objective is to be able to predict that impact and so evaluate alternative management strategies.

A model that could assist management would have to incorporate herbivores, vegetation, and rainfall; the model would thus represent, in some way, the behavior of the whole system. System models, however modestly they start out, tend to grow and often end up as large and complex undertakings. To keep track of the model and to maintain an overall perspective, it is essential to begin with a carefully thought out framework; one that ensures that the objectives of the model are always kept in mind.

A FRAMEWORK FOR THE MODEL

We want to predict how the cropping of one herbivore will influence the dynamics of the other herbivores. The model must therefore represent all the major herbivores. Our main assumption is that competition for food is the only interaction between the herbivores. It is therefore essential to represent each herbivore's food preferences in some way. This in turn will help us determine how to represent the vegetation. Finally, the amount of food available to the herbivores will depend on the rainfall, so once we have represented the vegetation in some fashion, we will have to model how it grows.

The sequence of calculations in the model will be in the reverse order. Rainfall drives the system, so we must begin by either specifying or simulating it. Once we know the rainfall, the next step is to simulate the growth of the vegetation. We have not yet decided what vegetation we are talking about, but we anticipate that we will have to introduce various classes (e.g., grasses and trees) and that they will compete for the rainfall. We also anticipate that the way in which the different classes of vegetation grow will depend on the soil type. Hence, our model, like the park itself, should contain five regions.

Next, we must simulate herbivory. Clearly the numbers of different herbivores and their food preferences will determine how much of each vegetation class is consumed. Finally, depending on how well the herbivores have eaten, we must compute an increase or decrease in numbers for each of the herbivore species and simulate movement from one region of the park to another for those species that are not sedentary. The flowchart in Fig. 5.1 depicts this sequence of calculations.

We should pause at this stage to confirm that the proposed structure will indeed meet the objectives of the model. The two management actions we anticipate are burning and cropping; the framework we have suggested can accommodate both.

The next step is to design the various segments or modules of the model one at a time. The appropriate level of detail may vary from one module to another, so we should begin by ranking the resolution required of each module. Our primary interest is in the herbivores, so we would expect the two modules dealing with the herbivores and what they eat to

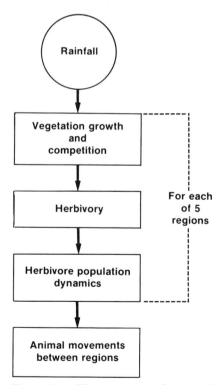

Figure 5.1   The sequence of calculations for one iteration of the system model.

be more detailed than the others. We are only interested in the vegeta-tion to the extent that it affects the herbivores, so here we expect our model to be cruder. Finally, the rainfall need only be represented in suf-ficient detail to facilitate the model of vegetation growth.

It is important to make these distinctions because, as we shall see, it is very easy to lose perspective while coping with the details of the various modules. This discussion also tells us that we should design the herbivore modules first, because they ultimately determine the level of resolution for the entire model. If we can be parsimonious but realistic in designing them, we may succeed in producing a lean and useful system model.

HERBIVORY

A good question to ask about the herbivores listed at the beginning of the chapter is whether we really need to include all nine species in the model. Since the interaction between species depends on what they eat, we might be able to group together herbivores with similar food preferences. Clearly giraffe must be in a class of their own; only they can browse on tall trees. The black rhinoceros and the kudu browse on shrubs and short trees, so we could group them together. Similarly, both the white rhinoc-eros and the zebra are grazers that can use relatively tall, coarse grass, while the wildebeest and warthog are grazers that both require short grass. Finally, the nyala and impala have similar feeding habits, utilizing short grass, shrubs, and short trees.

"Lumping" Variables

Can we model a black rhinoceros as a very large kudu, a warthog as a smaller wildebeest, and so on? The advantages of merging or "lumping" the herbivores into a few classes based on their habits are (1) that we reduce the number of variables in the model (which in turn reduces both the input requirements and computation time), and (2) that we reduce the amount of output from the model; this will emerge as an important consid-eration in due course.

Before we can go ahead and lump two variables we have to satisfy two conditions: We must have a formula for converting one variable into the other and we must make sure that both variables play a similar role in the model, both from the ecological and management points of view.

The concept of *equivalent animal units* enables us to convert, for ex-ample, a black rhinoceros into a kudu. One equivalent animal unit (EAU) is defined as an animal with the daily food intake of a domestic cow. On this basis a black rhinoceros is about 2.0 EAU (i.e., it consumes twice as much as a cow per day), while a kudu is only 0.4 EAU. Each black rhinoceros is therefore equivalent to about five kudu, so we can satisfy the first of the two conditions for lumping black rhinoceros and kudu.

Let us now look at the second condition. We have established that the two species have similar food preferences, but are they similar in other ways that are important for our model? Here we need to consider both the distribution and the population dynamics of the two species. Both kudu and black rhinoceros are found in fairly localized parts of the park and neither tends to roam over much larger areas; this facilitates the combination. However, mature kudu cows will produce one calf every year, while the rhinoceros will only produce a calf every four or five years. This discrepancy mitigates against merging, but we can get around it by arguing that if we look at the rate of increase in *biomass* of the two species, rather than in the number of individuals, then kudu and black rhinoceros are not that different.

Finally, we should consider whether merging kudu and black rhinoceros is likely to confound the management objectives of the model. While zoologists might at first be uncomfortable with this breach of taxonomic etiquette, a manager may welcome the flexibility it provides. If the model suggests that this lumped species needs to be cropped, the manager is free to implement it either by removing only kudu, only black rhinoceros (obviously in smaller numbers), or some mix of the two.

This discussion shows how careful we should be whenever we consider simplifying an important aspect of the model. On balance, the decision was taken to merge black rhinoceros into the kudu category, white rhinoceros into zebra, and nyala into impala. The wildebeest and warthog were not combined because warthog are sedentary, while wildebeest will, as we have mentioned, migrate from one region of the park to another. This was thought to be an important distinction.

Modeling Food Preferences

Having reduced our herbivore categories to six from the original nine, we now need to look more closely at what each category will eat. In so doing, we will also be defining the variables for the vegetation component of the model, so here too we should be as parsimonious as possible.

We have used terms such as short grass, coarse grass, shrubs, and short and tall trees in our previous discussion. We have always associated shrubs with short trees, so we might begin by defining three classes of vegetation: grass, shrubs (and short trees), and trees (meaning tall trees). We know, however, that within these classes, herbivores will select their food on a species basis, having strong preferences for some species and avoiding others unless there is a critical shortage of food. This selection can affect the competition between vegetation species, influencing what food will be available to the herbivores in future years. Modeling at the vegetation species level would be far too detailed for our purposes, but

TABLE 5.1   FOOD PREFERENCES OF THE HERBIVORES

Species	Preference 1	Preference 2	Preference 3
Giraffe	Palatable tall trees	Palatable shrubs	Unpalatable trees
Impala	Grass, palatibility >0.8	Palatable shrubs	Less palatable grass
Kudu	Palatable shrubs	Unpalatable shrubs	
Warthog	Grass, palatibility >0.8	Less palatable grass	
Wildebeest	Grass, palatibility >0.8	Less palatable grass	
Zebra	Grass, palatibility >0.6	Less palatable grass	

the distinction between species the herbivores prefer and those they tend to avoid is an important one.

The simplest way we can introduce this is by dividing each of our vegetation classes into two. We can think of them as palatable and unpalatable subclasses. Generally speaking, the leaves on an unpalatable shrub or tree species will always be unattractive to the browsers, but an unpalatable grass species can be attractive to grazers when the grass is short. We can simulate this by introducing a *grass palatibility factor* that varies from 0 (totally unpalatable) to 1 (enticingly palatable) as a function of grass height. The palatibility factor will be close to 1 for both palatable and unpalatable grasses when they are short, and will decrease as their height increases, slowly for the palatable subclass, rapidly for the unpalatable subclass.

We are now in a position to specify herbivore food preferences. This can be done in the form of a table such as Table 5.1. Here we suggest, for example, that impala will first choose palatable grass, then palatable shrubs, and, as a last resort, less palatable grass. Kudu, on the other hand, have only two preferences—first, palatable shrubs, then unpalatable shrubs. This shows us that we will have to interpret the table with care. It makes very little difference to an impala whether it is eating palatable grass or leaves, but the difference between palatable leaves and unpalatable leaves is a significant one for kudu. Also note how we have used the idea of a grass palatibility factor to differentiate between the grazing preferences of wildebeest and zebra, for example.

POPULATION DYNAMICS OF THE HERBIVORES

In previous chapters we modeled the population dynamics of animals in a number of different ways, depending on the species concerned and the objectives of the model. We will have to decide which aspects of these different models are important here, but because we are now concentrating on the interaction between six different species, we want to represent each population as simply as we can. Can we get by with a deterministic model? Can we ignore social and territorial behavior? What is the minimum population structure we need (in terms of sex and age classes)?

We have already decided to divide the park into five regions; all species, except for wildebeest and zebra, are confined to the region they are born in. We have no need to represent territorial or social behavior in any more detail than this. Populations are large enough to justify a deterministic model. Can we then use a single variable to represent the total population of a species in a region? This would imply no differentiation between sexes and age classes.

To decide whether this is realistic, we need to consider what impact food shortages are likely to have on the population. In general, the very young and the very old are the first to suffer. The loss of young animals does not immediately affect the breeding potential of the population but has implications for future years. This time delay could be important from the management point of view, so we definitely need to differentiate between adult and juvenile animals. This contrasts with the loss of old animals, which has no long-term implications and can be ignored.

If food conditions deteriorate even further, all age classes will be affected, and pregnant females may suffer more than adult males. This is likely to be a small effect, so we will not differentiate between the sexes.

We can thus represent a species in one of the regions of the park by two variables, one for the number of juveniles (usually less than two years old), the other for the number of adults. We will assume that food shortages have no impact on the number of births but, depending on severity, will first reduce the survival rate of juveniles, then reduce the survival rate of the adults. To see how this might work, let us take kudu as an example.

Suppose that at a certain time there are K adult kudu and k juveniles in one of the regions. We have not yet chosen a time step for the model, but let us suppose it is one month. If we estimate that an adult kudu requires B kg and a juvenile b kg of food per month, the kudu in that region would like to eat $KB + kb$ kg of leaves in the next month.

Moreover, we know from Table 5.1 that the kudu would prefer to eat leaves from palatable shrubs. Other herbivores (e.g., giraffe and impala) might also want a share of this browse. What we do, therefore, is calculate a demand for food, first assuming that every species eats only its first preference. If there is sufficient for all, we share the food out accordingly, but if there is a shortage, we allocate a share to each animal's second preference (and maybe third preference) as well. When the available food has all been shared out this way, there are three possible outcomes for the kudu:

1. They have managed to get all the palatable browse they need.
2. They have had to take some unpalatable leaves.
3. Not only have they had to take unpalatable leaves, but they were also unable to get the full $KB + kb$ kg of browse they required.

The effect of point 2 or 3 on the kudu will be cumulative; it will make a difference whether they have an inadequate diet for just one month or for a number of consecutive months. To keep track of this, we introduce the idea of a *condition index* with a scale (arbitrarily chosen) from 1 to 6. We calibrate this index by thinking of 1 as kudu in the peak of condition and 6 as kudu in extremely poor condition. An algorithm can then be developed for altering the condition index from one month to the next.

The amount by which the index is increased is determined by the extent to which kudu are unable to meet their total food needs or are forced to utilize their second food preference. The index is reduced fairly rapidly back to 1 once the kudu are again able to meet all their requirements with first-preference food. A table can then be constructed to relate the monthly rates of juvenile and adult mortality to the value of the condition index. Obviously mortality, especially juvenile mortality, will increase sharply as the condition index approaches 6.

In this discussion we have assumed a time step for the model of one month. Is this sensible? Competition for food is the key element of our model. It is likely to be crucial during the dry season, so the time step should not be longer than one season (three months). This is also a realistic time step from the management point of view. In practice, however, whenever a shortage of food occurred, we found three months to be too long a time step for adjusting populations and sharing resources. The model therefore performs its calculations using a time step of one month, but only prints out results every season. Except for zebra, all births take place during the first month of summer. It is assumed that zebra produce their young throughout the year. The annual birthrate (which is independent of condition index) varies from 0.20 for giraffe to 0.95 for warthog.

The preceding is by no means a complete description of the population dynamics section of the model. We have just highlighted those issues that were important in the design of the module. The following additional points should be noted.

The algorithm for sharing the available food resources is quite complicated. It contains two important assumptions. The first is that it makes no difference in the allocation process whether the resource being shared is one herbivore's first preference and another's second or third preference. All herbivores that need that resource have equal access to it. The second assumption is that the herbivores cannot eat all the vegetation. Only 80 percent of the browse is made available to them, and the grass cannot be grazed below a certain height.

The condition index is an artificial construct of the model. Its sole purpose is to keep track of accumulative diet deficiencies, and it is not designed to relate in any obvious way to actual measures of physiological condition. As so often happens with model constructs, however, we will find that the condition index helps us to interpret the results we get from the model.

Differences between species are built into the model in both obvious and subtle ways. Obvious differences are those of food preference (Table 5.1) and total food requirements. Less obvious is the fact that a different algorithm for adjusting the condition index was built for each species. Here, for instance, we allow for the observation that the second food preference for impala is quite acceptable to them, while the second preference for kudu implies a dietary deficiency.

Differences between species are also reflected in the numbers used for birthrates and are built into the table of mortality rates versus condition index. For example, warthog have a much higher birthrate than giraffe, but also a much higher juvenile mortality, particularly when their condition deteriorates. The numbers used are largely guesswork, but the guesswork tells a coherent story when the numbers are *compared* with one another.

Finally, note that even though we are desperately trying to keep our model as simple as possible, it is in fact becoming quite complicated.

MODELING THE VEGETATION

So far, by concentrating on what herbivores eat, we have managed to restrict ourselves to a model containing six types of herbivore and six types of vegetation (three classes, each with a palatable and unpalatable subclass). To get a feel for how to model the vegetation, let us consider one class, say palatable shrubs, in one of the five regions of the park.

The herbivory module of the previous section needs monthly information on how much food is available for browsers on all the palatable shrubs in the region; the leaf biomass on the shrubs is an essential variable. We therefore need to ask what will lead to changes in leaf biomass from one month to the next. Here are the important factors.

1. New leaf growth must depend on how many bushes there are and the extent to which leaves have already developed on them.
2. Rainfall will influence production, depending on the time of year and the soil type.
3. Herbivores will consume some of the biomass each month.

Let l_1 represent the total palatable leaf biomass in the region at a particular time—the subscript does not refer to the region but indicates that we are modeling the palatable subclass—and let Δl_1 represent the change in l_1 that occurs in the ensuing month. Points 1, 2, and 3 must then be incorporated into an equation for Δl_1.

Starting with point 1, we notice that we need to introduce another variable. Let S_1 represent the woody biomass of the palatable shrubs in the region. Then, when there are very few or only small leaves on the shrubs, we can argue that doubling S_1 will double the rate at which leaf biomass can potentially increase—i.e., when leaf biomass is low, Δl_1 will be proportional to S_1. We can then write

$$\Delta l_1 = r_l S_1 \qquad (5.1)$$

where r_l is a constant.

However, the potential for new production will be reduced if there is already a substantial bimomass of leaves on each bush. Suppose that q is the maximum leaf mass that one unit of wood mass can normally support. The maximum leaf biomass for the whole region will then be $q \times S_1$. We can therefore model the inhibitory effect of the existing leaf biomass by multiplying the right-hand side of Eq. (5.1) by the factor $[1 - l_1/(qS_1)]$. This expression satisfies the requirements that it is close to unity when l_1 is small; it approaches 0 as l_1 approaches qS_1, and it is negative if l_1 is greater than qS_1. Any other expression that satisfied these requirements would be equally plausible; we have used the simplest expression that came to mind. At this stage our equation is

$$\Delta l_1 = r_l S_1 \left[1 - \frac{l_1}{(qS_1)} \right]$$

We now need to address points 2 and 3. First, the change in leaf biomass will be modified by rainfall. We can model this by introducing a factor f_T (between 0 and 1) which, as we shall see later, depends on both the amount of rain and when it falls. Second, we subtract from the right-hand side of (5.1) an amount b_1 which represents the leaf biomass removed by the herbivores during the month. We then have

$$\Delta l_1 = r_l f_T S_1 \left[1 - \frac{l_1}{qS_1} \right] - b_1$$

The term b_1 can be computed from the herbivory module, but we need to compute S_1 in the vegetation module. It too can change with time, although we would expect it to change more slowly than the leaf biomass. As with the leaf biomass, we therefore start by listing the important factors that influence changes in the woody biomass of the palatable shrubs. They are:

1. Competition with all other woody vegetation (including itself) for space, soil nutrients, and ground water
2. Competition with grass and (indirectly) all green biomass for sunlight and rainfall
3. The rainfall itself

In the absence of competition, we can argue that the monthly change in woody biomass is

$$\Delta S_1 = r_S f_T S_1 \qquad (5.2)$$

where r_S is a constant and f_T is the rainfall factor. Comparing this with Eq (5.1) we notice that both leaves (l_1) and wood (S_1) grow from wood (S_1), but at different rates. However, while leaves only compete with themselves, we see from point 1 that the woody component must compete with all other bushes and trees. This suggests that we should multiply the right-hand side of (5.2) by an expression such as

$$1 - \frac{S_1 + S_2 + T_1 + T_2}{T_{\max}}$$

where $T_{\max}$ is the maximum woody biomass the soil in the region can support. The other variables are defined in Table 5.2.

The expression for competition with all other woody vegetation is negative when the total woody biomass in the region exceeds $T_{\max}$—i.e., shrubs will actually die. This makes sense, but we would expect the competition described in point 2 to be less drastic. Grass and other green biomass might inhibit woody growth, but is unlikely to actually reverse it. We can use a negative exponential function to represent this kind of com-

TABLE 5.2 VARIABLES AND PARAMETERS FOR THE VEGETATION GROWTH MODULE

Variables*	
A_1, A_2	Grass basal area (m²)
S_1, S_2	Woody component of shrubs (kg)
T_1, T_2	Woody component of trees (kg)
h_1, h_2	Grass height (m)
l_1, l_2	Shrub leaf biomass (kg)
L_1, L_2	Tree leaf biomass (kg)
G_1, G_2	Grass biomass consumed by herbivores (kg/month)
b_1, b_2	Shrub leaf biomass consumed by herbivores (kg/month)
B_1, B_2	Tree leaf biomass consumed by herbivores (kg/month)

Parameters	
r_A, r_S, r_T	Growth parameters for grass basal area, shrub woody component, and tree woody component respectively
r_h, r_l, r_L	Growth parameters for grass height, shrub leaf biomass, and tree leaf biomass respectively
f_g, f_T	Rainfall correction factors for grass and tree growth rates respectively (see Table 5.3)
$T_{\max}$	Saturation level for woody biomass
$h_{\max}$	Saturation height for grass
U	Saturation level for total green production
c	Converts grass volume to biomass
p	Modifies the degree of green biomass competition

*The subscript 1 refers to the palatable subclass. The subscript 2 refers to the unpalatable subclass.

petition. If U is a measure of the total green biomass the region can sustain, we can write the competition factor,

$$C = \exp - \frac{p\{c(A_1 h_1 + A_2 h_2) + l_1 + l_2 + L_1 + L_2\}}{U} \qquad (5.3)$$

where all the variables and parameters are defined in Table 5.2. This expression is close to unity when the green biomass is low but approaches 0 when the green biomass is high in relation to U. We can define what we mean by high in relation to U by our choice of the parameter p.

Multiplying the right-hand side of Eq. (5.2) by the various competition factors leads to the equation,

$$\Delta S_1 = r_S f_T \left[1 - \frac{S_1 + S_2 + T_1 + T_2}{T_{\max}} \right] C$$

Note that we needed two variables to describe the dynamics of palatable shrubs—one for the woody component, which changes slowly, and one for the leaf biomass, which depends on the woody component but can change more rapidly. Similarly, we need to introduce two variables each to describe the unpalatable shrubs, the palatable trees, and the unpalatable trees, and we can write down analagous equations to calculate changes in these variables from one month to the next.

The equations for the grasses will be somewhat different. Here, basal area is the slowly changing variable and grass height the more rapidly changing variable. We assume that only the green biomass competition factor C of Eq. (5.3) inhibits the spread of the basal area. Changes in grass height are assumed to be independent of the basal area, proportional to the height itself, and limited by a factor that tends to zero as the height approaches a characteristic upper limit we call $h_{\max}$.

In summary, the equations developed for monthly changes in the slowly changing variables are:

$$\Delta A_1 = r_A f_g A_1 C \qquad (5.4)$$

$$\Delta S_1 = r_S f_T S_1 \left[1 - \frac{S_1 + S_2 + T_1 + T_2}{T_{\max}} \right] C \qquad (5.5)$$

$$\Delta T_1 = r_T f_T T_1 \left[1 - \frac{S_1 + S_2 + T_1 + T_2}{T_{\max}} \right] C \qquad (5.6)$$

where C is defined by Eq. (5.3).

The equations for monthly changes in the more rapidly changing variables are:

$$\Delta h_1 = r_h f_g h_1 \left[1 - \frac{h_1}{h_{\max}} \right] - \frac{G_1}{cA_1} \qquad (5.7)$$

$$\Delta l_1 = r_l f_T S_1 \left[1 - \frac{l_1}{qS_1} \right] - b_1 \qquad (5.8)$$

$$\Delta L_1 = r_L f_T T_1 \left[1 - \frac{L_1}{qT_1} \right] - B_1 \qquad (5.9)$$

In these equations the subscript 1 refers to the palatable subclass and the subscript 2 to the unpalatable subclass. We have written only the equations for the rates of changes of the palatable variables. A similar set of equations for the unpalatable variables can be obtained merely by replacing the subscript 1, wherever it appears, with a 2, and vice-versa. Note that Eqs. (5.5), (5.6), (5.8), and (5.9) are written in units of biomass (kg), whereas (5.4) is in units of area (m²) and (5.7) is in units of height (m).

We still have to explain the rainfall factors f (i.e., f_g and f_T). Although the time step of our model is one month, we have already pointed out that we are really interested in changes from one season to the next. We will therefore only input rainfall to the model each season and we will only specify one of three rainfall classes: low, average, and high. By this we mean low, average, and high *for that season*, so 150 mm of rain may be average during the summer but would be high in winter. We then construct tables like Table 5.3, which defines the factor f_g for grass as a function of the rainfall and when it occurs. The table tells us, for instance, that low rainfall in spring is more beneficial to the grass than high rainfall in winter. A similar table can be constructed for f_T.

Equations (5.4) through (5.9) show only one of many possible ways of modeling the vegetation growth; all may be equally plausible. This is not to say that nothing is known about vegetation growth—there is in fact a large body of knowledge about it— but most of what is known is too detailed for our level of resolution. What is important, therefore, is that our equations should capture the gross effects of herbivory and the vegetation's competition for rainfall and sunlight in a manner that is consistent with what is known.

Whether the vegetation model we have built is adequate for our purposes can only be decided by testing it. Before doing so, however, we should be concerned, as we were at the end of the last section, about how complex our model is becoming, despite all our efforts to the contrary. Equations (5.4) through (5.9) may only be designed to model the gross features of vegetation growth, but note how many new parameters we have introduced. Remember, too, that there are another six equations for

TABLE 5.3 CORRECTION FACTOR f_g
FOR THE GROWTH RATE
OF THE GRASSES

Season	Rainfall		
	Low	Medium	High
Spring	0.3	0.5	0.8
Summer	0.4	0.6	1.0
Fall	0.2	0.3	0.4
Winter	0.0	0.1	0.2

the unpalatable subclass and that the various parameters can vary from
one region of the park to another. We will have to guess at values for virtually all of them!

ESTIMATING PARAMETERS AND TESTING
THE MODEL

It is impossible to formally validate the sort of model we have built, but it
is possible to test each individual module to see whether it behaves in an
acceptable manner. To test the modules we have to determine reasonable
estimates of the relevant parameters; testing and parameter estimation
thus go hand-in-hand.

The parameters of a model can, in theory, be estimated in one of two
ways. Either we have data relating directly to the model (e.g., field
measurements of fecundity and mortality) or we have data relating to the
output from the model (e.g., census data for the populations), in which
case we can deduce the parameters indirectly. Sophisticated techniques
are available in the latter case for making the best use of the available
data (see Spriet and Vansteenkiste, 1982).

In practice, however, we seldom have sufficient data to estimate
parameters in either of these two ways. What we do is piece together
some direct data, some indirect data, and whatever experience or intuition
is at hand, then test to see whether the output is plausible. This process is
similar to the informal way in which we explored the sensitivity of the
roan model in Chap. 3.

Three requirements are essential to tune a large system model in this
way:

1. The model must be broken down into modules that are tested
   one at a time. In the confined context of a module it is easier to
   see and understand which of two guesses at a parameter, for example, is more realistic.
2. We must have interactive computing facilities.
3. Biologists with experience of the system being modeled must be
   actively involved; if possible, they should estimate parameters
   and interact with the computer themselves.

All three requirements were met in the case of our model. The process of testing and tuning the first two modules (hervibory and herbivore
dynamics) went smoothly. The herbivory module was decoupled from
the rest of the code and was tested by varying the number of herbivores
in the different categories, varying the food available in the six vegetation classes, then seeing how the food was shared out.

Good estimates of how much the herbivores were likely to eat could be obtained from published data (Meissner, 1982). Considerably more guesswork was involved in the herbivore dynamics module, especially in the algorithms for calculating the condition indices. Good estimates were available for fecundity rates. The mortality rates (which are a function of the condition index) were found by asking questions such as, "Under such-and-such conditions, what percentage of impala lambs would you expect to survive?" At the end we had confidence that this module was robust for making *comparisons* between the various herbivores even if the actual numbers were not precise.

The vegetation growth module, however, led to difficulties. We understand unambiguously what is meant by a zebra (even if it incorporates a white rhinoceros), but it is harder to visualize the class of palatable grasses. This difficulty was overcome by identifying the most common palatable grass, unpalatable grass, palatable shrub, and so on in each of the five regions of the park, then basing the model on the behavior of those particular species. For example, this led to accurate estimates of the maximum grass height h_{max}, but to less accurate estimates of the various growth rates r. There was good field data for the saturation level U (data that suggested that the production of "green" biomass in African savannas at this level of rainfall was about 4000 kg per hectare), but no data for the woody biomass capacity T_{max}. All we could do was guess in such a way that the guesses reflected the differences between the five regions of the park.

Testing the vegetation growth module involved decoupling it from the rest of the code. As a result, we had to specify how much of each vegetation class was eaten each month. A good starting point was to see how the vegetation behaved in the absence of herbivores. The results showed the grass growing to its maximum height, the trees and shrubs sprouting as many leaves as possible, and then nothing changed; the grass and leaves stayed forever.

This is not a surprising result if we look at the equations. We have built in herbivory as the *only* mechanism that reduces grass height and the major mechanism for reducing leaf biomass. Is this realistic? If we assume that our trees are all evergreen and interpret the constant leaf biomass as a balance between leaf loss and new growth, this result is acceptable, but we cannot justify stands of perpetually tall, green grass.

What, besides herbivores, will have a negative effect on the grass? Three mechanisms were identified and incorporated into the model. The first recognized that if grass remained very short for a long time, this would have a negative effect on the basal area of the grass. The second was the action of termites. They are active in only three of the five regions, but were guessed to be capable of removing up to 50 percent of the grass under certain conditions. These conditions were built into the logic of the program. The third mechanism allowed long-standing grass to become moribund. This can only occur during winter, and then only if the grass is close to its maximum height and if the total rainfall over the past two or more years is appropriate.

The introduction of moribund grass turned out to be useful in a number of different ways. First, the standing moribund grass inhibited the growth of fresh new grass. Second, it led to a realistic simulation of the effects of fire. A *fuel load factor*, which depended on the amount of moribund grass and woody material in the shrubs, was introduced. The possibility of setting fire to the region, and the effect of doing so on grass, shrubs, and trees were all related to this factor. Last, the moribund grass was allowed to decay with time (the effect of reducing agents) and could even be grazed by herbivores, but only as a last resort.

With these changes, the vegetation growth module eventually gave results that were reasonable for the rapidly changing components (grass height and leaf biomass) but were not totally convincing for the slowly changing components (grass basal area and the woody component of shrubs and trees). We will comment on this last point in the discussion.

A LIST OF ASSUMPTIONS

We set out to build as simple a model as we could to predict how cropping one herbivore species would affect the other herbivores. Despite our attempts to keep the model simple, it has somehow managed to grow more and more complex. As it does so, it becomes more difficult to decide what to include and what to leave out. We are in danger of building a model that is unbalanced in the sense that parts of the model are described in too much detail and other parts in too little detail.

What is needed is a method for maintaining perspective while the model is being built. One way of doing this is to keep, update, and regularly refer to a list of the main assumptions built into the model. If an argument then develops about whether a particular effect should be included in the model, it can often be settled by ranking the importance of that effect relative to the assumptions already on the list. The following is a list of some of the assumptions built into our model:

- Adult and juvenile herbivores have the same food preferences, but a juvenile eats less than an adult.
- The condition of a herbivore is determined only by diet.
- The birthrate is independent of condition, but juveniles suffer much higher mortality when condition is poor.
- Only wildebeest and zebra can move between different regions of the park.
- There is always a part of the vegetation biomass that cannot be grazed or browsed.
- The growth of vegetation is driven by rainfall and season.
- Competition between the grass and woody components is indirect

and depends on how fast they grow and the carrying capacities for the different soil types.

- Shrubs and trees do not inhibit grass height, but the amount of woody biomass can inhibit the grass basal area.
- Short trees do not grow into tall trees. They are just a different type of vegetation, and the model does not attempt to simulate the population dynamics of trees.
- Termites have no preference between palatable and unpalatable grass.
- Moribund grass has no direct effect on the woody vegetation. Indirectly it has a positive effect by reducing the height and basal area of the grasses, and a potentially negative effect by facilitating burning.
- Burning decreases the basal area of grasses, as does over-grazing.
- Unpalatable shrubs are more susceptible to fire than palatable shrubs.

The reader should note how a list such as this conveys the essence of the model even though we have not explained how it has all been implemented. Not only does a list of assumptions help to control balance and resolution during the construction of a model, it helps to communicate the scope of the model to potential users (and to defend the model against potential critics) once the model has been built.

What is deliberately left out of a model is just as important as what is put into it.

USING THE MODEL

Once all the modules have been individually tested, we can put them together and see what kind of results the model as a whole produces. There is always a moment of euphoria in building a system model when, after struggling with the details and the separate parts of the model, we get our first results for the entire system. The euphoria is often short-lived; we discover that the problem of detail is still with us. Where before we had to worry about details of structure, now we have to worry about the details of input and output.

Apart from all the parameter values, so many numbers have to be fed in to describe the initial state of the system, and because the investment (in time or money) of performing a system simulation is not negligible, these numbers have to be chosen thoughtfully. There are also many numbers that we could print out or graph once the model is running, What should we look at, what can we ignore, how should we present the results, how do we interpret them? These suddenly become important questions, so important that it is worth spending a little time discussing them before we look at some results.

Coping with the Output

We agreed earlier in this chapter to look at our results every season. We could therefore print out the condition index, the number of juveniles, and the number of adults for each of the six herbivores in each of five regions in the park—i.e., 90 numbers a season to describe the state of the herbivores only. If we also want to describe the state of the vegetation we need to look at the slowly and rapidly changing variables for each of six vegetation classes as well as a fuel factor for each region—i.e., another 65 numbers. Obviously we have to be selective in what we look at.

It is important not to make the selection too early. Only *after* we have looked carefully at some of the output can we decide whether we should look at the other variables. The answer is to write *all* the output onto a computer file or disk, then interrogate that file selectively.

A Management Game

Unless standard graphing and data-handling software is used, it is worth spending a fair amount of effort in writing the code to interrogate the output file. If that code is written imaginatively, the system model can easily be converted into a management game. For example, one of the problems that managers face is how to allocate time and money to routine data collection in the park. Presumably the more time or money they allocate to a monitoring program, the better the quality of the data they will receive.

It is easy to simulate this. The graphing routines can be combined with a random number generator that can add different error levels (or "noise") to the actual output data. Those playing the management game then have to "buy" information from the model. The more they pay, the better the quality of the information they receive. All players have a limited "budget." The object is to see which players gain the best feel for the behavior of the system from their monitoring strategy. This can be an exciting technique for communicating the model results to a wider audience.

SOME RESULTS

The reader will have noticed that our description of the system model is, at best, sketchy. For example, we have not even described the algorithm for moving those herbivores that do move between regions. One of the problems with system models is that it takes a monograph to describe them in any detail. It takes a second monograph to present the results. All we will do here is give two examples. They have been chosen to show what kind of results can be obtained from the system model, and to underscore the point made in the previous section about the necessity of carefully choosing the output we look at.

An Example of Intraspecific Competition

All the diagrams in Fig. 5.2 refer to the first Cretaceous region, a region of clay soils supporting wooded grasslands (with a short grass layer) and thickets. The model was used to simulate what might happen over a period of 16 years (without management intervention) if a small population of about 70 giraffe were introduced into the region. Figure 5.2(d) shows the pattern of rainfall used for the simulation. Its important characteristics are two periods of low rainfall separated by six years of medium-to-high rainfall.

Figure 5.2(a) shows what happened to the giraffe population during those 16 years. It is interesting to see how the population continued to grow throughout the first period of low rainfall (when the giraffe population was only about 80), but declined during the second drought (by which time the population had grown to nearly 300). Other herbivore populations, such as kudu and impala, were also expanding during those years; that the giraffe were competing mainly with themselves can be deduced from Figs. 5.2(c) and (e). These show the leaf biomass on palatable and unpalatable tall trees respectively, both food resources that are utilized *only* by giraffe.

We see that during the first dry period the palatable browse was nearly depleted but the unpalatable browse was virtually untouched. During the second dry period the larger giraffe population first depleted the palatable browse, then (presumably because palatable browse on shrubs was already heavily used by kudu and impala) made large inroads into the browse on unpalatable trees. The effect this had on their condition index is shown in Fig. 5.2(b). There was a slight deterioration in condition during the first dry spell and a much more severe deterioration during the second dry spell.

We mentioned earlier that we often need to go back and look at additional output from the model. In this case it was interesting to ask how the mortality during the second dry spell occurred. The answer, when we retrieve more of the data, is that the reduction in population was largely due to juvenile mortality.

An Example of Interspecific Competition

The graphs shown in Fig. 5.3 tell a more complicated story of interspecific competition and the side-effects of cropping one herbivore species. In this case the results shown are for the region of old dunes, where there are deep, sandy soils supporting areas of short dry forest (with virtually no grass) and woodland with moderately tall grass.

The dotted-line graphs in Fig. 5.3 indicate what happened to the impala, kudu, and warthog populations, and to the leaf biomass on palatable shrubs, during a simulation of 16 years without management intervention. The graphs show impala and kudu populations that continue to

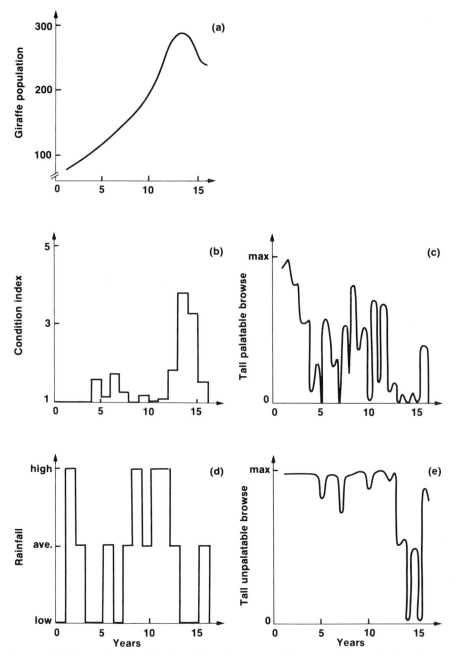

Figure 5.2 Results showing the effect of intraspecific competition: (a) the giraffe population, (b) the giraffe condition index, (c) the amount of palatable browse on tall trees, (d) the rainfall pattern, and (e) the amount of unpalatable browse on tall trees.

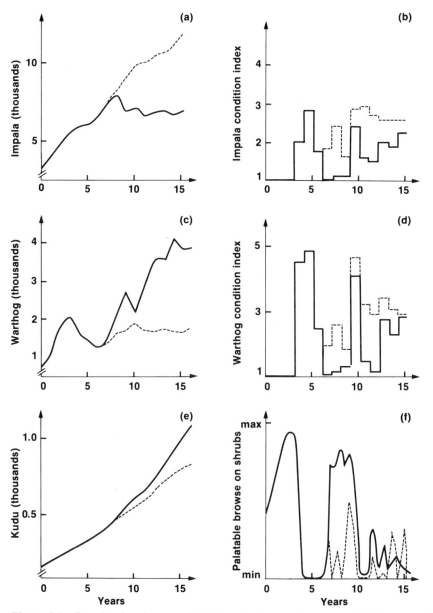

Figure 5.3   Results showing the effect of cropping impala on two of their competitors (warthog and kudu). The solid lines show what happens if the impala are cropped whenever their population exceeds 6000. The dashed lines are results obtained under similar circumstances without any cropping. (a) The impala population. (b) The impala condition index. (c) The warthog population. (d) The warthog condition index. (e) The kudu population. (f) The amount of palatable browse on shrubs and short trees.

grow at a steady rate throughout the 16 years. It is interesting to note that in neither case is the growth exponential.

After a few years the leaves on palatable shrubs are heavily utilized and the impala population, for instance, while still growing, is not in the peak of condition. The warthog population, after an initial period of very rapid growth, loses condition and fluctuates about a limit of approximately 1700. Evidently the warthog are unable to compete with the impala, who can utilize both the grass and palatable browse. Note that the' warthog condition deteriorates whenever *palatable browse* is in short supply.

The solid-line graphs in Fig. 5.3 show what happens if, under identical circumstances, a decision is made to crop impala. The cropping strategy is to reduce the population to 6000 whenever it exceeds that limit. Cropping first takes place in year 7 of the simulation, so for the first seven years the two simulations are indistinguishable. The graphs show that the consequences of controlling the impala population are:

1. An improvement in the impala condition index (which presumably has the side-effect of increasing impala production and increasing the number of impala that have to be removed each year)
2. A marked increase in the available browse on palatable shrubs, but only for a period of three to four years
3. A moderate increase in the rate of growth of the kudu population
4. A rapid increase in the warthog population until it reaches a new limit of about 3900—i.e., more than twice the previous limit

It was precisely to predict effects such as this that the model was built. It is therefore encouraging to see these results, but difficult to decide how much reliance we can place on them.

DISCUSSION

There are a number of points to be made about the system model we have built in particular and about system models in general.

Despite all our attempts to keep the model as lean and simple as possible, what has emerged is a relatively large and complicated model. If this is a disappointment, it should be pointed out that system models can be orders of magnitude larger and more complicated. It is worth speculating what might have happened if we had not built the model from the top down—i.e., if we had not used the management objectives to start modeling the herbivores down through the vegetation to the rainfall. The rainfall, after all, is what drives the whole model, so it looks like a logical starting point. The first question to ask would then have been, "What do we know about the rainfall?'' and the response would have been gratifying: There are good, extensive data on rainfall in the park. Given these data, it would have been difficult to resist the temptation to model the rainfall in some detail, and this false start could well have burgeoned into a model of fantastic complexity.

Notice, in contrast, how in our top-down approach we never even asked how good the rainfall records were; the question was not important. This underscores a vital point: *The initial structure of a model must be determined by the objectives, not by the available data.* However, as we saw in Chap. 3, the data may subsequently constrain that initial structure.

Nevertheless, it is worth asking whether we could have built a simpler model. It would be difficult, given our objectives, to make the herbivory and herbivore population dynamics modules any leaner. If there is any excess fat in the model, it is likely to be in the vegetation module.

The discipline we first impose on the design of a model often becomes more lax as the modeling exercise progresses. It is therefore prudent to review late additions to the model to decide whether they were really necessary. Introducing termites and the concept of moribund grass into our model certainly made the model look more realistic, but also made it more complicated. Could we have left them out? The answer must surely be no; both effects impinge directly on what is available for the herbivores to graze. Moreover, the introduction of moribund grass leads to a plausible routine for simulating the effects of fire, and burning is a management option we want to be able to exercise. It is likely, however, that if we had included these effects in the initial design of the model, we would have introduced them more elegantly.

Looking carefully at time scales is often a fruitful route to simplification. We built a model to investigate how a system changes with time, so we should be explicit about the time scale of interest to us. Although we have not actually said so, in this model we are not interested in changes that might occur from night to day. We *are* interested in seasonal changes, so we want to know how grass height and leaf biomass change from one season to another. We are also interested in time scales of a few years during which we might discern the effects of alternative management strategies, but if we look at our list of assumptions we realize that we have implicitly decided we are not trying to predict what might happen over periods as long as 20 or 30 years. On that time scale, trees could grow from seedlings and then decay, whereas we have assumed that the population dynamics of the trees can be ignored.

Our time scale is thus somewhere between 5 and 20 years, but we have not addressed the question of whether it is closer to 5 than 20. This is an important question. If the former, we should not expect to be able to model the impact of the herbivory on competition between the different classes of vegetation. If the latter, we would expect our model to predict changes, for example, in the number of shrubs in a region or the relative areas covered by palatable and unpalatable grasses. In fact, because we did not address this question, our model falls between two time scales. Let us see why.

The vegetation growth module contains some variables that change slowly and some that change rapidly. Our algorithm updates all these variables every month. Obviously the slowly changing variables (grass basal area and the woody component of shrubs and trees) do not need to be updated as often as the more rapidly changing grass height and leaf biomass. A time step of one year would be more suitable. In fact, if our model is only going to predict what will happen to the herbivores over a 5- to 10-year period, we can probably neglect the changes in basal area and the woody component altogether. Equations (5.4), (5.5), and (5.6) could then be deleted and we could specify A, S, and T (for both subclasses) as input to the model—i.e., they would be treated as parameters rather than variables. This would give us a leaner model that enables us to concentrate more effectively on the herbivores and what they eat.

On the other hand, if we are interested in how the herbivores will affect the vegetation over a period of, say, 10 to 20 years, our modeling of the slowly changing variables is too crude. Equations (5.4), (5.5), and (5.6) allow the rainfall (through the factors f_{g} and f_{T}) to influence the growth rate of the basal areas and woody components, but there is no allowance for the effect that herbivory might have on these growth rates. We remarked in a previous section of this chapter that the simulation results for the slowly changing vegetation variables were unconvincing; the reason is that the model in inadequate in this regard.

The discussion about time scales shows us that we were not as successful as we might have been in imposing the necessary intellectual discipline during the construction of our model. This is a common failing. One of the paradoxes of modeling is that discipline is most difficult to impose where it is needed most—in large system models. We often notice the weaknesses in the design of a large model only after it has been built. Given the effort that has gone into the model by that stage, it takes courage to point out those weaknesses and suggest how they should be rectified.

Given the choice between simplifying the system model or improving its capability to predict changes in the slowly changing vegetation variables, management will almost certainly opt for the latter, the argument being that management is indeed interested in the impact of the herbivores on the vegetation. This would probably be an unwise decision. A simplified version of our current model would eliminate its weakest component and allow us to explore its strengths. We are likely to learn a lot more about the effects of cropping on the herbivores in that way, and we could probably deduce whether they are having a longer-term impact on the vegetation from the values of the rapidly changing vegetation variables. If, for example, the palatable grass is grazed so that it is kept very short, this is bound to have a deleterious effect.

Broadening the objectives of a model usually dilutes its effectiveness in addressing the original, more limited objectives. This is a trade-off that should be remembered whenever we meet the temptation to do a little more with a system model.

The other temptation to be avoided is that of trying to make the model more realistic. Because there is often a fair amount of detail in a system model, the model may give the appearance of being realistic in parts. The temptation then is to try to make the rest of the model look equally realistic, irrespective of whether it is necessary in terms of the objectives of the model. In particular, if the system model is to be used directly by management (possibly in the form of a management game), it is often argued that unless the model is realistic, those interacting with it will have no faith in its results. This argument misses the whole purpose of modeling. The purpose is *not* to be realistic, *not* to inspire blind faith in the results, but to make people think. The proper approach is to educate management to use models that are patently abstractions and simplifications. Not only is this the intellectually sound approach, but it is far easier to do than to build models that really are realistic!

In the same vein, some would see the list of assumptions as a list of what still needs to be done to improve the model. On the contrary, the list of assumptions is there to help explain to others (and sometimes to oneself) what the model addresses and what it does not (and should not) attempt to simulate.

The results we eventually obtained from the model are interesting, plausible, perhaps even correct, but they are neither exciting nor surprising. If there is an element of surprise it is in the fact that when we put together all the components of the model, despite the assumptions and lack of data, what came out was actually meaningful.

There are two good reasons for this. First, the structure of the model is basically simple and sound. It consists of two trophic levels (herbivores and vegetation); the herbivores compete for vegetation and the vegetation competes for sunlight and water. Second, although much of the data we used in the model was guessed at, the guesses were intelligent and their *relative* values were plausible. What we get out of the model is therefore bound to be correct in a qualitative way.

There are also good reasons why the results are not surprising. We have not exercised this model as vigorously as we exercised the models in the previous chapters, partly because the model is large, but mainly because we do not know what to look for. We have not gained much insight into our model, so we do not know how to use it effectively. (Contrast this with our experiences with the simpler models of Chaps. 2 and 3, where one thing led, almost compulsively, to another.)

Moreover, if the results had been surprising we would have found it difficult to explain them. In fact, all the results that were thought to be surprising turned out to be caused by errors in the computer code or input data. (Yet another disadvantage of a large model is that one always has a suspicion that errors are still lurking in the code.)

RECAPITULATION

Our system model is not very large, but it is large enough to illustrate both the advantages and disadvantages of building large system models.

Here are the advantages we noticed:

1. We can indeed model a web of interactions and get plausible results.
2. A lot can be learned about the system we are modeling through the questions we are forced to ask in the process of building the model. Often, the process of building the model is more instructive than using it.
3. Building a large system model forces us to face the difficulties inherent in studying any complex system and to recognize the simplifications we have to make to gain any understanding at all. These difficulties can to a certain extent be ignored or underplayed in field work or when making empirical decisions, but the framework of a model imposes an intellectual honesty which, if nothing else, leads to an appreciation of the magnitude of the problem.

Here are the major problems we encountered:

1. It is difficult to keep the objectives firmly in mind and to control the growth of the model, particularly when the model is being built by a team rather than an individual.
2. It is equally difficult to refrain from adding to the objectives or changing the specifications for the model while it is being built.
3. Finding all the data needed to support the model is not easy. It follows that the sensitivity of the model should be explored extensively. Precisely because the model is large, this is difficult to do. First, there are a large number of input variables to change. Second, there are a large number of output variables that might be affected by those changes. Which should we look at? The pragmatic answer is that we should not talk about the sensitivity of the model in the abstract. We should rather test how sensitive a *decision*, based on the model, is to some of the input data. In other words, sensitivity analysis should be problem-oriented just as the design of the model is objective-oriented. This gives the sensitivity analysis a focus, but it still remains a formidable task.
4. It is asking too much to maintain an intellectual grasp of the entire model, so it becomes a "black box" on which we perform experiments in much the same way as we perform experiments on the real system—i.e., without quite knowing what the experiment is likely to produce. Sometimes this can be useful, but we

lose the real advantage of modeling—because we are experimenting on a structure of our own creation, we can truly *understand* the results.

The question to be asked whenever we contemplate building a large system model is whether the time and effort could not more usefully be spent in building a series of smaller models. The reader may want to think about this question after reading the next chapter.

FURTHER READING

Background material for this chapter can be found in the paper by Meissner (1982), which compares the forage intake of various African herbivores. Sinclair (1975) investigates when resources in an African savanna limit the herbivore populations.

Most system models are considerably larger than the one described in this chapter and more concerned with defining processes than with questions of management. Innis (1978) contains material on a large grassland simulation model, including a chapter on sensitivity analysis. Phipps (1979) describes a management-oriented model used to predict the effects of flood frequency and the depth of the water table in a wetlands forest.

How to cope with detail in an organized fashion is described in Swartzman (1979). Overton (1975) discusses a structured, hierarchical approach to large system models. Goodall (1972) provides an overview of large ecosystem models. He believes, as did many of those working on large system models, that the model improves as we add more and more detail—a different philosophy from that espoused in this book.

When we have a large model, the sensitivity analysis must be designed in much the same way as a series of field experiments; this is discussed in Reed et al. (1984). When we have the appropriate data, we can also be more sophisticated in the way in which we estimate parameters, as described in the section on parameter estimation in Spriet and Vansteenkiste (1982).

There are examples of less ambitious system models and system models with well-defined management-oriented objectives. Walters and Bunnell (1971) describe how system models can be useful as management games. Botkin et al. (1972) present a computer model of forest growth that is a good example of a system model with a carefully chosen level of resolution. Milner (1972) describes a reasonably complex compartmental model and uses it to look at the interaction between sheep and vegetation. Pellew (1983) is another good example of a small, management-oriented system model.

6

Variations on a Theme: Analytical Models

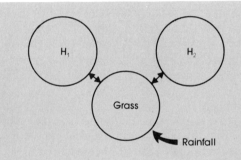

In Chap. 1 we drew the distinction between *simulation* models (which use the language of mathematics but depend on the computer for step-by-step calculations) and *analytical* models, where the aim is to draw conclusions from the mathematics itself. All the models described so far have been simulation models; this chapter is devoted to analytical models. They will be illustrated by a variety of problems that relate to subsections of the system model described in Chap. 5. Our purpose is (1) to introduce the reader to analytical models and show how they make use of mathematical concepts, and (2) to show what one can learn from a few small models, each relevant to only a part of a much larger system model.

ANALYTICAL MODELS AND DIFFERENTIAL EQUATIONS

In simulation models we give the computer an algorithm that enables it to calculate how the variables change from one time step to the next. In mathematical terms, the rate of change of a function is called the *derivative* of that function with respect to time. It follows that if we can write the algorithm that describes how a variable changes as a mathematical expression, we will have an equation for the *derivative* of the variable. This is called a *differential* equation, and many analytical models take this form.

The way in which we build an analytical model and then deduce its behavior is best illustrated by an example. Let $H(t)$ represent the size of a zebra population at time t. Then dH/dt represents the rate at which that population is growing at time t. We will assume that the population is restricted to a small, closed park, so that there is no immigration or emigration. It follows that the only changes that can occur in the population are births and deaths, so dH/dt must be equal to the rate at which zebra are born minus the rate at which they die.

In some climates, zebra have no preferred breeding season but reproduce throughout the year. We will assume that our park has such a climate. We can then argue that the larger the size of the zebra population, the more births there will be, on average, at any time—i.e., the rate at which zebra are born is proportional to H. The rate at which they die (assuming there are no predators) will also be proportional to H. This leads to an equation of the form

$$\frac{dH}{dt} = bH - mH \qquad (6.1)$$

which is a differential equation. Note that the parameters b and m can be interpreted as the number of births per zebra per year (if t is measured in years) and the number of deaths per zebra per year respectively.

In practice, b and m will not be constants in time but will depend on a number of factors such as the quality and quantity of the food supply, weather conditions, and diseases and parasites. But let us for the moment assume that both b and m are indeed constants. If we look at Eq. (6.1) we see that if $b > m$, then dH/dt will *always* be positive, irrespective of whether H is small or large. It follows that the population will *always increase*. If $b < m$, the population will always decrease, while if $b = m$, new births will exactly compensate for deaths and the size of the population will never change.

This is the type of information we can infer just by looking at differential equations. It is essential to do this, if only to make sure that the mathematics behaves as we expect it to. (In this particular example we should be uneasy that Eq. (6.1) permits the zebra population to keep on growing unchecked, no matter how large the population.) Once we are convinced that the differential equation has the properties we expect, we can try to actually solve it. It should be stressed, however, that a lot of effort can go into finding the mathematical solution—in some cases it cannot be found and we say that the equation is *intractable* —so it pays to infer as much as possible from the form of an equation before trying to solve it.

In the case of Eq. (6.1), the solution can easily be found. If we know that there are H_0 zebra at some time we will call $t = 0$, the solution tells us that the number of zebra at some subsequent time t will be

$$H(t) = H_0 e^{(b-m)t} \qquad (6.2)$$

The model we have proposed thus leads to either exponential growth (if $b > m$) or exponential decay (if $b < m$).

What more does the solution tell us? We could graph it, as in Fig. 6.1, and see how it looks and perhaps compare it with field data, if we have any, or we could look for distinctive properties of the solution. For instance, if we put $H(t)$ equal to $2H_0$ in Eq. (6.2), a little manipulation leads to the result $t = [\ln 2]/(b - m)$. Since this does not depend on the value of H_0, we infer that one of the properties of our model is a characteristic doubling time that depends only on b and m.

Obviously the population cannot go on doubling indefinitely. The model we have proposed is therefore bound to be inadequate at large values of H. (We were uneasy about this before we even solved the differential equation.) To remedy this, let us suppose that the birth parameter b is independent of H but that the mortality parameter m increases with increasing H. For simplicity we will assume that the relationship between m and H is a straight line of slope α:

$$m = m_0 + \alpha H \qquad (6.3)$$

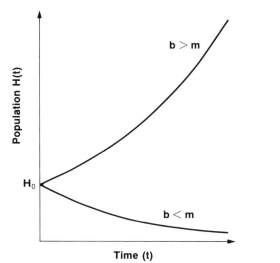

Figure 6.1 Exponential growth ($b > m$) and decay ($b < m$).

This is called a *density-dependent* effect. Substituting (6.3) into (6.1) we get

$$\frac{dH}{dt} = bH - (m_0 + \alpha H)H$$

or

$$\frac{dH}{dt} = H(c - \alpha H) \qquad (6.4)$$

where we have written c for $b - m_0$.

Looking at Eq. (6.4) we notice that dH/dt will be 0 if H is equal to c/α; the population will therefore remain constant if it ever reaches that value. Moreover, if H is greater than c/α, dH/dt will be negative, so the population will decrease until H is exactly equal to c/α, and will remain constant thereafter. Similarly, if H is less than c/α, dH/dt will be positive and will increase until it reaches the value c/α. Thus, no matter what our initial population may be, it will eventually reach the value c/α and stay there. We call c/α the *asymptotic* population.

Equation (6.4) is called the *logistic* equation. If H has the value H_0 at time $t = 0$, its solution is

$$H(t) = \frac{H_0 c e^{ct}}{c - \alpha H_0 (1 - e^{ct})}$$

and one can confirm that for large times the solution tends to the value c/α. A graph of the solution is shown in Fig. 6.2, and the shape of H versus t is the characteristic S-shape normally associated with the logistic equation. For small times at low populations, the solution looks very much like exponential growth. But as the population increases, the density-dependent mortality plays an ever-increasing role, the rate of growth is slowed, and eventually the population stabilizes.

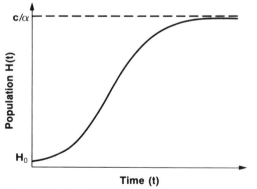

Figure 6.2 Logistic (density-dependent) growth.

It is not very satisfactory, particularly if we are trying to manage the zebra population, to postulate a density-dependent mortality without understanding why it occurs. In later sections of this chapter we will induce a density-dependent effect, not by the mathematical device we have used here (making the mortality increase with increasing population), but indirectly by making the herbivores compete for food. The purpose of introducing the logistic equation here is only to show how the model of exponential growth can be modified. In fact, from the examples described, we can generalize to the following procedure for building, modifying, and manipulating analytical models:

1. First, for each variable in the model, make a list of those processes that will increase the value of the variable and those that will decrease it. From this list, write in words a *conservation law* or equation that balances what comes in with what goes out. For example, the list for the herbivore variable might contain (1) births, (2) deaths, (3) immigration, and (4) emigration; the conservation law would be:

   Rate of change of herbivores = rate of birth
   + rate of immigration − rate of emigration − rate of deaths

2. Deduce a mathematical expression for each of these rates. An example of how to do this is the way in which we argued that the birth rate was proportional to the size of the zebra population. This step is the most important in the development of any model. It is here that we model the mechanisms that bring about changes in the system. The examples in the rest of this chapter will provide further illustrations of how to do this.

3. Combining steps 1 and 2, we can write a differential equation for each variable in the model.

4. See how much can be deduced about the behavior of the variables without actually solving the differential equations. This usually means testing to see when the derivatives or rates of change are 0, when they are negative, and when they are positive. These tests serve two purposes: First, they alert us to possible inadequacies or misrepresentations in the model (which we can then try to rectify). Second, if the behavior of the equations is plausible, they may teach us something pertinent about the system we are modeling. Noticing that for $b > m$ the model in Eq. (6.1) led to an ever-increasing population is an example of the first point. Inferring that the population will stabilize at a value of c/α for the model in Eq. (6.4) is an example of the second.

5. Once we are comfortable with the gross behavior of the model, we can try to solve the differential equation or equations. As

mentioned earlier, there are many differential equations that even the best mathematicians cannot solve. In these cases we have to resort to the computer and solve the equations numerically. We will see how to do this later in the chapter.

6. Interpret the solution. This is the most important part of the exercise. Here we discover the mathematical properties of the model we have built and try to relate them to our field data and what we know of the real system. It is vital to remember that the properties of the solution are a direct consequence of the mathematical structure. That structure in turn is something *we* created when we made various assumptions and put together our model. The solution can give us useful information about the structure that may enable us to understand our problem better or, if we are skeptical, to rebuild our model. An example of this is the characteristic doubling time of the exponential growth model. This is a useful piece of information about populations experiencing exponential growth. It is also a warning that our model must eventually break down.

MODELS OF VEGETATION GROWTH WITH CONSTANT HERBIVORY

One of our objectives in this chapter is to try and reproduce some of the effects and interactions we noted in the system model of Chap. 5 by focusing specifically on those interactions and ignoring the rest of the ecosystem dynamics. The interactions of interest to us are those related to rainfall and its effect on the vegetation, herbivory and the interaction between the vegetation and the herbivores, competition between herbivores for similar food resources, and the effect of different control measures on herbivores and vegetation.

We are going to build up our models to investigate these interactions step by step, starting with vegetation growth with constant rainfall, adding a constant grazing pressure, looking at the effect of fluctuating rainfall, and, finally, allowing the herbivore populations to respond to the state of the vegetation.

A Preliminary Model

We begin, therefore, with a model for the vegetation. We can think of this either as a single class of vegetation (in which case we will ignore competition from other classes of vegetation) or as a representation of the total edible biomass. In either case we let $V(t)$ represent the green biomass at time t. Our differential equation for dV/dt will then be a statement of the fact that the rate of change of V is equal to the growth rate minus the decay rate (and, when we introduce herbivory, minus the rate at which the vegetation is eaten). Noy-Meir (1975) has argued that plant growth is a good example of a natural process that indeed satisfies the logistic equation—i.e., an equation of the form

$$\frac{dV}{dt} = gV\left(1 - \frac{V}{K}\right) \tag{6.5}$$

If we draw a graph of this expression for dV/dt versus V, we get an inverted parabola, as in Fig. 6.3(a). Noy-Meir argues that when the biomass is low, any new leaf area will improve the capacity for photosynthesis, so dV/dt will at first increase with increasing V. As the biomass increases, effects such as shading and competition or self-interference become important and the growth rate levels off and eventually decreases. Finally, when V is equal to K, maintenance losses exactly balance photosynthesis and no further growth takes place. We can therefore think of K as the maximum biomass that can be supported. It will depend on the type of vegetation, on the soil, and on average weather conditions. The general shape of Fig. 6.3(a), if not the exact form of Eq. (6.5), has been verified experimentally in pastures.

What happens if we superimpose a constant grazing pressure on this model—i.e., we assume we control the herbivores in such a way that they consume the vegetation at a constant rate of G units of vegetation per unit of time? Equation (6.5) then becomes

$$\frac{dV}{dt} = gV\left(1 - \frac{V}{K}\right) - G \tag{6.6}$$

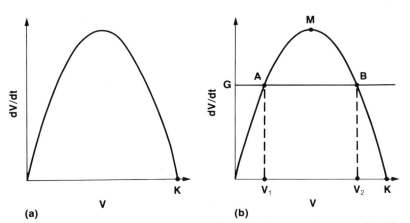

Figure 6.3 Vegetation growth rate dV/dt plotted versus the vegetation biomass V for the logistic model: (a) no grazing and (b) showing the line of constant grazing pressure G.

We will not actually solve this differential equation, but we can argue the effect of herbivory very effectively from Fig. 6.3(b). Here we graph Eq. (6.6) in two parts: First, we redraw the parabola $dV/dt = gV(1 - V/K)$ of Fig. 6.3(a), then we superimpose the straight line $dV/dt = G$. The growth rate in Eq. (6.6) will then be the *difference* between the parabola and the straight line. If we look at a value of V where the parabola is above the straight line ($V_1 < V < V_2$), the growth rate will be positive. If the straight line is above the parabola ($V < V_1$ or $V > V_2$), the growth rate will be negative. It follows that where the straight line intersects the parabola, herbivory will exactly match new growth and there will be no net change in the vegetation. This occurs at points A and B in the figure.

Stability of the Preliminary Model

It is illuminating to look at points A and B more closely. Suppose the system is in equilibrium at point B, where the vegetation is V_2. What happens if for some reason—perhaps the termites are more active this year—the vegetation drops slightly below V_2 while the grazing rate G remains unchanged? We would then move to the left of V_2 in Fig. 6.3(b), so we know that dV/dt would be positive. That in turn tells us the vegetation would recover until it was in equilibrium with the herbivory at B again. Similarly, if a perturbation led to a slightly higher value of V, we would move to the right of V_2 where dV/dt is negative, so the vegetation would decline until it reached its equilibrium value V_2 once again. It follows that B is a *stable* equilibrium point; the system returns to B when it is perturbed.

If we repeat this exercise for point A, we can confirm that it is an *unstable* equilibrium point. For example, if V drops below V_1, we move into a region where dV/dt is negative, so the vegetation will continue to decrease unless the grazing pressure is reduced. It is important to note that this distinction between a stable and an unstable equilibrium point does not depend on the precise form of Eq. (6.6). We can expect to find both types of equilibrium points as long as the general shape of the dV/dt versus V graph (in the absence of herbivory) is something like a parabola.

Finally, we can use Fig. 6.3(b) to define an upper limit to the grazing rate G. As we increase G, points A and B will move up their respective sides of the parabola until they merge at point M. If we increase G any further, the herbivores will always graze faster than the grass can grow, which is an unstable situation. The upper limit on G is therefore just below point M (below, because at M itself the system could be unstable). It can easily be shown that at point M, $dV/dt = gK/4$, so we know that G must be less than $gK/4$. (This value is sometimes called the maximum sustainable yield or MSY.) This result *does* depend on the precise form of Eq. (6.6).

Varying the Rainfall

So far we have assumed that our climatic conditions are identical from one year to the next. In practice it is the change in rainfall that is so important in African savannas. How should we modify Eqs. (6.5) and (6.6) to reflect variations in rainfall from one year to the next?

Let us look at Eq. (6.5) first and introduce herbivory later. There are two constants in (6.5), a growth parameter g and a carrying capacity K. Presumably an increase in rainfall will lead to an increase in both constants: The vegetation will grow faster and the carrying capacity will increase. Suppose, however, that the previous year was so dry that the herbivores reduced the vegetation to a very low level. If the current year is very wet, because V itself is so low it will make very little difference in (6.5) if we increase both g and K—dV/dt will still be low. Experience tells a different story: Even if V is very low, there is likely to be a spurt of new growth with the first rains. Where does our model diverge from reality?

If we retrace our argument for the shape of the dV/dt versus V graph, we will recall that when V is low, the leaf area available for photosynthesis is low, so dV/dt is correspondingly small. If we think about what happens in practice, we must conclude that the spurt of new growth is fueled from the underground reserves or woody component of the vegetation. Our model only considers the green biomass. This discussion should remind us of the way we modeled the various classes of vegetation in the previous chapter. We had *two* variables to describe each class, one that changed quite quickly (analagous to the green biomass) and one that changed more slowly (analagous to the reserves). We have been trying to model with only *one* variable, and that is the cause of our confusion.

Moreover, if we think carefully about the field evidence we used to justify Eq. (6.5), we will realize it was based on day-by-day observations in a pasture during one particular growing period—i.e., it was a model of growth during a season. That is the wrong time scale for the model we are trying to build. We are really interested in what happens from one year to the next.

Our mistake has been in using intraseasonal data to build an interseasonal model. All the analysis and discussion in this section may therefore be relevant to the grazing pressure in a pasture during any one growing season, but it has no relevance at this level of resolution to longer-term interactions between rainfall, vegetation growth, and herbivory.

An Interseasonal Model of Vegetation Growth

We have two options at this stage. The first is to develop a two-variable model for the vegetation—one variable to describe the logistic type of behavior during the growing season and one that models the reserves from one year to the next. The second option is to derive a completely new model of the green biomass, one that is meaningful on a time scale of years and therefore implicitly reflects the role of the reserves. One equation is always easier to work with than two, so on the grounds of parsimony we will try the second approach first.

Going back to first principles, we can argue that if V is the green biomass, dV/dt will be equal to the difference between the rate of new growth and the rate at which the vegetation decays. Provided we have sufficient reserves, the rate of new growth will depend on rainfall (and perhaps temperature) and will be largely independent of the value of V itself. However, the decay rate will depend on V in much the same way as the death rate in the herbivore model of the previous section depended on the size of the herbivore population. This leads to an equation of the form

$$\frac{dV}{dt} = a - pV \qquad (6.7)$$

where the rate of new growth a is a function of rainfall and p is a decay constant. Before we explore the properties of this new model, there are a number of points to make about our modeling experience in this chapter so far.

Interlude

The way we analyzed the logistic model of vegetation growth with constant herbivory is an excellent example of what we can learn from an analytical model without even solving the equations. The reader should note how we drew conclusions at two different levels. Some results (e.g., on stability) depended only on the general shape of the graph in Fig. 6.3, not on its precise equation, while others (e.g., the maximum value for G) were less robust because they depended on the precise equation.

The logistic model of vegetation growth is one of the few models in this book to be built on the basis of really good field data. Unfortunately, as we discovered, those field data were at the wrong level of resolution for the type of model we were trying to build. The logistic model is not wrong, but it is inappropriate to the problems we are trying to solve.

In the context of the new model we have built, the discussion about photosynthesis is a second-order effect; the first-order effect is the influence of rainfall on new growth. That is why we have specified that the coefficient a in Eq. (6.7) is a function of rainfall only. We could argue that p depends on rainfall too (grass becomes moribund faster in dry conditions), but that would also be a second-order effect.

We must not forget that our new model for vegetation growth has a built-in assumption—that there are always sufficient reserves to respond to rainfall. We have seen how easy it is to forget the premises that underlie a model, and we must be careful not to use this new model in situations where we really need a vegetation model with two variables. Examples of such situations might be an extended period of overutilization that leads to depletion of the reserves, or a herbivore that is capable of uprooting the vegetation on a large scale. It would also be inappropriate to try to model competition between two types of vegetation without using two variables to represent each type.

The New Vegetation Model with Constant Herbivory but Fluctuating Rainfall

If we introduce a constant grazing rate G into our new model, Eq. (6.7) becomes

$$\frac{dV}{dt} = a - pV - G \tag{6.8}$$

and the reader should, using the techniques of the previous sections, be able to confirm that provided $G < a$ (i.e., provided the herbivores consume the vegetation at a rate that is less than the rate of new growth), there will only be one equilibrium point, that the value of the vegetation at equilibrium will be $(a - G)/p$, and that the equilibrium is always stable.

Suppose now that the rainfall fluctuates. The simplest way to represent this is to assume a smooth cycle of good and bad years, in which case we could replace the new growth rate a by the expression

$$a[1 + \beta \sin(\omega t)] \tag{6.9}$$

where $0 \le \beta < 1$. From the properties of the sine function, it follows that the new growth rate will fluctuate between the values of $a(1 - \beta)$ in the worst year of the cycle and $a(1 + \beta)$ in the best year. One full cycle will have a period of $T = 2\pi/\omega$ years.

Substituting (6.9) in (6.8) leads to the differential equation

$$\frac{dV}{dt} = a + a\beta \sin(\omega t) - pV - G$$

This equation can be solved, and the solution, after a few cycles, settles down to the form

$$V(t) = \frac{a - G}{p} + \frac{a\beta}{\sqrt{p^2 + \omega^2}} \sin(\omega t + \delta) \tag{6.10}$$

where δ, the so-called phase angle, will be explained shortly. The minimum value of the vegetation will occur when the sine term in Eq. (6.10) is equal to -1, so we can write

$$V_{min} = \frac{a - G}{p} - \frac{a\beta}{\sqrt{p^2 + \omega^2}}$$

Multiplying throughout by p and rearranging the terms in the above expression, we see that to ensure that V_{min} is always greater than 0, G must be less than a maximum value:

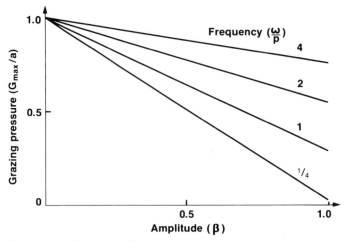

Figure 6.4   The reduction in the maximum constant grazing rate G_{max} as a function of the amplitude and frequency of regular fluctuations in the rainfall. (*Note:* All quantities are in dimensionless form.)

$$G_{max} = a - \frac{a\beta}{\sqrt{1 + (\omega/p)^2}} \tag{6.11}$$

When $\beta = 0$ (which means that the rainfall is always constant), Eq. (6.11) reduces to $G_{max} = a$, which is what we would expect. Figure 6.4 shows how the right-hand side of Eq. (6.11) varies with β and ω/p. It tells us that if our policy is to have a constant grazing rate (which is almost, but not quite, the same as a constant number of herbivores) despite the fact that the rainfall fluctuates from year to year, then the maximum grazing rate we can sustain drops off as the amplitude of the rainfall oscillations increases. Since a longer cycle implies a smaller value of ω, Fig. 6.4 also tells us that long cycles in the weather are more deleterious than short cycles—i.e., we would have to reduce our grazing pressure for a weather pattern that repeats itself every 20 years compared with a weather pattern that repeats itself every 2 years. This makes sense intuitively. The longer cycle implies longer sustained periods of dry conditions.

The phase angle δ in Eq. (6.10) tells us that the fluctuations in the vegetation are out of phase with the fluctuations in rainfall. It can be shown that $\tan \delta = -\omega/p$. The minus sign implies that the vegetation lags behind the rainfall, so the vegetation will reach its lowest value not in the year of lowest rainfall, but later in the cycle when the rainfall is already beginning to pick up and approach its average value. This too makes sense if we remember that we are keeping our grazing pressure constant throughout the whole cycle.

Obviously, fluctuations in rainfall do not occur in smooth cycles and do not repeat themselves in a precise number of years. Nevertheless, our analysis gives us a feel for the effect that fluctuations in rainfall can have

on the vegetation when the rate of grazing is kept constant, and how this limits the maximum grazing rate.

In the next section we will see what happens when we allow the number of herbivores (and hence the grazing rate) to respond to changes in vegetation.

MUTUAL INTERACTION BETWEEN VEGETATION AND HERBIVORES

Functional Response of the Herbivores

If we let $H(t)$ represent the number of herbivores at time t, and if each herbivore grazes (if it possibly can) at a rate q (measured in units of biomass per herbivore per unit time), the total grazing rate G in Eq. (6.8) will be $qH(t)$. However, the state of the vegetation can affect the rate at which a herbivore grazes. If V is very low, the herbivore may spend a great deal of time finding food and its rate of consumption will drop. Conversely, if the herbivore prefers short grass, when V is large it might have trouble finding food and its consumption rate will also drop. We therefore need to modify q in some way depending on the value of V and the type of herbivore. We can do this by introducing a function $f(V)$, which is 0 when V is 0 and has a maximum value of 1. We then postulate that the consumption rate of each herbivore is in fact $qf(V)$. We call $f(V)$ the *functional response* of the herbivore to the state of the vegetation. The shape of the functional response will differ from one species of herbivore to another, as illustrated in Fig. 6.5.

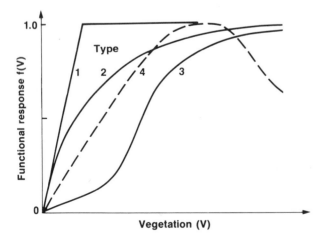

Figure 6.5 Four examples of how a herbivore might respond to the available vegetation. (*After Holling, 1965, and Caughley, 1981.*)

Caughley (1981) discusses what is known from pasture measurements about functional response curves. The concept itself is obviously an oversimplification. The herbivore's response will depend on the composition of the vegetation, for instance, and on whether there are patches of short or tall grass. However, these are effects we have ignored in our model, so the concept of a functional response fits well with our level of resolution. Introducing this concept into Eq. (6.8) we get

$$\frac{dV}{dt} = a - pV - qf(V)H(t) \qquad (6.12)$$

The concept of a functional response also provides a neat way of modifying the population dynamics of the herbivores in terms of their food intake. If we look back at Eq. (6.1),

$$\frac{dH}{dt} = bH - mH$$

we can postulate that the birth coefficient b is unaffected by the herbivores' diet, but that mortality increases to the extent that the herbivores have not met their consumption requirement q—i.e., we write

$$m = m_0 + s[1 - f(V)]$$

where s is a constant. Equation (6.1) then becomes

$$\frac{dH}{dt} = bH - m_0H - sH[1 - f(V)]$$

or

$$\frac{dH}{dt} = sf(V)H - rH \qquad (6.13)$$

where we have written r for $m_0 + s - b$. Note that we would expect both r and s to be positive with $s > r$—i.e., the herbivore population would normally increase, but could decrease if the functional response were low. Note too that we could argue that the function $f(V)$ in Eq. (6.13) is not necessarily the same as the functional response in Eq. (6.12): The herbivores could conceivably eat less grass, but the nutritional quality may not be proportional to the amount eaten. This distinction is unimportant in the following discussion, so we will assume that the two functions are identical.

Phase Diagrams and Stability

Equations (6.12) and (6.13) are differential equations that describe the mutual interaction between the vegetation and an unmanaged herbivore population. We will discuss their solution later. First we will see what can be gleaned from them without solving them. From (6.13), dH/dt will be 0 when

$$f(V) = \frac{r}{s} \tag{6.14}$$

and from (6.12), dV/dt will be 0 when

$$H = \frac{a - pV}{qf(V)} \tag{6.15}$$

These equations tell us that the herbivore population will be steady when the vegetation is such that their birth rate exactly matches their death rate, while the vegetation biomass will be steady when the rate of new production matches the rate of decay plus the rate of consumption. For equilibrium, dH/dt and dV/dt must be 0 at the same time, so we can use Eq. (6.14) to determine the equilibrium value for V, then substitute that value in (6.15) to find the equilibrium value for H.

It is pertinent to ask whether the equilibrium is stable. We cannot talk about an equilibrium point unless the rainfall is constant. It follows that a, the rate of new production, must also be constant. Let us assume for the moment that this is so. Then we can test for stability by looking at what is called a *phase diagram* for the two differential equations. Normally we would represent the solution to Eqs. (6.12) and (6.13) by drawing two graphs, one a plot of V versus time and the other a plot of H versus time. In a phase diagram we plot H directly versus V, as in Fig. 6.6. The figure shows, as we move from one time to another, how we trace a curve in the phase diagram. That curve is called the *phase trajectory*.

It is sometimes possible to sketch the phase trajectory roughly without ever actually solving the differential equations. This is done as follows. In Fig. 6.7(a) the vertical line AB represents Eq. (6.14)—namely, $f(V) = r/s$, while the curve CD represents Eq. (6.15). We call these two graphs *isoclines*. On AB we know that dH/dt is 0, and we can remind ourselves of this by drawing little horizontal lines on AB (horizontal because that implies H is not changing). Also, by inspecting Eq. (6.14) we can see that if $f(V) < r/s$, then dH/dt will be negative and so H will decrease with time. We can represent this by drawing arrows 1 and 2 to the left of AB to denote *decreasing H* and arrows 3 and 4 to the right of AB to denote *increasing H*. Similarly, the vertical lines along CD remind us that dV/dt is 0 on CD, arrows 5 and 6 denote that V is *increasing* ($dV/dt > 0$) below CD, and arrows 7 and 8 denote that V *decreases* above CD.

dV/dt and dH/dt are both 0 simultaneously at point E where the two isoclines cross. E therefore represents our equilibrium point. If a small perturbation moves us away from equilibrium to any point P in the diagram, we will know that equilibrium is stable if the phase trajectory traces a path that leads back to E. In Fig. 6.7(b) we sketch the phase trajectory. Starting at P, we follow the sense of the arrows, making sure that whenever the trajectory crosses CD it is vertical and whenever it crosses AB it is horizontal. The reader should try to do this; it is difficult to draw a trajectory that does not spiral back to E. This suggests that equilibrium is stable.

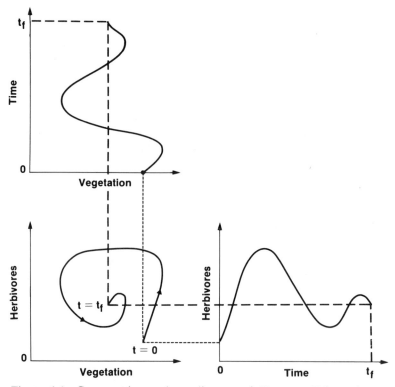

Figure 6.6 Constructing a phase diagram of *H* versus *V* from the graphs of *H* versus *t* and *V* versus *t*.

There are a number of points to note about this use of the phase diagram:

It is not always possible to tell unambiguously from the phase diagram whether an equilibrium point is stable. There are, however, mathematical tests for stability that are infallible even when the phase diagram is ambiguous. It can, for instance, be proved that E in Fig. 6.7(b) is a stable equilibrium point.

Point E is not the only equilibrium point in the diagram. From Eq. (6.13), dH/dt is also 0 when $H = 0$, so the V-axis in Fig. 6.7 is also an isocline. It follows that point D is also a point where both dH/dt and dV/dt are simultaneously 0. The reader can confirm that it is an unstable equilibrium point in the sense that with the introduction of only a few herbivores, the phase trajectory will move away from D toward E.

The fact that the phase trajectory spirals inward instead of tracing a more direct curve from P to E tells us that the vegetation biomass and herbivore population will oscillate, but with decreasing amplitude, before reaching their equilibrium values.

In sketching the isoclines we have implicitly assumed a type 1, 2, or 3 functional response (see Fig. 6.5). For a type 4 response, there could have been *two* values of V satisfying $f(V) = r/s$ and we could have had two equilibrium points. It can be shown that the equilibrium point corresponding to the lower value of V (where the slope of the $f(V)$ curve is positive) is always stable, while the other value is always unstable.

Once the phase trajectory has traced a path from some initial condition to the equilibrium point E, it will stay there unless the rainfall changes. It follows that the graph of H versus time t will also eventually reach a particular value and stay there. This would look like the solution to Eq. (6.4), as shown in Fig. 6.2. Equation (6.4) completely ignores the vegetation, but does contain a density-dependent term. We argued when we wrote (6.4) that this density-dependent term was artificial and that it would be preferable to have an underlying mechanism that produced much the same effect. Our model of mutual interaction between the vegetation and the herbivores does that.

The concept of an equilibrium point loses its meaning when we allow the rainfall to fluctuate from one year to the next and we cannot then easily sketch phase trajectories. The only way to probe the behavior

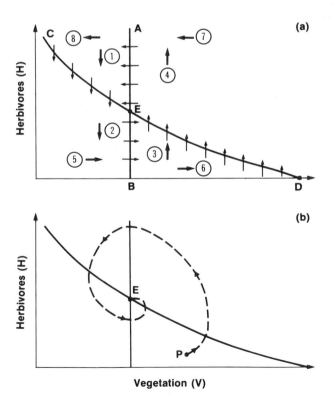

Figure 6.7 Constructing a phase trajectory without solving the differential equations. (a) Preparation (the numbered arrows are referred to in the text). (b) The phase trajectory.

of the model under those circumstances is to solve the differential equations (6.12) and (6.13), recognizing that a is now a function of time. We mentioned earlier that there are many differential equations that even the best of mathematicians cannot solve. Equations (6.12) and (6.13) are mathematically intractable. In the next section we will see how they can be solved numerically using a computer and we will explore how our model behaves when rainfall is not constant.

Numerical Solutions and Fluctuating Rainfall

For the sake of convenience, let us rewrite the differential equations (6.12) and (6.13):

$$\frac{dV}{dt} = a(t) - pV - qf(V)H(t)$$

and

$$\frac{dH}{dt} = sf(V)H - rH$$

where we have written $a(t)$ to emphasize that the rate of new growth a will change with time.

These equations cannot be solved mathematically for arbitrary $f(V)$. To find out how V and H respond to different rainfall patterns, we therefore have to somehow generate the solution to the equations. The simplest technique for doing this is known as *Euler's method*. Suppose we know the values of V and H at some time t. We can then get good estimates of V and H a little later, say at time $t + \Delta t$, by moving along the tangents (at time t) of the graphs of V and H versus time respectively. We can write these estimates as

$$V(t + \Delta t) = V(t) + \Delta t \frac{dV}{dt}$$

and

$$H(t + \Delta t) = H(t) + \Delta t \frac{dH}{dt}$$

and substituting for dV/dt and dH/dt (at time t) from Eqs. (6.12) and (6.13) we get

$$V(t + \Delta t) = V(t) + \Delta t[a(t) - pV(t) - qf\{V(t)\}H(t)] \quad (6.16)$$

and

$$H(t + \Delta t) = H(t) + \Delta t[sf\{V(t)\}H(t) - rH(t)] \quad (6.17)$$

If we are given the growth rate $a(t)$, (6.16) and (6.17) enable us to step from the solution at any time t to the solution at the next time $t + \Delta t$. Starting with known values for V and H at time $t = 0$, we can use these equations to estimate V and H at time Δt, then use those estimates to calculate V and H at time $2\Delta t$, and so on. This is Euler's method and it is very easily implemented on a computer. The solution is only approximate because we assume that dV/dt and dH/dt do not change during the time interval t to $t + \Delta t$. In theory, therefore, the smaller we choose Δt, the more accurate our approximation. But in practice, if we make Δt very small, we run into problems with the precision of the computer.

We refer to Euler's method as a numerical method because it only enables us to solve the equations if we actually substitute numerical values for all the coefficients and variables on the right-hand side of Eqs. (6.16) and (6.17). Thus we can only obtain a solution for one particular set of values of p, q, r, s, and so on, at a time. If we want to know what happens if we change s, for instance, we have to compute the solution all over again. This is the price we pay for not being able to solve the differential equations mathematically; we lose the overall perspective an analytical solution provides. Unfortunately, when the equations are intractable, we have no option but to solve them numerically.

Figure 6.8 is an example of the kind of result one can get using Euler's method. It shows the way in which a small herbivore population grows over a period of some 20 years during which there are two cycles of good and poor production. The results were obtained using a time step Δt of 0.2 years. The figure shows how the herbivores are unaffected by the first drought, when their numbers are low, but not so during the second drought, when their population has grown. This is reminiscent of the kind

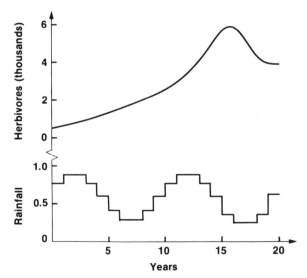

Figure 6.8 A numerical solution for changes in a herbivore population during years of fluctuating rainfall.

of result we noted when we were exercising the system model in Chap. 5. The reader should refer back to Fig. 5.2; the two figures obviously tell the same story.

This is exciting because we have taken the herbivore and vegetation out of the context of the complex system model and represented their interaction by a pair of relatively simple differential equations. The type of result we get is indistinguishable from the results obtained using the complex model. This is encouraging evidence in support of our contention that one can often successfully model parts of a complex ecosystem in isolation. We will see another example of this shortly.

Before looking at more complex models of herbivore-vegetation interaction, there are a few points to make both about the results we get when we solve the equations with fluctuating rainfall numerically and about numerical solutions of differential equations in general.

Euler's method is the simplest available for solving differential equations numerically. We have chosen to present it here because it is so intuitively obvious and simple to explain. More accurate numerical solutions of differential equations (see, for example, Conte and de Boor, 1972) can be obtained using any one of the more sophisticated methods readily available in the form of computer packages. However, we will argue later in this chapter that Eqs. (6.16) and (6.17) may actually be a better model of the system than the original differential equations (6.12) and (6.13), in which case the use of a more sophisticated package would not be warranted.

It is always useful to check the choice of the time step Δt whenever we use a numerical method. A suitable value of Δt is one that is small enough so that the results do not change significantly if we make Δt any smaller, but not so small that we run into trouble with the precision or power of the computer.

We lose perspective when we are unable to solve equations mathematically. Note, for instance, how we were able to look at Eq. (6.11) in the previous section and deduce that the grazing pressure had to be reduced more drastically for longer rainfall cycles than shorter cycles. The only way we could reach that kind of conclusion via a numerical solution would be by performing a set of computations for different rainfall cycles, and comparing results. Even then we could never be sure (as we can when we have a mathematical expression) that any trend we notice is robust. We would have to change all the other parameters in the model to see if they affect the trend. The way in which we think with a numerical solution is more like the way we use simulation models than the way we use an analytical solution.

It follows that if the equations cannot be solved mathematically, the only advantage of building a model in terms of differential equations lies in the analyses we can perform (such as those associated with the phase diagram in the previous section) *before* we actually solve the equations. These analyses are usually concerned with questions of equilibrium and stability, which can be very important, but are in fact obscured as soon as we allow the rainfall (and hence the rate of new vegetation growth) to change with time.

Figure 6.9 illustrates this. It shows two trajectories, both drawn from the results of numerical solutions of Eqs. (6.12) and (6.13). The first shows the trajectory obtained when the rainfall is cycled as in Eq. (6.9). The second shows the trajectory obtained when the rainfall varies randomly, but within the same limits as Eq. (6.9). The diagram also shows the equilibrium point E we would obtain if the rainfall were constant at its average value.

It is obvious that the concept of equilibrium has lost its meaning, but analyses for equilibrium and stability are not entirely wasted. They do at least indicate (but do not guarantee) that the solution for fluctuating rainfall will meander within the region of the phase diagram that contains the equilibrium point.

A MODEL WITH TWO TYPES OF HERBIVORE

In this section we will look at two different species of herbivore, both competing for the same food resource. We will assume that there is no direct aggression between the two species and that the competition is indirect and is determined only by the limited food resource.

To be more specific, we begin by building a model of warthog and

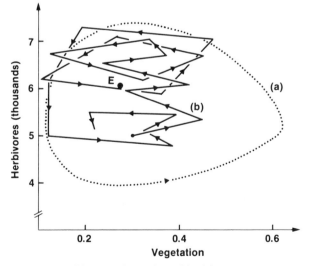

Figure 6.9 Phase trajectories of herbivores versus vegetation when rainfall fluctuates: (a) regular rainfall cycles, and (b) rainfall varies randomly. (E is the equilibrium point for constant rainfall.)

impala competing for grass. This could be interesting, because while the warthog are totally dependent on the grass for their food supply (if we think of grass in a very broad sense), the impala will utilize browse as well. In order not to introduce too many variables into our model, we will make two assumptions about the impala:

1. That their numbers are controlled by management, so we do not have to model their population dynamics.
2. That the component of grass in the impala diet is independent of the relative availability of grass and browse. This may be a weak assumption, but since it enables us to ignore the browse completely, we will make it and then consider what effect it may have at the end of our analysis.

With these assumptions we can modify Eqs. (6.12) and (6.13) as follows:

$$\frac{dV}{dt} = a - pV - qf(V)H(t) - uI \qquad (6.18)$$

and

$$\frac{dH}{dt} = sf(V)H - rH \qquad (6.19)$$

where $V(t)$ now refers specifically to the grass biomass and $H(t)$ to the warthog population at time t. $f(V)$ is the functional response of the warthog, u is the rate at which impala consume grass, and I is the number (as determined by management) of impala.

Figure 6.10(a) shows the phase diagram for these two equations. It is very similar to Fig. 6.6. The only difference is that as we increase the number of impala, the isocline CD moves down and to the left. It follows that we have a different equilibrium point corresponding to each value of I, and by the same arguments as we used on Fig. 6.6 we can deduce that each of the equilibrium points E_0, E_1, and E_2 is stable. However, if we allow the impala population to increase to the level I_3, the equilibrium point will be E_3 on the V axis. (Note that dH/dt in Eq. (6.19) is also 0 when $H = 0$, so the line $H = 0$—i.e., the V axis—is also an isocline.)

The reader can confirm that this too is a stable equilibrium point, but one that excludes warthog from the system. In practice, of course, it is unlikely that the warthog would be completely eliminated. A small warthog population would always be able to utilize some food resources not available to the impala.

We can do a rather interesting experiment with the help of Fig. 6.10(b). Suppose that for some time the impala population has been kept at the level I_2 and that the system is in equilibrium at E_2. (We are, of course, neglecting rainfall fluctuations in this analysis.) Suppose, next, that management decides to reduce the impala population to I_1. What will

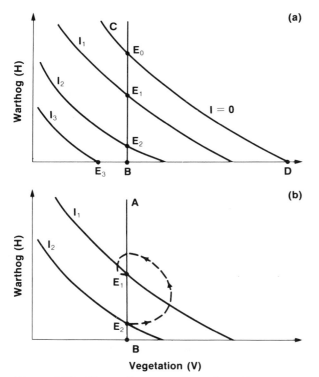

Figure 6.10   Phase diagrams of warthog H versus vegetation V: (a) shows the isoclines for different levels of the impala population I, where $I_3 > I_2 > I_1$ while (b) shows the phase trajectory when the impala grazing pressure is suddenly reduced from I_2 to I_1.

happen? E_2 will no longer be an equilibrium point. The reader should confirm that the phase trajectory from E_2 will move first to the right, curve upward, cross the isocline corresponding to I_1, then curve in to the new equilibrium point E_1. The end effect of reducing the impala population will therefore be an increase in the warthog population, but the vegetation, after an initial increase, *will decrease to its previous value*. Figure 6.11 shows the results obtained in a specific case by solving Eqs. (6.18) and (6.19) numerically.

Figure 6.11 is reminiscent of Fig. 5.3 in the previous chapter. Here too we have managed to reproduce a result we obtained from the complex system model, again using only a simple model of the interactions between the main variables.

Let us now go back to our second assumption, that the component of grass in the impala diet is independent of the relative availability of grass and browse. If this is a poor assumption, its effect is likely to be most noticeable when the green biomass is very low. It follows that the parameter u in Eq. (6.18) may not be constant when V is very low. This will affect the shape of the isoclines $dV/dt = 0$, but only when V is very

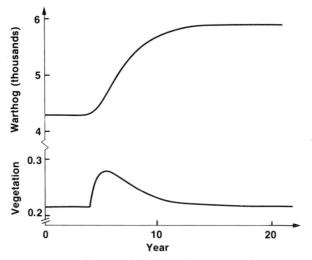

Figure 6.11   Changes in the warthog population and vegetation when the impala population is suddenly reduced (in year 4) from one level to another, then kept at the lower level.

low, and that does not materially change any of our arguments. The assumption may be poor, but it is not important at the level of resolution in this model.

More importantly, in this analysis we have assumed that rainfall is constant. As in the discussion at the end of the previous section, we hope that the general conclusions drawn from the analysis for constant rainfall will still hold in principle, if not in detail, when we allow the rainfall to fluctuate. But we cannot guarantee this will be true.

Some numerical solutions were therefore obtained for fluctuating rainfall. They confirmed that on average a reduction in impala numbers left the vegetation unchanged but facilitated an increase in warthog. They also suggested that a reduction in the number of impala reduced the amplitude of the oscillations in the vegetation but increased the amplitude of the oscillations in warthog.

This is interesting because it shows how an external factor can mediate in the interaction between rainfall, vegetation, and a herbivore. It also sounds plausible, but, as discussed in the previous section, it would require a great deal more computation to establish this as a general principle.

A MORE COMPLEX MODEL WITH TWO HERBIVORES

To show what can happen when we allow both herbivore populations to react to changes in the vegetation, we will consider a very small park. We will suppose the vegetation is homogeneous and ideal for zebra, but only marginally satisfactory for buffalo. The management objective is to maintain healthy populations of both zebra and buffalo in the park.

Because the park is small and homogeneous, we will assume that the zebra and buffalo will be competing for the same food resources. We will also assume that this indirect competition for food is the only way in which they influence each other. If we let $V(t)$ represent the biomass at time t of the food resource, $Z(t)$ represent the zebra population, and $B(t)$ the buffalo population, then by arguments analogous to those used in deriving (6.12) and (6.13) we can write,

$$\frac{dV}{dt} = a - pV - qf(V)Z - ug(V)B \qquad (6.20)$$

$$\frac{dZ}{dt} = sf(V)Z - rZ \qquad (6.21)$$

and

$$\frac{dB}{dt} = \sigma g(V)B - \rho B \qquad (6.22)$$

The meaning of the new constants (u, σ, and ρ) introduced in these equations should be obvious. It should be noted that the equations now contain two response functions—$f(V)$ for the zebra and $g(V)$ for the buffalo. Zebra will fare better than buffalo when the grass is short; buffalo will fare better than zebra when the grass is tall. We can model this by choosing a type 2 response curve for zebra and a type 3 response curve for buffalo, as shown in Fig. 6.12.

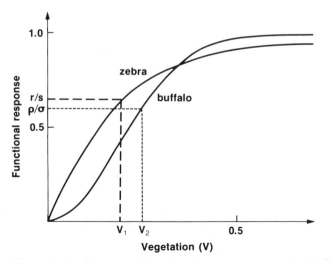

Figure 6.12 Suggested functional response curves for buffalo and zebra.

With these shapes for the response functions, it is impossible to actually solve Eqs. (6.20), (6.21), and (6.22) mathematically. We can (and will) solve them numerically, but first we will see what can be said about the behavior of the system in general terms directly from the form of the three equations. For instance, we see from (6.21) that dZ/dt will be 0 either when $Z = 0$ (i.e., when there are no zebra, which we do not want to happen) or when $f(V) = r/s$. Let V_1 be the value of V (there can only be one value) that satisfies this equation—i.e., $f(V_1) = r/s$. Similarly, from (6.22), dB/dt will be 0 when $B = 0$ (which we also do not want to happen) or when $g(V) = \rho/\sigma$. Let V_2 be the value of V that satisfies $g(V_2) = \rho/\sigma$.

The system can only be in equilibrium if dV/dt, dZ/dt, and dB/dt are all zero *simultaneously*. It is extremely unlikely that V_1 will equal V_2, so unlikely that we can assume it will never occur. It then follows from the previous paragraph that dZ/dt and dB/dt can only both be 0 simultaneously when $V = V_1$ and $B = 0$ or when $V = V_2$ and $Z = 0$, so the two species cannot coexist in this small park. Figure 6.12 shows that V_2 is likely to be greater than V_1, in which case the buffalo will die out, as can be seen from the argument in the next paragraph. If in fact $V_2 < V_1$, the same argument can be used to show that the zebra will die out.

There are three cases to consider.

1. If V lies between V_1 and V_2, the zebra population will increase while the buffalo population declines $(dZ/dt > 0$ and $dB/dt < 0)$. Equation (6.22) tells us that dB/dt is proportional to B, so that as buffalo numbers decline, their rate of decline will slow down. On the other hand, from (6.21), dZ/dt is proportional to Z, so as zebra numbers increase, their rate of increase will accelerate. Eventually the effect on the vegetation of the increase in zebra must outweigh that of the decline in buffalo. So although the vegetation may begin by increasing, in due course it must decrease and will eventually approach the value V_1. As this happens, the zebra will tend to equilibrium while the buffalo continue to decline. Eventually there will be so few buffalo left that for all practical purposes we can ignore them.

2. If $V < V_1$, both dZ/dt and dB/dt will be negative and both species will decline. As a result of this reduction in herbivory, the vegetation must increase, until eventually $V > V_1$. We can then argue as in case 1.

3. If $V > V_2$, both the zebra and buffalo populations will flourish. This will lead to a reduction in the vegetation until eventually $V < V_2$, and again we can argue as in case 1.

It follows that the stable equilibrium point for the park is one where there are no buffalo, where $V = V_1$, and where the zebra population can be found by putting $dV/dt = 0$, $B = 0$, and $V = V_1$ in Eq. (6.20). This is the only stable equilibrium point. Our model thus implies that the park is too small and homogeneous to support buffalo as well as zebra. If we solve the equations numerically, the solution confirms this result. But, depending on the values of the various parameters and the exact shapes of the two response functions, it may take many years before the buffalo actually die out. The problem might thus not be urgent.

What can management do to maintain a viable buffalo population? It really has only three options: (1) to separate the zebra and buffalo so they cannot compete for food, (2) to feed the buffalo artificially, or (3) to crop zebra.

It might be possible to implement the first option without fences —e.g., by dividing the park into regions that are deliberately burned in different ways. This might promote a mosaic of shorter and taller grass that would encourage the two species to segregate naturally. We will not consider this option here, mainly because it would require a different model. Nor will we consider the second option. Instead, we will suppose that a decision is taken to crop zebra, and we will use our model to compare three different cropping strategies.

Strategy 1. Crop zebra at a constant rate of C zebra per year.

Equation (6.21) must be modified to

$$dZ/dt = sf(V)Z - rZ - C$$

As before, $dB/dt = 0$ when $V = V_2$. It follows that dZ/dt is 0 when

$$Z = \frac{C}{sf(V_2) - r}$$

Since we have assumed $V_2 > V_1$, $sf(V_2) - r$ is positive, so we can indeed have buffalo and zebra in equilibrium at the same time. Putting this value for Z into Eq. (6.20) and putting $dV/dt = 0$ and $V = V_2$ would lead to an expression for the size of the buffalo population at equilibrium. We could in theory use these expressions to choose a suitable value for C.

It is never sufficient to show that we can find a suitable equilibrium point; we also have to show that the equilibrium is stable. It is possible, but not easy in this case, to draw diagrams that are the equivalent, in three variables, of phase diagrams, and to argue questions of stability from them. It is also possible to use standard mathematical techniques that test for stability. They show that the equilibrium is *unstable* in this case. Any slight increase in the zebra population will cause the buffalo to decline and eventually die out, while any slight decrease in the zebra population will initiate a decline in their numbers that will eventually cause them to die out (unless, of course, the cropping rate C is adjusted). This can be confirmed by solving the equations numerically.

Strategy 2. Crop zebra at a rate proportional to the number of zebra.

Suppose we crop at a rate equal to k times Z zebra per year. Then (6.21) becomes

$$\frac{dZ}{dt} = sf(V)Z - rZ - kZ$$

or

$$\frac{dZ}{dt} = sf(V)Z - (r + k)Z$$

from which it can be seen that if k is chosen so that $(r + k)/s = f(V_2)$, both dZ/dt and dB/dt could be 0 at the same level of vegetation V_2. This is not really practical. We cannot control k so precisely. If it is even a little too small the buffalo will die out, while if k is a little too large the zebra will die out.

Strategy 3. Crop zebra at a rate proportional to the square of the number of zebra.

Suppose we crop at a rate equal to K times Z^2 zebra per year. Then (6.21) becomes

$$\frac{dZ}{dt} = sf(V)Z - rZ - KZ^2$$

and both dB/dt and dZ/dt will be 0 when

$$Z = \frac{sf(V_2) - r}{K}$$

The equilibrium buffalo population can be found by putting this value for Z into Eq. (6.20) with $dV/dt = 0$ and $V = V_2$. A suitable value for K can then be chosen. It can be shown mathematically that this equilibrium point is indeed stable.

We have not discussed these three strategies with the idea that management might actually implement one of them, but rather to highlight the type of analysis we can make using models of this kind. The mathematical results are crisp and clear, but not their interpretation. Nobody, for instance, who set out to implement strategy 1 would continue to crop C zebra per year once it was obvious that the zebra population was in a major decline. A more sensible strategy might be to crop C zebra per year, but only when the zebra population is above a particular threshold. (This is not easy to analyze mathematically, but numerical results suggest that it could be an effective strategy.)

However, setting aside the limitations of strategy 1, the analysis nevertheless tells us that it is fundamentally unsound to think of cropping a fixed number of zebra per year. This is useful as a principle, particularly because there may be pressure from management to implement a strategy of this kind. Similarly, the analyses relating to strategies 2 and 3 should also be interpreted broadly. They could be summed up in rules such as, "If the zebra population doubles over a period of time, do not double the cropping quota (which might seem the reasonable action to take) but quadruple it" As a general principle, a linear response to zebra population changes is inadequate.

Even this discussion on how to interpret the mathematical results is too clear cut. So far we have ignored fluctuations in rainfall from one year to the next. If the annual production is not constant, the only way to explore the consequences of the different strategies is to solve the differential equations (6.20), (6.21), and (6.22) numerically. Figure 6.13 shows results obtained from a number of numerical solutions. The results suggest some interesting points.

No management action was taken in three of the situations graphed in Fig. 6.13. Those three situations are identical except for the way in which new production in the vegetation is modeled. In one case, new production is kept constant, in the next it varies cyclically, and in the third it varies randomly. Comparing the three solutions demonstrates how the simplest of them—the solution for constant production—manages to catch the main trend in the population dynamics of both zebra and buffalo. This is important because it is only the simplest case we can properly analyze mathematically. Figure 6.13 shows that the mathematical analysis is relevant even when rainfall and new production vary from one year to the next.

By contrast, it is illuminating to look carefully at the solution for random rainfall through the eyes of the park manager. The graphs would only be revealed to the manager year by year as data came in from game counts. (The reader should place a blank sheet of paper over Fig. 6.13(c) and move it slowly to the right to simulate this.) For the first seven years the field data would indicate a satisfactory growth in both populations. Seven years is a long time in the life of a manager, so if any theoretician suggested that zebra and buffalo could not coexist in the park, the manager might well scoff at the suggestion on the basis of hard field data.

The rainfall would be more erratic during the next seven or eight years, and this would provide a plausible explanation for the fact that the buffalo were not doing quite as well as before. In fact there would be no cause for alarm until the eighteenth year: even then it would not be obvious that the buffalo were in serious trouble. The manager might wonder whether the census had underestimated the number of buffalo, or could point to the drought and the simultaneous decline in the zebra population as evidence that the buffalo would recover when the rainfall improved —after all, nearly 20 years of experience had "proved" that buffalo and zebra could coexist in the park!

This highlights how difficult it can be to interpret even the best field

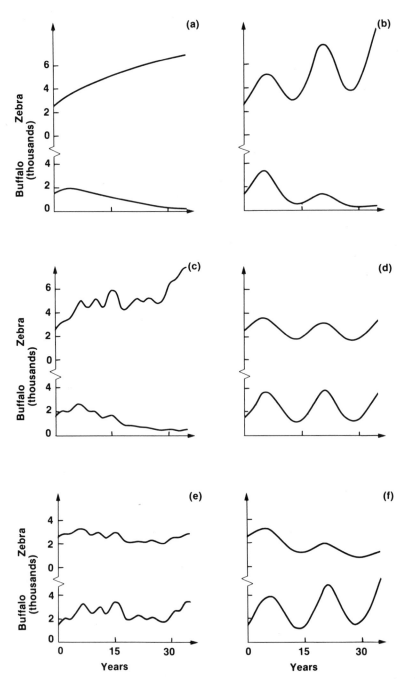

Figure 6.13   Predicted interaction between buffalo and zebra competing for the same vegetation. (a) Constant rainfall. (b) Cyclic rainfall. (c) Rainfall varies randomly. (d) Cyclic rainfall as in (b) but the zebra are cropped according to strategy 3. (e) Random rainfall as in (c) but the zebra are cropped according to strategy 3. (f) Random rainfall as in (c) but the zebra are cropped according to strategy 1.

data. Earlier in this section the reader will find a sentence that says in essence that nobody would continue to implement strategy 1 once it became obvious that the zebra population was in a serious decline. It should now be apparent that a serious decline is not always obvious. (An example can be found in Chap. 2, where the wildebeest were cropped despite a drop in their numbers.) It should also be apparent that fluctuations in rainfall can mask, over a period of time, the fundamental dynamics of a system.

There are two conclusions to be drawn from this. First, one has to be wary of basing an understanding of the system dynamics even on data from periods as long as 20 years—it may take much longer to discern the important trends. Second, the level of modeling described in this section can be of value even if its only purpose is to make us speculate about potential trends in the system dynamics.

Although the concept of an equilibrium point loses its meaning when the rainfall varies from year to year, it is encouraging to note that our analyses of the different cropping strategies are nevertheless relevant. Strategy 3, which is the stable strategy when rainfall is constant, is also successful when rainfall varies, as borne out by Figs. 6.13 (d) and (e), while strategy 2 is unstable even when the rainfall fluctuates.

We cannot assume that this will always be the case. For instance, if one herbivore has a type 3 functional response and the other a type 4, it can be shown that under certain conditions one herbivore will die out if rainfall is constant, while the other will die out if the rainfall varies sufficiently. It follows that the mathematical analyses for constant rainfall should be used to generate strategies that are *likely* to be successful, but these strategies must still be tested carefully via numerical solutions for the case of variable rainfall.

The mathematics of strategy 2 is interesting if we interpret it from a slightly different point of view. Suppose that the term $-kZ$ in the equation for dZ/dt represents deaths due to predation rather than losses due to cropping. This would be a good model if the park contained a predator with the following characteristics:

1. It does not kill buffalo (or we would have to introduce a term of the form $-\gamma B$ in the equation for dB/dt).
2. Zebra are not an important component of its diet (so that the population dynamics of the predator is independent of the zebra population).
3. It will kill zebra if the opportunity arises (which explains why the rate at which zebra are taken is proportional to Z).

It follows from point 3 that the coefficient k will be proportional to the predator population. If that population is originally small, k will be a low number, and despite the predation the zebra will thrive while the buffalo die out. We can confirm this by looking at Fig. 6.12 and noting that dZ/dt will now be 0 when $f(V) = (r + k)/s$. Provided k is small, this will lead to a value V_1 that is still less than V_2, so it will still be the buffalo that die out. Suppose, however, that the predator population thrives too (on its independent food resource). k will then increase, $(r + k)$ will increase, and it should be apparent from Fig. 6.12 that eventually V_1 will be greater than V_2, in which case it is the zebra that will die out.

A predator with the described characteristics may thus tip the balance in favor of the buffalo. As the coefficient k increases, it eventually passes through a critical value (when $V_1 = V_2$) and completely changes the dynamics of the vegetation-zebra-buffalo system. For small k the only stable equilibrium point in the system is when $V = V_1$ and $B = 0$. For large k the only stable equilibrium point is when $V = V_2$ and $Z = 0$. This switch from one type of system behavior to another is called a *catastrophe,* and the concept is important. In this example, management action (cropping too high a proportion of zebra) would have had the same effect, but the situation is reversible (it could crop fewer zebra). Conceptually, management action could, directly or indirectly, cause a system to switch from one equilibrium point to another irreversibly.

We have seen from the mathematical analysis and the numerical solutions that the addition of the term $-KZ^2$ in Eq. (6.21) stabilizes the system. It is pertinent to ask whether a term of this kind might be inherent in the system even when there is no management intervention. If, for instance, there were an explicit density-dependent effect in the zebra (one that was independent of the density dependence induced by the vegetation V), the buffalo and zebra could indeed coexist. Such an effect could conceivably be induced by limitations in a food resource other than V—i.e., a food resource not utilized by buffalo.

DISCRETE ANALYTICAL MODELS

In Chap. 1 we drew the distinction between continous models (those that lead to differential equations) and discrete models (leading to difference equations). In this chapter we have so far only used continuous models to describe vegetation growth and the dynamics of the vegetation-herbivore interaction. We have not justified this use of continuous models. Nor have we asked whether discrete models might not be equally plausible or perhaps even more realistic. We will briefly address these questions here.

Our continuous model for vegetation growth in the absence of herbivory is Eq. (6.7),

$$\frac{dV}{dt} = a - pV$$

The equivalent discrete model is

$$V_{t+1} = V_t + a - pV_t \tag{6.23}$$

where a now represents the new production between times t and $t + 1$ and p is the fraction of the vegetation that decays during this period.

Equation (6.23) is not meaningful until we specify the interval between time step t and the next time step, $t + 1$. Depending on how we plan to use the equation, an appropriate time interval could be a season (three months) or a year. It would not be appropriate to choose a time interval of a few days or weeks because on that time scale the appropriate model is the logistic equation (6.5). Equation (6.23) models vegetation changes *between* seasons, not during a season.

There are subtle differences between the differential equation and Eq. (6.23). In the differential equation, a represents a growth rate (if t is measured in years, a will have the units of biomass per year) and at *any* time the equation assumes that the vegetation is growing at that rate—i.e., growth takes place continuously throughout the year. In Eq. (6.23) time is not continuous, and a represents net growth, not a growth rate (it has units of biomass). Moreover, the model does not care how the growth actually takes place between t and $t + 1$ as long as the total new production during that time is equal to a. The difference equation also makes it easy to "switch on" the growth for one season of the year (if the time step is a season) and switch it off for the remaining three seasons. We will explore this idea shortly.

We now introduce herbivory. Suppose our time step is one year and that the herbivores consume an amount of vegetation G each year. Equation (6.23) then becomes

$$V_{t+1} = V_t + a - pV_t - G \qquad (6.24)$$

which is the discrete version of Eq. (6.8). In differential equations, as we have seen, it can be useful to draw a graph of dV/dt versus V. For difference equations it is often useful to plot V_{t+1} versus V_t. The result in the case of Eq. (6.24) is a straight line of slope $1 - p$ with intercept $a - G$ on the V_{t+1} axis, as shown in Fig. 6.14. Equilibrium will be reached when V_{t+1} is identical to V_t. We therefore draw the line $V_{t+1} = V_t$ on the graph, and the point E where it intercepts the line representing (6.24) is the equilibrium point. We can confirm that at E,

$$V_{t+1} = V_t = \frac{a - G}{p}$$

Only positive vegetation values are meaningful, so G must be less than a.

We can use Fig. 6.14 to argue that equilibrium is stable. Suppose we perturb the vegetation to the value represented by V_1 on the V_t axis—i.e., the vegetation is greater than its equilibrium value. We can then predict the vegetation V_2 in the following year by moving vertically upward from V_1 until we hit the graph that represents Eq. (6.24) at point P. Moving horizontally from P we can read off the value of V_2 on the V_{t+1} axis. However, if we stop when we hit the line $V_{t+1} = V_t$ (at Q), then drop down vertically, we can read the value of V_2 on the V_t axis instead. Note that V_2 is closer to

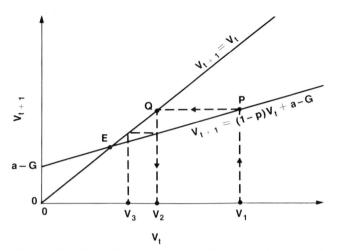

Figure 6.14 The difference equation for vegetation growth with constant grazing pressure is a straight line on a graph of the vegetation V_{t+1} at time $t + 1$ versus the vegetation V_t at time t. Where this line crosses the line $V_{t+1} = V_t$ is the equilibrium point E. The diagram shows how the vegetation returns to equilibrium if it is perturbed to a value V_1.

equilibrium than V_1. Using a similar construction, starting at V_2, we can find V_3, which is even closer to equilibrium, and so on. The reader can confirm that the solution also approaches equilibrium from the left.

Suppose that we now introduce a herbivore H with functional response f and allow it to interact with the vegetation. The difference equation versions of (6.12) and (6.13) will be

$$V_{t+1} = V_t + a - pV_t - qf(V_t)H_t \qquad (6.25)$$

and

$$H_{t+1} = H_t + sf(V_t)H_t - rH_t \qquad (6.26)$$

Putting $H_{t+1} = H_t$ in (6.26) leads to the equation $f(V_t) = r/s$. Let us call the value of V_t that satisfies this equation V^*. Similarly, putting $V_{t+1} = V_t = V^*$ in (6.25) leads to the result

$$H_t = \frac{s[a - pV^*]}{qr}$$

We will call this H^*. It follows that the system will be in equilibrium when V has the value V^* and H has the value H^*. The stability of this equilibrium point can be investigated mathematically. If the response function of the herbivore is type 1, 2, or 3, it can be shown that the stability condition is

$$p + qH^*f'(V^*) < 2$$

Recall that the differential equations (6.12) and (6.13) are always stable at equilibrium for functional-response types 1, 2, and 3. We thus see that the condition for stability in the difference equation model is more restrictive than in the corresponding differential equation model. As a rule, difference equation models of a system are less stable than differential equation models of the same system. The explanation here is that in the differential equation model herbivores react instantaneously to changes in vegetation, and vice versa. The difference equation model has a built-in time delay of one time step, which is destabilizing.

The question that should then be asked is whether the time delays built into Eqs. (6.25) and (6.26) are biologically realistic. Suppose we use the equations with a time step of one season. The term containing $f(V_t)$ in (6.26) then implies that the survival rate of the herbivores during the three months between times t and $t + 1$ depends on the vegetation biomass at the beginning of that time period. This may well be a better assumption than one that implies a continuous and instantaneous reaction on the part of the herbivores to changes in vegetation. However, the term in H_t in (6.25) implies that the amount of vegetation consumed by the herbivores during the same period depends on the number of herbivores at the beginning of the period. This can be a poor assumption, especially if there is a significant drop in the herbivore population during the season. At a critical time, the model could implicitly assume that dead herbivores are still consuming vegetation. It would be better to write (6.25) in the form

$$V_{t+1} = V_t + a - pV_t - q\frac{f(V_t)H_t + f(V_{t+1})H_{t+1}}{2}$$

which assumes an average rate of herbivory. This has no effect on the stability at equilibrium, but it does affect numerical results away from equilibrium. In particular it influences how far the system can be perturbed from equilibrium and still return to it.

It is difficult (often impossible) to solve nonlinear difference equations mathematically, but they are trivial to solve numerically. Note that (6.25) and (6.26) are already in a form that could be built directly into a computer program.

If we choose a time interval of one year, note too that (6.25) and (6.26) are identical to Eqs. (6.16) and (6.17) with a time step of one year. It follows that when we use Euler's method to solve differential equations we are really converting those differential equations into difference equations. The same holds true if we choose a time interval of three months. [It may not be immediately obvious that the equations are still identical, but if the reader looks carefully at the units implicit in each pair of equations it will be apparent that $\Delta t \times a$, $\Delta t \times p$, etc., in (6.16) and (6.17) must be numerically equal to a, p, etc., in (6.25) and (6.26).]

There is, however, a subtle difference in the way we interpret the two sets of equations. We have already argued that it would be a mistake to choose a time interval of a few days or weeks for the difference equation model because we would then be modeling interseasonal growth, which is better described by a logistic equation. However, we could legitimately choose a very small time step in Euler's equations because there is no implied biological interpretation of those equations. Their sole purpose is to obtain an accurate numerical solution of the differential equation model.

This raises an interesting question. If we can interpret Euler's equations in biological terms when we choose a time step of three months, but not when we choose a time step of three days, then even though a time step of three days leads to a more accurate solution of the differential equations, would it not make more sense biologically to choose a time step of three months? In other words, is a difference equation model better than the differential equation model of this particular system?

In general, the answer depends on the important characteristics of the system being modeled and on how the model is to be used. For example, if time delays are an important feature of the system, difference equations are clearly a better mathematical tool for constructing the model. If they are not important, differential equations have the practical advantage, at this level of modeling, of being easier to investigate mathematically. The answer also depends on the level of resolution of the model. For a broad overview, the continuous model will be easier to manipulate and may still capture the essential features of the system dynamics (except where time delays are crucial), while the discrete model is more realistic and easier to build if we want to include more detail in the model.

We could, for example, easily develop a discrete model that permits different effects in each of the four seasons. At the beginning of this chapter we introduced the idea of a differential equation by looking at the dynamics of a zebra population. The form of that differential equation depended on the argument that zebra have no preferred breeding season. We then used that model, or variations on it, throughout the rest of the chapter and for many different species without ever asking whether they had a preferred breeding season.

This was an oversight on our part, but if we had asked the question, even if the answer had been that the species concerned (like wildebeest) had a very short and distinctive calving season, we still would not have changed our model for the simple reason that we were already neglecting seasonal effects in the vegetation growth. So the assumption of a constant birth rate (throughout the year) was not a poor assumption within the resolution of our model. However, once we introduce different effects in each of the seasons into our model, we have to be sure that our assumptions are consistent at this new level of resolution.

This means that not only will we model seasonal growth patterns in the vegetation, but we must also, where necessary, model seasonal differences in the herbivore population dynamics. In this way we build more realism into the model, but as we do so, its character will change. It will soon become a simulation model, to be used in the spirit of the models described in Chaps. 2 through 5, rather than an analytical model conceived in the spirit of this chapter.

THE ROLE OF ANALYTICAL MODELS

The results we discover in any model are predetermined by the way we have built it and the assumptions we have made en route—i.e., the results we obtain from a model follow directly from its structure, *not* from the structure of the real world. However, if we have been astute in building the model and if we interpret the results at the appropriate level, the model should tell us something useful about the real world.

In simulation models, particularly larger simulation models such as those described in Chaps. 4 and 5, the thread that connects the way we have built the model to the results we obtain from it is often lost. If we obtain an interesting result it often requires a good deal of detective work to discover how that result relates to the internal workings of the model. It is vital to do this detective work, because it is only by understanding *why* we get a result that we can guard against the possibility that the result is more a consequence of what we left out of the model, or misrepresented in it, than of its robust features.

The beauty of analytical models is that the connection between the structure we postulate and the results we discover is so clear.

We have seen in this chapter that there are a number of different techniques for investigating the link between the structure and the consequences of analytical models.

1. There are conclusions we can draw with a minimum of mathematical manipulation from the differential or difference equations that constitute the model.
2. There are extremely useful ways of representing the equations diagramatically.
3. There are the results we obtain by actually solving the equations.

In all these activities, our intellectual control over what we are doing is far easier to maintain than when we are working with large simulation models. Mathematical models thus serve the very important purpose of showing us how we should try to use all models.

Analytical models are lucid because they contain a minimum of confusing detail. This lack of detail extracts a penalty—we are not able to draw very specific conclusions from them and we should be wary of trying to do so. However, this is a small price to pay for the advantages they offer in helping us discern important issues, principles, and trends. Analytical models are useful for generating hypotheses we can then investigate either in computer experiments on a more realistic simulation model of the same system, or by direct observation in the field.

The mathematical results are always crisp and unambiguous. For example, the stability condition for an equilibrium point will draw a clear line between those parameter values for which the point is stable and those for which it is unstable. If we investigated stability in a more complex model of the same system, we would expect that clear line to blur into a gray area where, depending on some of the factors we have left out of the analytical model, we would sometimes have stability and sometimes not. That gray area in turn would become even more fuzzy in the real world.

A number of points follow from the previous paragraphs.

Analytical modeling promotes conceptual thinking. We have, for instance, introduced the concept of stability. An equilibrium point is stable if, when we perturb the system away from equilibrium, it eventually returns to the same point. We have not asked how far we can perturb the system and still have it return to the same point. Asking that question leads to the concept of a *region of stability* and the possibility that if we perturb the system too far, it may move into a region associated with a different and perhaps less desirable equilibrium point—i.e., we might change the whole character of the system dynamics.

This is akin to the idea of a catastrophe. We saw in the zebra-buffalo model how predation could act as a sort of switching device: At one level of predation we had one stable equilibrium point in the system, but at a slightly higher level of predation that point became unstable and we had a completely different stable equilibrium point. Thinking in these terms colors the way we approach practical problems.

Because analytical models lack detail, it would be unrealistic to expect to validate them by making field measurements that depend on detail. We have to test the models more broadly by looking in the field for examples of the principles or trends suggested by the model. This is easier to say than to do. The discussion about how a manager might interpret the data contained in Fig. 6.13(c) shows how difficult it can be to find evidence to support a trend even when we have built that trend into the model we are testing. This highlights two lessons learned from Chaps. 2 and 4: That we can *never* really validate a model (we can only hope to gain confidence in it) and that we have to be just as wary in our interpretation of field data as we are in our interpretation of modeling results.

The reason we build models is precisely because the real world is so complex. We are often unable to perform those experiments in the real world (either through lack of money, time, or the ability to control all the variables) that would really help us to understand how a system functions. Even if we could perform the experiments, the results might turn out to be ambiguous.

By trying to understand the workings of the models, we hope to gain some insight into the behavior of part or all of the real system. We have seen, particularly in Chap. 5, that the models in turn can become so complex that we have difficulty in understanding how they function. The analytical models in this chapter can be thought of as "models of the model" because they help us discover how parts of the simulation model function, or the generalizations implicit but obscured in the model.

This suggests a two-step approach. We can use analytical models to look for the properties of the underlying structure, then try to understand how those properties are diluted by complexity. The graphs in Fig. 6.13 illustrate this point.

One of the ways we try to understand the workings of simulation models is by seeing how sensitive the results are to changes in the values of the various parameters in the model (examples of this can be found in Chaps. 2 and 3). Because of the clear link between the structure and the results in analytical models, we can take the idea of sensitivity analysis one step further and see how sensitive the results are to changes in the structure of the model itself. In this chapter we have done this in a number of different ways.

We have ignored an interaction or component of the model in the first instance, then subsequently discussed what its effect might be on the conclusions we have drawn. For example, in the interaction between warthog and impala we first ignored the browse component in the impala diet and subsequently argued how it might affect the rate at which impala consumed the grass.

In that example we decided our basic results were not affected by the assumption we had made. It would have been equally useful if we had discovered how the basic results were modified by the assumption. When something is potentially important but difficult to fit into a model, it is often good modeling practice to leave it out of the model provided we subsequently ask how it could affect the outcome.

We have modified or added terms to our differential equations. Because these terms (or rather their mathematical representation) can be interpreted in a number of different ways, this sort of sensitivity analysis, used with a little imagination, can open up a wealth of new ideas. In the zebra and buffalo model, for instance, we interpreted a term in k times Z as a predation term; this led us to the idea of a catastrophe. We also noted that a term in k times the square of Z stabilized our system of equations; this led us to ask whether this might represent a hitherto unrecognized stabilizing factor inherent in the system.

We have changed the form of our model from differential to difference equations and noticed that the latter, because they imply certain time delays in the system, are less stable. This has led us to question whether those time delays were realistic.

RECAPITULATION

This chapter has the title "Variations on a Theme" because all the models we have built relate in some way to the interaction between herbivores and vegetation. The emphasis, however, is on what happens to the herbivores rather than what happens to the vegetation, and the structure of the models reflects that emphasis. For example, if we had wanted to study the effect of herbivory on competition between different classes of vegetation, on the basis of our experience in the last chapter we would have needed more than one variable to describe each class of vegetation. We can get by with one variable in the present context provided we remember that herbivory must never be so severe that it reduces the growth potential of the reserves.

The title also reflects the fact that we have built a number of smaller models rather than one large model. Each has a particular, limited purpose. Analytical models lend themselves to this sort of exercise. If we think of detailed simulation models as large oil paintings, then analytical models can be thought of as quick sketches, each trying to capture the essence of some part of the larger picture. This analogy is fruitful because an artist has a commitment to a large oil painting that is completely different from the approach to quick sketches. As the oil painting progresses, the artist becomes locked into the initial design. While a detail here or there may be changed, it is a formidable task to restructure the whole painting. Sketches, on the other hand, can be drawn quickly. If they do not succeed in conveying what the artist had in mind, they can be thrown away and drawn again. However, they can, even with little detail, dramatize a mood or posture. This is the spirit in which we build and use analytical models.

FURTHER READING

An introduction to differential equation models, stability analysis, and the uses of phase diagrams can be found in books by Maynard Smith (1974), Pielou (1977), Jeffers (1978), and Vandermeer (1981). The application of these techniques to problems of either a practical or more theoretical nature are developed in books by Bartlett and Hiorns (1973) and May (1973 and 1981) and in the paper by Murdoch (1978). Comins and Hassell (1974) and Beddington et al. (1976) develop and analyze discrete models of the interaction between predators and prey. Noy-Meir (1975 and 1981) shows how phase diagrams can be used to analyze sets of up to three differential equations, and the ideas of multiple equilibrium points and catastrophes are discussed and illustrated in Jones (1977) and May (1977). Goel, Maitra, and Montroll (1971) have written a mathematically sophisticated book on nonlinear models of interacting populations, and the book by Nisbett and Gurney (1982) provides sophisticated mathematical analyses of fluctuating populations.

Caughley (1976 and 1981) analyzes the interaction between herbivores and vegetation using differential equations, but with a logistic model for vegetation growth. Noy-Meir (1978) investigates the stability of grazing models.

Analytical models lend themselves to approaches that aim to optimize the harvest or yield from a system. The concept of a maximum sustainable yield (briefly introduced when we looked at the maximum stable grazing rate in our logistic model for vegetation growth) is important and is discussed in the book by Clark (1976), which uses techniques similar to those introduced in this chapter to investigate the optimal exploitation of renewable resources. The paper by Clark and Tait (1978) looks at sex selection in the harvesting of wildlife populations, while Beddington and May (1977) address the problem of harvesting populations in a fluctuating environment.

model for vegetation growth. Noy-Meir (1978) investigates the stability of grazing models.

Analytical models lend themselves to approaches that aim to optimize the harvest or yield from a system. The concept of a maximum sustainable yield (briefly introduced when we looked at the maximum stable grazing rate in our logistic model for vegetation growth) is important and is discussed in the book by Clark (1976), which uses techniques similar to those introduced in this chapter to investigate the optimal exploitation of renewable resources. The paper by Clark and Tait (1978) looks at sex selection in the harvesting of wildlife populations, while Beddington and May (1977) address the problem of harvesting populations in a fluctuating environment.

Cropping Strategies and Linear Programming

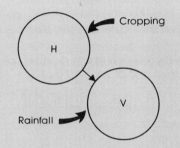

The last two chapters were concerned with how to control herbivore populations in relatively small, enclosed game parks with few, if any, major predators. In both chapters we constructed models to simulate the dynamics of the vegetation and the herbivores, but the models were constructed with the problem of herbivore control, or cropping, firmly in mind. The two chapters simulated the ecosystem dynamics at two different levels of resolution—in Chap. 5 we included considerable detail; in Chap. 6 the models were less detailed and more abstract. In this chapter we will look at the problem from the point of view of the manager to see if we can provide general guidelines about when and how to crop. To do this we will take an even simpler view of the ecosystem dynamics.

A good starting point was to speak to managers of small parks about their perceptions of the problems they face. The following points emerged:

1. A major concern, and for many the first priority, was to minimize soil

losses and maintain the quality of the vegetation. Heavy rains after a long dry period can wash away large quantities of top soil if the vegetation cover is depleted. Managers stressed the importance of preventing the herbivores from destroying vegetation cover during dry periods.

2. Managers also want to maintain healthy and viable herbivore populations. Within this context, some emphasized tourism and the need for both a variety of species and a large total population. Others were more concerned with the logistical problems they faced in controlling the population. They either wanted to crop as lightly as possible or maintain animal numbers at predetermined levels.

3. Preserving the vegetation cover during dry periods and maintaining large herbivore populations are conflicting objectives. This was highlighted by the fact that some managers were anxious to provide sufficient water for the animals during droughts, while others were more concerned with the damage suffered by the vegetation and soil base in the vicinity of the watering places.

4. All agreed that at times it would be necessary to remove some of the herbivores. Some of the practical difficulties associated with cropping were:

   a. Bureaucratic or logistical time delays between the decision to crop and the implementation of that decision.

   b. Difficulties associated with cropping in some years and not in other years, particularly if an emergency developed and animals had to be cropped drastically.

   c. Problems in public relations and the need to justify and defend all policies and practices.

In this chapter we will suppose that reliable watering points are scattered throughout the park. Acting like consultants, we can then formulate the remaining management objectives as follows:

1. Prevent the vegetation cover from ever dropping below a certain threshold value, the actual value to be chosen to prevent erosion and a deterioration in the quality of the vegetation.

2. Aim to maintain, on average, as large a herbivore population as possible. Alternatively, aim to minimize, on average, the number of herbivores that will have to be removed.

3. Try to plan ahead to avoid having to reduce the herbivore population drastically.

4. Have a policy that can be easily implemented and defended.

Economists, politicians, wildlife enthusiasts, or ecologists might disagree with some of these objectives. Our purpose in this chapter is not to argue the merits of the manager's viewpoint, but to develop modeling techniques that will help meet these objectives. The same techniques will still be useful even if the objectives are modified.

THE SIMPLEST POSSIBLE MODEL

Since our emphasis here is on broad questions of policy, we want to make our model of the ecosystem as simple as possible, but not so simple it is trivial. We should therefore use the objectives listed at the end of the previous section to define the minimal components of a model. To meet objective 1, the model must describe in gross terms how vegetation grows in response to rainfall, how it decays, and how it is consumed by the herbivores. To meet objective 2 it must also describe how the herbivore population grows in the absence of cropping and what happens if it is cropped.

Since the vegetation is our first priority, we should begin building the model by introducing a variable V to denote the green biomass. Considering the manager's calendar and the ecosystem dynamics, there are four important times during a year: when the decision to crop is made, when it is implemented, when (just before the first rains) the vegetation cover is at its minimum, and when the herbivores produce their young.

The crucial time of the year for the herbivores is just before the first rains. We therefore let V denote the vegetation biomass at that time. Suppose that V_0 is the value of V just before the start of the last rainy season, and V_1 is the value we predict for just before the start of the next rainy season. Our simplest model must calculate V_1 from V_0. An equation that does this is

$$V_1 = a_1 + V_0 - pV_0 - qf\{V_0\}H$$

where $a_1 = $ the new growth during the rainy season

$p = $ a decay rate for the standing grass left over from the previous year

$H = $ the average number of herbivores grazing during the year

$q = $ the total amount of grass a herbivore would like to eat during a year

The function f reduces the amount eaten if the vegetation is such that the herbivores will not be able to eat their fill. We should recognize this as Eq. (6.25) from the previous chapter.

Can we make this equation any simpler? We cannot neglect any of the terms; each represents an important process. We can, however, put the response function f equal to 1. This is tantamount to assuming that the herbivores will be able to eat as much, or very nearly as much, as they require, and since a management priority is to maintain a healthy herbivore population, it should be a good assumption. It also has the important mathematical advantage that the equation then becomes linear:

$$V_1 = a_1 + kV_0 - qH \tag{7.1}$$

where we have written k for $1 - p$. This simplification might appear trivial, but later in the chapter we will see how the linearity of (7.1) can be exploited.

Suppose now that there are H_0 herbivores just before the start of the last rainy season. Suppose too that the decision to crop (or not to crop) is made when it is possible to estimate the production a_1 with some confidence, and that it is implemented before the calving season. This timetable may not be easy to implement in practice, but we will assume it can be done. Then, if x_1 herbivores are cropped, there will be $H_0 - x_1$ herbivores just before the calving season and $(1 + b)[H_0 - x_1]$ herbivores just afterward (where b is related to the birth rate). If a fraction s of these survive until just before the next rainy season, we can write

$$H_1 = s(1 + b)[H_0 - x_1]$$

or

$$H_1 = wH_0 - wx_1 \qquad (7.2)$$

where we have written w for $s(1 + b)$. Thus w is a measure of how fast the population grows (it is sometimes called the *growth multiplier*). Since we have assumed the population is healthy, we would expect w to be greater than 1. It follows from (7.2) that the herbivore population will grow geometrically (almost exponentially) in the absence of cropping. Our implicit assumption is that management will intervene before food becomes limiting.

Since most of the grazing takes place between the end of the growing season and the next rains, we will be conservative if we ignore mortality and put H equal to $(1 + b)[H_0 - x_1]$ in Eq. (7.1). Writing c for $q(1 + b)$ we get

$$V_1 = a_1 + kV_0 - c[H_0 - x_1] \qquad (7.3)$$

Equations (7.2) and (7.3) can be used to make management decisions. Suppose that V_{min} represents the lower threshold to the vegetation—i.e., management has decided that if the biomass ever drops below V_{min} there will be undesirable consequences. We have postulated that management will have a good estimate of the new production a_1 when it makes its decision. We can assume that it also has good estimates of V_0 and H_0 and plausible values for the constants k and c. Equation (7.3) can then be used to predict V_1 on the assumption that x_1 is 0. If the predicted value of V_1 is greater than V_{min}, there is no need to crop. If the predicted value of V_1 is less than V_{min}, we can use Eq. (7.3) to calculate the value of x_1 that ensures V_1 is exactly equal to V_{min}:

$$x_1 = H_0 - \frac{a_1 + kV_0 - V_{min}}{c} \qquad (7.4)$$

This tells us how many herbivores to crop. There is, however, one potential complication: What happens if Eq. (7.4) gives a value for x_1 that is very close to or perhaps even greater than H_0? This situation would arise if, even in the absence of herbivores, the vegetation left standing at the end of the year was likely to be close to or below V_{min}.

It is an unlikely situation, and incidentally gives the lie to our assumption about good management. But, particularly if we are writing a computer program to calculate x_1, it is a special case we must provide for. The best we can do, pragmatically, is reduce the herbivore herds to some minimally viable level H_{min} and accept the consequence that the vegetation biomass will drop below the critical value V_{min}. The number to be cropped will than be

$$x_1 = H_0 - H_{min}$$

Figure 7.1 depicts a flow chart for implementing this strategy on a year-by-year basis. How well does it work? The only way to tell is to test it. It would obviously be both premature and irresponsible on the basis of a few simple equations to go out and test the strategy in the field. In any case, a proper field test would require decades of carefully controlled measurement and would be almost impossible to implement. What we can do, however, is devise a *computer experiment*. Such an experiment will be incomplete because it cannot simulate all the imponderables of the real world, but it can at least test the strategy we have devised in the context of the model it is supposed to serve.

TESTING THE STRATEGY

Parameter Estimation

To run an experiment on the computer we have to put actual numbers into the equations in the previous section. A good way of doing that is first to look at the units the various constants and variables will be measured in. Our two main variables are the vegetation V and the number of herbivores H. The level of resolution of our model is such that we do not know exactly what we mean by the vegetation—we have vague idea that it is some sort of biomass—nor do we know what species of herbivore, or mix of species, we have in mind. In the absence of an intuitive feeling for what these numbers should be, we are free to invent our own units. Suppose we measure the herbivores in "animals" and that we imagine 5000 to 10,000 animals to be reasonable for the total herbivore population of the park. Suppose too that we invent a unit, the "veg," to measure the vegetation, and that we calibrate it by forming a mental picture of the vegetation in the park in the absence of any herbivores, just before the rainy season, under average conditions. We will call this 1 veg.

If we now look at Eq. (7.3),

$$V_1 = a_1 + kV_0 - c[H_0 - x_1]$$

we notice that the left-hand side is measured in vegs, so each group of

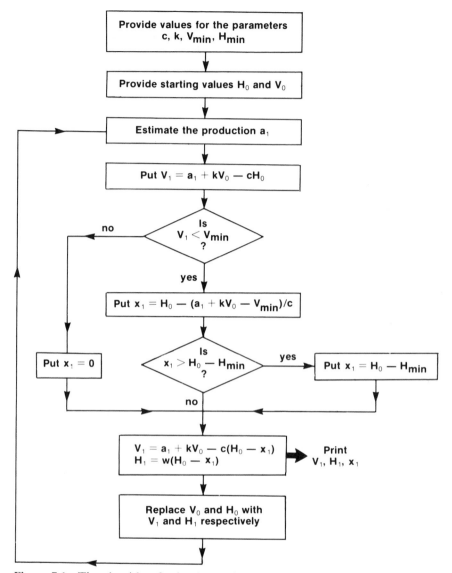

Figure 7.1   The algorithm for implementing a simple cropping strategy.

terms on the right-hand side must also be measured in vegs. If we start at the end of the equation and work backward, since H_0 is measured in animals, x_1 must also be measured in animals and $c[H_0 - x_1]$ must be measured in vegs. It follows that c has the dimensions of veg per animal, and we can deduce a reasonable value for c as follows. We know there are about 5000 animals in the park and that before the rains, in the absence of any animals, the vegetation will be 1 veg. What proportion of that vegetation would 5000 animals eat in a year? Fifteen percent, or 0.15, is a plausible guess, which means that 5000 c is roughly equal to 0.15, or c is equal to 0.00003 veg per animal. This is the number we will use in our computer experiment.

The next term to consider is kV_0. V_0 is already measured in vegs, so k is in fact dimensionless. It is just the proportion of the previous year's vegetation that would be left standing a year later in the absence of herbivores. The value of k thus depends on factors such as fire, termites, and rates of decomposition, but to consider those factors is to read too much into our model. We will estimate that 40 percent of the vegetation would still be left after one year if there were no herbivores, so we choose $k = 0.4$.

Finally, we must consider the annual production a_1. This too will be measured in vegs and will vary from year to year depending on rainfall. We must think of both an average value and how it will vary. The average value is implicit in our previous definition. Suppose there are no herbivores and that the rainfall and hence production never change from year to year. In that case the vegetation just before the rainy season would be the same every year; in terms of our definition of the veg, it would be exactly 1 veg. Making these substitutions in Eq. (7.3) we get

$$1 = a_1 + k \times 1 \qquad \text{or} \qquad a_1 = 1 - k$$

Since we have already chosen k to be 0.4, it follows that our average annual production should be 0.6 veg. In other words, the new production during the rainy season is on averge about 60 percent of the total biomass we would expect to find, again on average, just before the next rainy season, in the absence of herbivores.

It remains for us to choose a statistical distribution from which we can generate a sequence of values for the annual production over any number of years. We have already decided that the distribution must have a mean of 0.6, but we still have to choose its shape. For simplicity we will assume a flat distribution between the values 0.2 and 1.0. This implies that the annual production in any given year is equally likely to be any number between 0.2 and 1.0. Again, we try to evaluate whether this is reasonable. It implies that the new growth in the best of years is similar to the total amount of vegetation to be found, on average (when there are no herbivores), just before the rainy season. It also implies that the new growth in the best of years is about five times greater than the new growth in the worst of years. We will assume that these statements are plausible.

Note how in these paragraphs we have managed to get a feeling for what the numbers we intend to use actually mean. It is essential to do this.

Simulation Results

We are now ready to simulate the changes in vegetation from one year to the next. We begin with the vegetation left over from the previous year (V_0), then use a random number generator to calculate the new production. From this we compute the new vegetation using Eq. (7.3). If we do this with H_0 and x_1 both equal to 0 we will get some idea of how the vegetation would have responded to changes in rainfall over a number of years in the absence of herbivory. Figure 7.2 shows a typical (generated) sequence for new production over 18 years and the corresponding (calculated) changes in the vegetation.

The next step is to include the herbivores and allow the computer to decide when and how many to crop according to the strategy we developed in the previous section and summarized in Fig. 7.1. We must now include Eq. (7.2) and choose values for the initial herbivore population, the minimally viable population H_{min}, and the growth mutiplier w. We will start with 7000 herbivores and assume they can increase by 20 percent per year—i.e., $w = 1.2$. If we put h_{min} equal to 700, the population could then recover from that low number to about 5000 in nine years, which is reasonable. We must also choose a value for the vegetation threshold V_{min}. If we put V_{min} equal to 0.3 we are in effect saying that our management objective is to ensure that the vegetation (just before the rains) never drops to less than 30 percent of its average value. This is probably conservative.

Using the 18-year sequence of production data from the no-herbivore simulation and applying our algorithm with the preceding numbers, we get results that are also shown in Fig. 7.2. The dotted lines in the herbivore graph indicate that the herbivores were cropped during that year. We should note that cropping took place five times during the 18 years, and that in the worst year over 9000 herbivores had to be removed! Few managers would be happy with a strategy that allowed the population to fluctuate so widely and necessitated such drastic reductions. Moreover, if we look at the vegetation graph, we see that it was very close to the minimum value of 0.3 in six of the eighteen years; this too would probably be undesirable.

One cannot, of course, draw conclusions from a single computer experiment with only one set of randomly generated production data. However, similar experiments with different annual production sequences show very much the same results, so we are forced to the conclusion that this is a management strategy we would not want to implement.

A STRATEGY THAT LOOKS AHEAD ONE EXTRA YEAR

So far we have only attempted to predict what will happen to the vegetation and the herbivores one year into the future. The management strategy that follows logically from that prediction is unsatisfactory because it allows herbivore populations to build up without anticipating the possibility of low rainfall and low production in the future. It might therefore be useful to develop a model and strategy that tries to look ahead one extra year.

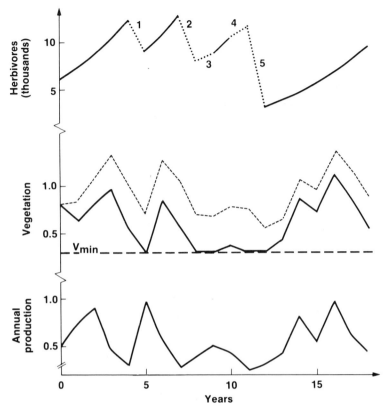

Figure 7.2 Implementing the simplest cropping strategy when annual primary production varies randomly. Two graphs are shown for the vegetation biomass: The dashed line indicates how the biomass would have responded to the annual production in the absence of herbivores, while the solid line indicates its response when herbivores were present and were controlled according to the strategy outlined in Fig. 7.1. The five dotted line segments on the herbivore graph indicate when herbivores were cropped. The actual numbers removed in each case were: (1) 4968, (2) 6201, (3) 723, (4) 813, (5) 9029.

In our simplest possible model we started with vegetation V_0 and herbivores H_0 just before the start of the last rainy season. Given the production a_1 during that rainy season, we predicted the vegetation V_1 and herbivores H_1 just before the next rainy season. Now suppose that the production during the next rainy season is a_2, and let us try to predict V_2 and H_2 just before the following rainy season. Since we are still trying to keep our model very simple, we will assume that the parameters in our model (the decay rate of old grass, herbivore birth and survival rates, and the amount of grass eaten by an average herbivore) do not change during this period. Only the annual production may change significantly. By analogy with Eqs. (7.2) and (7.3) we then write

$$H_2 = wH_1 - wx_2 \qquad (7.5)$$

and

$$V_2 = a_2 + kV_1 - c[H_1 - x_2] \qquad (7.6)$$

where x_2 is the number of herbivores we crop just before the H_1 herbivores produce their young.

If we use (7.2) and (7.3) to substitute for H_1 and V_1 in (7.5) and (7.6), we can calculate H_2 and V_2 directly from H_0 and V_0:

$$H_2 = w^2 H_0 - w^2 x_1 - wx_2 \qquad (7.7)$$

and

$$V_2 = a_2 + k[a_1 + kV_0 - cH_0 + cx_1] - cw[H_0 - x_1] + cx_2 \qquad (7.8)$$

We want both V_1 and V_2 to be greater than the specified value V_{min}—i.e., mathematically we want

$$V_1 \geqslant V_{min} \qquad \text{and} \qquad V_2 \geqslant V_{min}$$

We call these two inequalities our *constraints*. Substituting for V_1 and V_2 from (7.3) and (7.8) and rearranging terms, the constraints can be written

$$x_1 \geqslant \frac{V_{min} - a_1 - kV_0}{c} + H_0 \qquad (7.9)$$

and

$$(w + k)x_1 + x_2 \geqslant \frac{V_{min} - a_2 - ka_1 - k^2 V_0}{c} + (k + w)H_0 \qquad (7.10)$$

The advantage of writing the constraints in this form is that we have our unknown values x_1 and x_2 on the left-hand side and, with a few assumptions, we can put numbers to everything on the right-hand side of both (7.9) and (7.10). (The major assumption is that we can estimate not only the production a_1 from the last rainy season but also the production a_2 for the next rainy season.) For simplicity, let us call the right-hand side of (7.9) P and that of (7.10) Q. Then,

$$x_1 \geqslant P \qquad (7.9a)$$

and

$$(w + k)x_1 + x_2 \geqslant Q \qquad (7.10a)$$

Depending on the values we choose for V_{min}, a_1, a_2, etc., in (7.9) and (7.10), P and Q could turn out to be positive or negative numbers. Suppose that both P and Q are positive and that $P < Q/(w + k)$. We can then graph the two inequalities (7.9a) and (7.10a) as in Fig. 7.3(a). Note that in so doing we have first drawn the two straight lines

$$x_1 = P \qquad \text{(the line ABC)}$$

and

$$(w + k)x_1 + x_2 = Q \qquad \text{(the line DBE)}$$

then shaded the region represented by the inequalities $x_1 \geqslant P$ and $(w + k)x_1 + x_2 \geqslant Q$. (We have only shaded the region that corresponds to positive values for both x_1 and x_2 since negative cropping is meaningless.) Note too that the slope of the line DBE is $-(w + k)$. We recall that w (the growth mutiplier) is greater than 1, while k (the proportion of grass left standing from the previous year) lies between 0 and 1, so that $w + k$ must be greater than 1 but less than $1 + w$.

Each point in Fig. 7.3(a) represents a pair of values (one for x_1 and one for x_2) and hence a possible cropping strategy. Those points in the shaded region represent strategies that, if we are correct in our estimates of the production a_1 and a_2, will ensure the vegetation for both this year and next year never falls below $V_{\min}$. How do we decide which point in the shaded area to choose? This is where the management objective comes in. If, for instance, the objective is to crop as little as possible, this implies that we want to make the sum $x_1 + x_2$ as small as possible. How

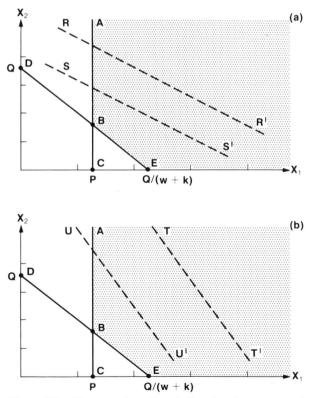

Figure 7.3 Constructing the solution for the strategy that looks one year ahead: (a) with the objective of minimizing the number of herbivores to be cropped and (b) with the objective of maximizing the average number of herbivores. (*Note:* The scale on the x_1 axis is twice the scale on the x_2 axis).

small can we make $x_1 + x_2$ and still be in the shaded region? The dotted line RR′ represents the straight line

$$x_1 + x_2 = \text{a constant}$$

and SS′ represents

$$x_1 + x_2 = \text{a smaller constant}$$

Note that the slopes of RR′ and SS′ are the same and both equal to -1, which is *less* steep than the line DBE. Note too that as we reduce the value of $x_1 + x_2$ we move the line SS′ closer to the boundaries of the shaded region until, as SS′ passes through the point E, it is about to move out of the shaded region altogether. E thus represents the *minimum* value of $x_1 + x_2$ that will satisfy our constraints. At E, x_1 has the value $Q/(w + k)$ and $x_2 = 0$, so if our objective is to minimize cropping, the graph tells us to crop $Q/(w + k)$ herbivores this year and none next year.

Management might, however, have expressed its objective differently. It might have said that, on average, it wants to make the total number of herbivores as large as possible—i.e., it wants to maximize $H_1 + H_2$. To use the approach developed in the previous paragraph, we must express management's objective $H_1 + H_2$ in terms of x_1 and x_2. From (7.2) and (7.5),

$$
\begin{aligned}
H_1 + H_2 &= H_1 + w[H_1 - x_2] \\
&= (1 + w)H_1 - wx_2 \\
&= (1 + w)w[H_0 - x_1] - wx_2 \\
&= w(1 + w)H_0 - w[(1 + w)x_1 + x_2]
\end{aligned}
$$

Since the values of w and H_0 are given, the first term in their expression is constant. The way to make $H_1 + H_2$ as large as possible is therefore to make the term we subtract—i.e., $(1 + w)x_1 + x_2$, as *small* as possible.

Figure 7.3(b) shows the same shaded region as Fig. 7.3(a). Here TT′ represents the line

$$(1 + w)x_1 + x_2 = \text{a constant}$$

and UU′ the line

$$(1 + w)x_1 + x_2 = \text{a smaller constant}$$

Note that the slope of UU′ is $-(1 + w)$. Since $k < 1$, this means that UU′ is *steeper* than the line DBE. If we now follow the same argument as before, moving UU′ down closer to the boundaries of the shaded region, UU′ will be just about to move out of the shaded region as it passes through the point B. It follows that B represents our cropping solution if our objective is to maximize the number of herbivores. At B,

$$x_1 = P \qquad \text{and} \qquad x_2 = Q - (w + k)P$$

which tells us to crop some herbivores this year and more the following year.

Let us now try to interpret the mathematics from a practical point of view. When P and Q are both positive, the implication is that the vegetation could drop below the threshold V_{min} at the end of this year and the end of next year. If $Q/(w + k) > P$, next year is going to be more critical than this year. Figure 7.3(a) tells us that under these circumstances, if our objective is to minimize the number of herbivores we have to crop, we must crop this year (and only this year) in such a way that nearly two years from now the vegetation will just be at V_{min}. This makes sense. By cropping before the herbivores breed we anticipate the problem and so crop fewer now rather than more next year.

On the other hand, if we want to maximize the number of herbivores, Fig. 7.3(b) tells us that we should first let the population grow, then crop a year from now. But if we did that, the vegetation would still drop below V_{min} this year, so we have to crop some herbivores this year too (just enough to get by) and crop again later. This too makes sense.

There are a number of points to note about this analysis.

Managers are very often vague about whether their objective for the herbivore population is to maximize the population or minimize the numbers they have to crop. Although these two objectives may appear to be similar, our analysis shows that they lead to different management strategies. In the first case we anticipate and act now; in the second we try to postpone any action.

We have made the assumption that we know what the production will be in a year's time; at best we can only guess at it. Our analysis has nevertheless been useful. It has highlighted the differences between alternative management objectives and, even if we do not have enough confidence in it to follow its advice on how many herbivores to crop, it has provided a basis for deciding whether to crop now or to postpone the decision for a year. How we can use this, despite our ignorance about a_2, will become clearer in the next section.

The case we have considered, where both P and Q are positive and $P < Q/(w + k)$, is only one of four cases. Figure 7.4 depicts the other three. The following are the results obtained from them:

1. $P < 0$ and $Q < 0$: $x_1 = 0$ and $x_2 = 0$ for both management strategies.
2. $P > 0$ and $P > Q/(w + k)$: $x_1 = P$ and $x_2 = 0$ for both management strategies.
3. $P < 0$ and $Q > 0$: $x_1 = Q/(w + k)$ and $x_2 = 0$ to minimize cropping, and $x_1 = 0$ and $x_2 = Q$ to maximize the number of herbivores.

As in the simplest possible model, this strategy could on occasion require us to crop all or nearly all the herbivores. If this happens, we should modify it in the same way as before—i.e., crop to reduce the herbivore population to a small but viable level H_{min}.

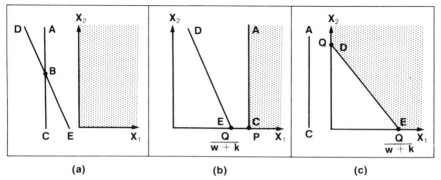

Figure 7.4 Three additional cases that might arise when implementing the strategy that looks one year ahead. (a) $P < O$ and $Q < O$. (b) $P > Q/(w + k)$ and $P > O$. (c) $P < O$ and $Q > O$.

The method of solution we have described in this section is a simple example of a more general technique called *linear programming*. We will have more to say about it as a modeling technique later in this chapter.

IMPLEMENTING AND TESTING THE NEW STRATEGY

Although our new strategy tells us how many herbivores to crop in two years, we should only act on what it tells us to do during the first year. The reason for this is that we have to guess at the production a_2 during the second year. By the beginning of that year, however, we should be able to estimate the production rather than guess at it. At that stage we can therefore think of the second year of the first calculation as the first year of a second calculation, so we can guess ahead one more year, calculate the corresponding x_1 and x_2, and again only implement the x_1. In this way we recalculate the number of herbivores we crop each year, not only on the basis of what we know at the time, but also on the basis of what we think will happen a year later.

The question then arises how to guess at a_2, the production for the following year. If we consistently guess high, a large a_2 in the right-hand side of Eq. (7.10) will make the expression we have called Q negative, which in effect means that our new strategy reduces to the old strategy where we only look at one year at a time. It follows that in the absence of any indications to the contrary, our guesses for a_2 should be conservative.

Figure 7.5 shows what happens if we use exactly the same data as in Fig. 7.2 but apply our new strategy with the objective of minimizing cropping. Each year we assume that a_2, the new production in the following year, will be equal to 0.35. (Recall that on average, a_2 will be equal to 0.6, so this is a conservative guess.) The figure shows that the new strategy is a marked improvement over the old. Herbivore numbers do not fluctuate as

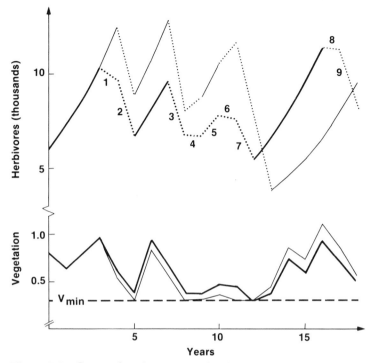

Figure 7.5 Comparing the strategy that looks one year ahead (bold line) with the simplest cropping strategy (light line). The dotted line segments in the herbivore graphs indicate when herbivores were cropped. The numbers removed for the simplest strategy are the same as in Fig. 7.2, while for the new strategy they are: (1) 2272, (2) 4078, (3) 4125, (4)1097, (5) 287, (6) 1461, (7) 3000, (8) 1996, (9) 4179.

widely, cropping takes place more frequently (but fewer animals are cropped at each stage), and the vegetation approaches the minimum threshold only once during the 18 years. The differences between the two strategies are shown up more dramatically in Fig. 7.6, where we have shaded the area of the phase diagram (a plot of herbivore numbers versus vegetation) traversed during the 18-year simulation. Figure 7.6 shows how the first strategy leads to minimal vegetation levels over a wide range of herbivore numbers, while the second strategy confines the solution to a far more acceptable region of the phase diagram.

Other simulations with different random sequences of annual production confirm these general observations. However, if we repeat the exercise with the objective of maximizing the number of herbivores rather than minimizing the numbers to be cropped, we find that our new strategy differs very little from the old. This is not an unexpected result because we have already seen that we tend to postpone cropping if our objective is to maximize the population.

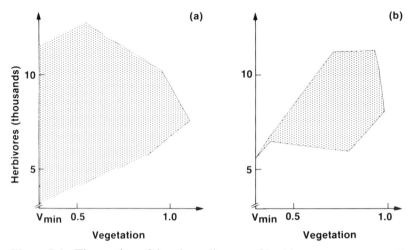

Figure 7.6   The portion of the phase diagram of herbivores versus vegetation that is traversed when implementing (a) the simplest cropping strategy and (b) the strategy that looks one year ahead.

Comparing the two strategies, we conclude that it is prudent to look ahead, even only for one additional year and even if we can only guess the new production for that year. We also conclude that it is prudent, when guessing about the future, to guess conservatively and use a strategy that is conservative in the sense that we choose to crop now rather than later.

LINEAR PROGRAMMING

The graphical technique we used to find a strategy that looked ahead one extra year is known as *linear programming*. It is one of several approaches that fall under the general heading of optimization techniques. An optimization technique does not look for just any solution to a problem (any point in the shaded area of Fig. 7.3 could have been a solution), but specifically seeks a solution that *maximizes* or *minimizes* a clearly stated objective (such as minimizing the total number of herbivores cropped).

Optimization techniques are used extensively in many different fields, and computer codes that implement them are readily available. If a management problem can be stated in a form that is compatible with a particular optimization technique, one of these computer codes can be used directly and there is no need to write a computer program to solve the problem. In this section we will introduce the language of linear programming and show how standard linear programming codes can be used in the context of our cropping problem.

The Standard Linear Programming Problem

Consider a problem with N variables. In standard notation we write these as $x_1, x_2, \ldots, x_N$ and formulate the problem in such a way that all the variables are greater than or equal to 0. In our problem there were only two variables, x_1 and x_2, and since they represented the number of herbivores to be cropped, they were indeed greater than or equal to 0. Various physical, economic, or other considerations may limit (or constrain) the relationships between the variables. In general we will suppose that there are M such *constraints*, each consisting of a linear combination of the variables on the left-hand side. Each combination will be less than, equal to, or greater than (i.e., constrained by) a constant on the right-hand side. We had two constraints, Eqs. (7.9) and (7.10), both linear in the two variables.

A standard linear programming problem has an *objective function*, which is again a linear combination of some or all of the variables. Depending on the problem, this function must be maximized or minimized. In our problem the objective function was defined by management goals. In one case these led to the objective function $x_1 + x_2$, and this had to be minimized. The *solution* to the problem is the set of values for the variables that satisfies all the constraints and maximizes (or minimizes) the objective function.

When there are only two variables, a linear programming problem can be solved graphically, as we saw in Fig. 7.3. When there are more than two variables, an algorithm known as the *simplex method* has to be used; it can be found in standard linear programming computer codes. In practice, therefore, there are three steps in developing a linear programming model:

1. Formulate the model as a linear programming problem.
2. Use a standard code to solve it.
3. Interpret the solution. This may involve formulating and solving the problem again. Many linear programming codes provide an extensive sensitivity analysis that can be very useful at this stage.

An Example

As an example of how to formulate a model as a linear programming problem, we will extend the analysis for looking ahead one extra year and ask what we would do if we try to look ahead *two* extra years. On the face of it, this would extend the linear programming problem from two variables to three (how many to crop in three successive years) but in fact it will turn out to be an eight-variable problem. The reason is that in our previous analysis we managed to express all our vegetation and herbivore variables (V_1, V_2, H_1, and H_2) in terms of the initial values H_0 and V_0. As we extend this to more years, the substitution becomes clumsy and it is easier to treat the vegetation and herbivore variables as linear programming variables too. This means that we actually build the structure of our model into the constraints. This is done as follows:

As in Eqs. (7.3) and (7.6) the vegetation equations will be

$$V_1 = a_1 + kV_0 - c[H_0 - x_1]$$
$$V_2 = a_2 + kV_1 - c[H_1 - x_2]$$

and

$$V_3 = a_3 + kV_2 - c[H_2 - x_3]$$

Suppose we define additional linear programming variables,

$$x_4 = V_1, x_5 = V_2, x_6 = V_3, x_7 = H_1, x_8 = H_2$$

We can then rewrite the vegetation equations as

$$-cx_1 + x_4 = a_1 + kV_0 - cH_0$$
$$-cx_2 - kx_4 + x_5 + cx_7 = a_2$$

and

$$-cx_3 - kx_5 + x_6 + cx_8 = a_3$$

(Note that we have moved all our variables to the left-hand side, and these three expressions are not just equations, they are also linear programming constraints.)

The requirement that the vegetation always be greater than or equal to V_{min} adds the additional three constraints.

$$x_4 \geqslant V_{min}$$
$$x_5 \geqslant V_{min}$$

and

$$x_6 \geqslant V_{min}$$

The herbivore equations (7.2) and (7.5) add another two contraints:

$$wx_1 + x_7 = wH_0$$

and

$$wx_2 - wx_7 + x_8 = 0$$

so that there is a total of eight constraints.

Finally, if the management objective is ιο minimize cropping, the objective function is to minimize $x_1 + x_2 + x_3$.

Once the equations have been written in this form, all we have to do is substitute numbers for c, k, V_0, V_{min}, a_1, etc., and we are ready to use a standard linear programming code. We will not actually run a three-year model. The purpose of developing it is first to show how the model becomes a part of the linear programming constraints, and second, to point out that once we see the pattern in the constraints, we can easily add to them to formulate a 4-, 5-, or even a 10- or 20-year model.

It is interesting to show what happens when we try to run a larger model. For example, consider what happens when we try to minimize cropping using the first nine years of production data from Fig. 7.2. (This leads to a linear programming problem with 26 variables and 26 constraints.) The results show that with *perfect* knowledge of the rainfall and production during all nine years, it is possible to crop only 4036 herbivores.

This is considerably less than the number of herbivores we have had to crop during the first nine years of any of the experiments with other strategies we have run using this series of production data. We might be tempted to conclude that our other strategies are not very good, but a closer look at the linear programming solution gives us a different perspective. We see that cropping only takes place once—in the first of the nine years. The linear program has in fact reduced the herbivore population to 2356 in that first year, then allowed it to grow naturally thereafter. The net effect of this is that the vegetation remains good until the drought in year 8, when it drops to 0.38. In year 9 it actually drops to the limit of 0.3.

If we think about this, it is *mathematically* a perfectly reasonable solution. The linear programming code has indeed found the best way to do what it was told to do—i.e., minimize the total number of herbivores cropped. However, from the point of view of the management problem we were trying to solve, the result is meaningless. It is totally impractical to crop now just because we anticipate problems in eight or nine years.

Comments on the Example

This example shows how careful we have to be whenever we use more sophisticated modeling tools. The mathematics may be consistent and hence mathematically correct, but the problem the mathematics solves may not be quite the problem we want to solve. What the linear programming solution really tells us is that it is futile to formulate our problem in this way. This is brought home even more strongly if we try to solve exactly the same nine-year problem but change the value of V_{min} from 0.3 to 0.6. The linear program cannot solve this problem and tells us that the solution is *infeasible*, meaning it is impossible to satisfy all the constraints.

There is a good reason for this. We noted in our previous strategies that we could not always ensure that the vegetation remained above V_{min}. Sometimes all we could do was reduce the number of herbivores to a minimum value H_{min}, accepting that the vegetation would drop temporarily below V_{min}. The linear programming formulation has no such flexibility. When we defined the constraints we told the computer the vegetation would always be greater than or equal to V_{min}. When the computer cannot satisfy this condition, it tells us that the solution is infeasible.

It is not uncommon, when formulating complex models, to discover there is no feasible solution. There is always an explanation, if we look for one, and frequently that explanation implies a discrepancy between the linear programming formulation (i.e., the problem we have told the computer to solve) and the problem we are trying to solve. Either the linear programming model is too rigid or the problem itself has not been correctly formulated.

There are two ways around this rigidity. One is to be subtle in the way in which we formulate the linear programming model and to make good use of sensitivity analysis to interpret the answer. The other is to use extensions of linear programming, or other related optimization techniques, that allow us to be more flexible in setting up the constraints. We will use a slightly different management problem to explore both approaches.

Formulating the Problem in a Different Way

Suppose management argues that it is impractical to make cropping decisions every year and that the bureaucratic and logistical constraints dictate a policy of keeping the herbivore population fixed at a predetermined level, no matter how the rainfall and production may vary from year to year. The main advantage of this policy is that the number of herbivores to be cropped will remain more or less constant, so the whole cropping procedure will become routine. If we accept this argument, it remains for us to determine an appropriate size for the herbivore population. We can formulate this as a linear programming problem in which the objective is to maximize the (constant) herbivore population subject to the usual constraint that the vegetation never falls below V_{min}, and we can test the solution over a number of years, using typical or historical data for annual production.

For example, if we let x_1 represent our constant herbivore population, and consider a three-year model, the vegetation equations are:

$$V_1 = a_1 + kV_0 - cx_1$$
$$V_2 = a_2 + kV_1 - cx_1$$

and

$$V_3 = a_3 + kV_2 - cx_1$$

Writing x_2 for V_1, x_3 for V_2, and x_4 for V_3, and rearranging the equations so that all our variables are on the left-hand side, we get:

$$cx_1 + x_2 = a_1 + kV_0$$
$$cx_1 - kx_2 + x_3 = a_2$$
$$cx_1 - kx_3 + x_4 = a_3$$

which give us three constraints. In addition we must have

$$x_2 \geq V_{min}$$
$$x_3 \geq V_{min}$$
$$x_4 \geq V_{min}$$

and our objective function is to maximize x_1.

We thus have a problem with four variables and six constraints, and having written down the constraints for a three-year model, it is easy to see how to extend them to a 10 or 20-year model. What happens if we test this formulation for an 18-year model using the same sequence of annual production figures as in our previous tests? The results of five separate runs are summarized in Table 7.1 and discussed next.

The first run gives 5270 as the maximum number of herbivores that can be sustained continuously over the 18-year period. If we compare this with Fig. 7.5 we see that it is considerably lower than the populations we are able to sustain if we follow a strategy that allows numbers to fluctuate. This linear programming exercise thus gives management some idea of the cost (in terms of potential animal numbers) that we pay if we follow a strategy of keeping herbivore numbers constant.

The solution is likely to be sensitive to the parameters k (the proportion of vegetation surviving from one year to the next) and w (the growth multiplier.) We will not explore that sensitivity here, but in runs 2 and 3 we show what happens if we vary V_{min} by 10 percent.

Looking at the first three runs, we note that the vegetation in year 12 is always crucial. A good question to ask is how much difference it would make if we relaxed the constraint on V_{12} without relaxing any of the other constraints. This is equivalent to saying that perhaps in the worst of the years we will allow the vegetation to drop below V_{min}. The result is quite dramatic: The number of herbivores goes up to 6908 (which begins to be comparable with the results of Fig. 7.5) and the vegetation in year 12 only

TABLE 7.1 MAXIMIZING THE CONSTANT NUMBER OF HERBIVORES THAT CAN BE SUSTAINED OVER A PERIOD OF 18 YEARS WITHOUT DAMAGING THE VEGETATION
$V \geq V_{min}$ Always

Run	Constraint, V_{min}	Maximum herbivores	Minimum value of the vegetation
1	0.30	5270	0.30 in year 12
2	0.27	5870	0.27 in year 12
3	0.33	4671	0.33 in year 12
4	0.30*	6908	0.22 in year 12
5	0.30†	4983	0.30 in year 14

*Except in year 12.
†Using a different set of production rates.

drops to 0.22. It follows that we can sustain a considerably higher constant herbivore population if, occasionally, we allow the vegetation to drop below V_{min}.

We might at this stage wonder to what extent the points suggested by these results are dependent on the sequence we used for the annual production. Run 5 is a repeat of run 1, but with a completely different and randomly chosen sequence for the annual production. It suggests that the kind of result we are getting is not overly influenced by the data sequence we have used. Many more runs of this type confirm that general conclusion.

This exercise illustrates how we can overcome the rigidity of the linear programming formulation. First, the problem we posed (what is the maximum number of herbivores we can sustain if we keep the herbivore population constant?) lends itself to a linear programming formulation using a model that spans nearly two decades of data. It is a more sensible question to ask of the linear programming model than the type of question we previously asked. Second, we do not perform just one run of the model; a sensitivity analysis on the crucial constraint gives us a good idea of how that constraint affects our results. A logical extension of this is to relax the crucial constraint altogether.

The value of the whole exercise ultimately lies in these variations on the initial run. They lead us to tentative conclusions or hypotheses we can then test on different data sequences. Optimization is thus seen to be just another form of modeling. The fact that we have a program that optimizes is incidental; what is really important is that the program makes it easy for us to perform a useful series of computer experiments.

GOAL PROGRAMMING

The second way around the rigidity of linear programming is to use a more versatile optimization technique. *Goal programming* is an extension of linear programming with considerably more flexibility. It has two features that makes it especially attractive:

1. It allows for more than one objective function to be considered simultaneously in the formulation of the model.
2. It permits what were previously regarded as "fixed" constraints to be more loosely formulated as goals that are desirable (but no longer essential).

We will show how these features can be exploited by reformulating the problem discussed in the last section. There, the variable x_1 represented the constant number of herbivores in a game park, while x_2, x_3, and x_4 represented vegetation levels for three successive years. Our objective was to maximize x_1 subject to the constraints $x_2 \geq V_{\min}$, $x_3 \geq V_{\min}$, and $x_4 \geq V_{\min}$. To obtain sensible solutions to problems such as this, we found that we sometimes needed to relax the constraints. Perhaps a more realistic goal for the vegetation would be to minimize how frequently and how far the vegetation drops below the critical value $V_{\min}$. Goal programming allows us to address this more loosely formulated constraint.

Suppose that we are willing to allow the vegetation to drop below $V_{\min}$ in each of the three years. Let d_2^-, d_3^-, and d_4^- measure the *deviation* below $V_{\min}$ in each case. Then we can write

$$x_2 = V_{\min} - d_2^-, \; x_3 = V_{\min} - d_3^-, \text{ etc.}$$

and replace the constraints

$$x_2 \geq V_{\min}, \; x_3 \geq V_{min}, \text{ etc.}$$

by the objective:

$$\text{Minimize } d_2^- + d_3^- + d_4^-$$

This captures the spirit of our newly stated goals for the vegetation.

Note how we have replaced some of our constraints by a new objective expressed in terms of deviations from those constraints, and how the new objective aims to minimize the extent to which we violate the replaced constraints. However, we still want to maximize x_1. We thus have more than one objective. The goal programming algorithm requires us to rank the objectives in order of priority. It then attempts to meet them one by one, starting with the first priority, moving to the second, and so on.

Like all linear programming variables the three *deviation variables* d_2^-, d_3^-, and d_4^- must be greater than or equal to 0. By writing $x_2 = V_{\min} - d_2^-$, etc. we make it impossible for the vegetation to ever attain a value above $V_{\min}$. To redress this we have to introduce three more deviation variables, d_2^+, d_3^+, and d_4^+. We then write $x_2 = V_{\min} - d_2^- + d_2^+$, etc., and our goal programming algorithm must ensure that d_2^- is 0 if d_2^+ is not 0, and vice-versa. This ensures that $x_2 = V_{\min} - d_2^-$ if the biomass drops below $V_{\min}$, while $x_2 = V_{\min} + d_2^+$ if the biomass is above $V_{\min}$. The reason for writing the deviation variables with positive or negative superscripts should now be obvious. Note that in this example we impose no restraints on d_2^+, d_3^+, or d_4^+.

Deviation variables and multiple ranked objectives are thus the hallmarks of a goal programming formulation. Our example has so far illustrated how they allow us to be more flexible. They also permit a richer description of our problem. For example, our stated goals (in rank order) might be to (1) maintain an economically acceptable number of herbivores; (2) avoid degradation of the vegetation, and (3) if possible, maintain larger numbers of herbivores.

We could express the first goal by writing

$$x_1 = N_1 + d_1^+ - d_1^-$$

where N_1 represents a lower limit to the number of herbivores. The first objective would then be to minimize d_1^-. We have already seen that the second goal can be written as: minimize $d_2^- + d_3^- + d_4^-$. The third goal leads to the objective: maximize d_1^+.

We noted previously that managers were often uncertain whether their objective was to minimize cropping or to maximize the size of the herbivore population. We also showed, using a linear programming model, that these two objectives led to very different cropping policies. In a goal programming formulation we could use multiple ranked objectives to reach a compromise solution. Our first priority might be to keep the number of herbivores to be cropped *below* a certain level; our second priority, to keep the total number of herbivores *above* a certain level, and so on. As part of the sensitivity analysis we could then examine the effect on the solution of making changes to these levels or interchanging priorities. This would allow us to explore the trade-offs between the objectives.

Alternatively, there are formalized techniques that allow the user to interact with the solution procedure and so guide it toward a desirable result. These techniques are referred to as interactive goal programming. Often, especially in larger optimization models, it is difficult to decide whether the objectives are reasonable until we have explored their consequences. Interactive goal programming facilitates that exploration.

DISCUSSION

In the first chapter of this book we outlined how a system could be modeled at a number of different levels. Each level, we argued, has its appropriate amount of detail, so it follows that the different levels have different data requirements. It follows too that some questions are meaningful at one level but cannot be asked at another and that the type of answer we hope to get from a model depends on the level at which the model is built.

This chapter has been built around a model that contains the barest minimum of ecological detail. We have introduced a single variable to describe all the vegetation and another variable to describe all the herbivores that live off that vegetation. The data required by the model are correspondingly simple. We need to specify the annual production of the vegetation, a decay rate for old vegetation, a growth rate for the herbivore population, and the amount of vegetation consumed by the average herbivore in a year. Nothing could be simpler than that, but because the annual production varies from one year to the next and because we are unable to predict how it will vary, the questions raised by the model are fascinating and important.

However, because the model is so simple, we have to be very careful indeed to match the level of these questions to the level of resolution of the model. We have done this by looking at the model from the point of view of broad management objectives. In that context we have been able to ask some pertinent, but general, management questions, and to get some equally pertinent and general management answers or principles.

The first of these is that it is important to look ahead when making cropping decisions. Even if we cannot predict rainfall and production, we make better decisions if we analyze what is likely to happen not only this year but also a year from now.

A second principle is that it pays to be conservative. This applies both to the choice of objectives—trying to minimize the number cropped is more conservative than trying to maximize the number of herbivores—and to estimates of future rainfall and production.

A third principle is that there is an implicit cost associated with strategies that try to keep herbivore populations constant in a fluctuating environment. The constant population that can be sustained is considerably lower than populations that could be supported if fluctuations were allowed but controlled. However, if the decision is taken to maintain a constant herbivore population, the number that can be sustained is much higher if we are prepared to allow the vegetation to drop below the minimum threshold occasionally.

In deriving these principles we have assumed very clear-cut management objectives; the principles are in fact a direct consequence of those objectives and the structure of the model. In one sense, because the principles depend on such scant input, they are very robust—the broad principles are independent of detail. In another sense, because the principles ignore ecological detail, they cannot and should not be used to determine detailed strategies in a specific case—there are too many questions that our level of modeling does *not* address.

For example, we do not ask whether it really is necessary to ensure that the vegetation never drops below a certain threshold. Nor do we ask what damage the herbivores will do when the vegetation is low. We do not even know whether the herbivores can only crop the grass or whether they will root it out. These are important questions, but they are at a different level of resolution.

How then can the results and techniques introduced in this chapter be used? First, there is a level of decision-making where only gross decisions are addressed—for example, whether to keep the herbivore population constant. Questions of economy, politics, and logistics are as important at this level as the ecological considerations. It is in discussions such as these that the approach taken here can be useful. It provides, for example, a basis for arguing the trade-off between the potential economic advantages of a larger herbivore population and the potential ecological damage due to occasional overutilization of the vegetation. We need only think of a game farm rather than a game park to appreciate this sort of application.

Second, we can use the techniques developed here to generate approaches that can subsequently be modified and tested in a more specific and data-rich situation. For example, we could take the cropping strategy that always looks two years ahead and try to apply it in the system model of Chap. 5. In so doing we would immediately raise a number of questions. For example, which of the vegetation classes are we most concerned about? If we have to crop, should we crop all species or only impala and warthog, for example? Questions such as these force us to interpret the general principles within a specific context.

Finally, there is the situation where a management plan has to be formulated in a park where the infrastructure of research and monitoring is weak or even nonexistent. In this type of situation, management often chooses a cropping quota without even stating a clear management objective. The approaches we have developed in this chapter *start* with an objective and then suggest guidelines. The guesswork is at least done within a properly defined framework.

RECAPITULATION

In this chapter we have a fairly sophisticated mathematical technique (linear programming) as an interface between a very simple model and broadly but explicitly defined management objectives. The following points are worth highlighting.

As in previous models, the important step here has been to clearly state management objectives. Once these have been stated, the model allows us to explore their consequences. This in turn helps us to clarify objectives and draw distinctions between them (for example, between minimizing cropping and maximizing the herbivore population). The model also highlights the potential trade-offs between conflicting management objectives (e.g., increasing the number of herbivores but maintaining the integrity of the vegetation).

Because the model is simple, the results that emerge are general principles rather than specific remedies. They help the manager to think about a problem, formulate objectives, and perhaps make decisions of broad policy. They do not absolve the manager from looking at every particular decision in far greater detail.

As with any modeling exercise, the results obtained in this chapter are open to abuse. There are those who would apply them indiscriminately, without questioning whether the model is sufficiently detailed to be applied in a particular case, and those who would ignore them because the model lacks convincing biological detail, without asking whether that detail is really necessary. Both abuses can be avoided if we clearly understand the resolution of the model and the level at which its answers should be interpreted.

The mathematical technique we have used in this chapter is an example of an optimization technique. There is a temptation when using these techniques (perhaps because they promise to find the best answer, perhaps because we use them in the form of ready-to-run computer codes) to assume that they only need to be used once, that whatever answer they provide is indeed *the* answer to the problem. This temptation must be resisted; optimization techniques should be thought of as just another type of modeling. We have learned that we gain the greatest insight from modeling by playing with the model and testing its assumptions. In linear programming we can usefully explore what happens if we change our objective or relax our constraints, and in extensions of linear programming, such as goal programming, we can see the consequences of changing our priorities.

Optimization techniques are most useful in ecology when they are used interactively. It is precisely because playing with the model is so important that, on the one hand, direct interaction is so effective, and on the other hand, just formulating a problem, then relying on the computer to find a meaningful solution, is so dangerous.

It is difficult to formulate large optimization problems. We are often unsure of the precise objectives and uncertain whether or not we have included all the relevant constraints. Both of these problems can be reduced if we use interactive optimization codes. It is futile, for example, to rack one's brains trying to think of *all* the constraints. It is far more sensible to solve the problem taking into account all the obvious constraints, then look carefully at the solution. If the solution is practically or intuitively unacceptable, asking "why?" should suggest additional constraints.

Linear programming codes are sometimes unable to provide a solution that satisfies all the specified constraints (particularly in large models). The solution is then said to be "infeasible." This can often be interpreted as a discrepancy between the problem the biologist is trying to solve and the mathematical formulation of the problem. Linear programming can also produce answers that make good sense mathematically but do not make good sense biologically. A case in point is the example where the solution required us to crop now in anticipation of a very dry year eight or nine years from now. It is always important to look closely at the solution and reinterpret it in biological terms.

In simplifying the model of rainfall-vegetation-herbivore interaction we have concentrated on changes in the most important variable—the vegetation biomass. In the terminology of Chapter 1, this is the first-order effect. Changes that might occur in the herbivore population dynamics or in their food intake as a consequence of changes in the biomass are second-order effects and have therefore been ignored. It should be noted that these simplifications are all *conservative:* We assume that the herbivores eat as much as they can and increase at the same rate, irrespective of the vegetation.

The simplified model is, fortunately, linear in the sense that the objective function and all constraints can be represented by straight lines. If the model were made slightly more complex, this would no longer be true and we would be unable to use linear programming as our optimization technique. There are, however, other optimization techniques, such as *dynamic programming*, which can be used to analyze nonlinear problems.

It should be noted how often it pays to be adventurous in modeling. We might easily have rejected the idea of developing the strategy of looking ahead one extra year on the grounds that it was impossible to estimate the rainfall or production during the extra year. By assuming we could do this, we developed a viable strategy. So often, by assuming we have all the data, we discover what data we really need, or we learn how to compromise with our ignorance.

Finally, it should be stressed that it is very difficult, if not impossible, to prove results of this kind of analysis in the field. The results are general, while what happens in the field depends on details the analysis ignores. Even if we could design a controlled experiment, it would be many years before we could draw any conclusions from it. In the meantime, managers must make decisions. There are two ways around these difficulties. First, if we have very little data and cannot experiment in the field, we can at least experiment on the computer. We will never be entirely satisfied with the results of those experiments, but it is essential to test conclusions as thoroughly as possible from the theoretical, if not from the practical, point of view. Second, we can develop a strategy of adaptive management: Starting with general principles, one can apply them and modify them in the light of experience. This is the theme of the next two chapters.

FURTHER READING

Sposito (1975) has written an introductory text on linear programming and other optimization techniques, and the book by Williams (1978) explains how to formulate problems for solution by an optimization code.

Beneke and Winterboer (1974) have written a book on the applications of linear programming in agriculture. Applications of linear and dynamic programming to problems in range management are described in Swartzman and Singh (1974), Hunter et al. (1976), Miller et al. (1978), and Nelson (1978). Bell (1977) describes applications of linear programming in forest management, and Everitt et al. (1978) discuss the use of optimization techniques in a fishery.

Dynamic programming is introduced simply and effectively in a paper by Watt (1963). Walters et al. (1981) show how a fairly complex simulation model can be simplified for incorporation in a dynamic programming model. Silvert (1978) uses dynamic programming to explore the differences between short and long-term management considerations, and Shoemaker (1977) describes a dynamic programming approach to pest management. Stochastic dynamic programming and its application to fisheries is described in papers by Walters (1975) and Walters and Hilborn (1976). Anderson (1974) discusses the use of stochastic dynamic programming for optimizing an animal harvest in a fluctuating environment, while Stocker and Walters (1984) apply the technique to a herbivore-vegetation model that is similar to the models described in the last chapter.

Applications of goal programming in forest management are to be found in Porterfield (1974), Bottoms and Bartlett (1975), and Schuler et al. (1977). Charnes et al. (1975) discuss applications in land-use management. Two books on interactive and multi-objective decision making are Spronk (1981) and Goicoechea, Hansen, and Duckstein (1982), and an application of interactive goal programming to watershed management is described in Goicoechea et al. (1976).

dence to suggest that it might be a dominating factor. The lion model, on the other hand, was constructed to reflect the importance of social and territorial behavior. Male lions, for example, were a crucial component of the model because they affected the survival of cubs. We suspect that, as in the roan model, we can ignore kudu males altogether, and since the social behavior of kudu is similar in some respects to roan, if any of our previous models can serve as a prototype for kudu, it will be the roan model of Chap. 3.

There are, however, differences in the two species. Roan are not limited by their food supply but rather by their social behavior; kudu, we suspect, are limited by their food supply. There is also a major difference, not between kudu and roan per se, but in what we know or hope to know about the two species. In the case of roan we had some information on their social behavior, but no data whatsoever. The lack of data forced us to abandon our original plan to build a model that contained different age classes and to concentrate instead on the dynamics of roan herds. In the case of kudu we expect to have accurate age-specific mortality and fecundity data for the female section of the population. Here, at last, we have an opportunity to build a model that divides the population into distinct age classes and predicts what will happen to each age class from one year to the next. This fits well with our objectives. Changes in one age class rather than another will have implications for subsequent changes in the population.

We will therefore build an age-specific model of the female section of the population with a time step of one year. Since kudu have a distinct calving season, a suitable time to look at the population, from the modeling point of view, would be shortly after the end of the calving season (although, as we shall see, this is not the best time to take a census of the population).

The next decision we have to make is whether to build a deterministic or stochastic model. If we build a deterministic model we will be able to predict the average numbers in each age class, but not the variance; a stochastic model, if we ran it many times for each year, could give us a variance as well. However, unlike roan, the number of kudu in each age class is not so small that this variance will be significant compared with the uncertainty in the data for our model. Moreover, the model we are thinking of, at least at this stage, has no complex interactions (as in the lion model) where stochastic effects may be important. We will therefore build a deterministic model.

How many age classes do we need? In the wildebeest model of Chap. 2 we argued that all wildebeest aged three years or more could be modeled as a single unit, so we had only four age classes. That argument depended on the assumptions that predation by lions was the only cause of adult wildebeest mortality and that all adult wildebeest had about the same chance of being caught by a lion. Predation, we have hypothesized, is not the major cause of kudu mortality, so kudu may well die of old age.

It follows that very old kudu are likely to have lower survival rates, so we must model *all* age classes. As we shall see, the field data indicated that very few kudu lived beyond 12 years. Starting with new-born calves (aged 0) and allowing for all ages up to and including 12 years would give us a model with 13 age classes.

The Structure of the Preliminary Model

We want to predict what will happen to the number of female kudu in each age class from one year to the next. If we look at the population structure at the end of the calving season, the model must (1) calculate how many in each age class have survived the preceding year, and promote them to the next age class, and (2) compute the number of female calves born to these newly promoted females.

Suppose $k_{x,t}$ represents the number of female kudu that are x years old at the end of the calving season in year t. If a proportion p_x of these survive to the next calving season, we can write

$$k_{x+1,t+1} = p_x k_{x,t} \qquad (8.1)$$

Knowing $k_{0,t}$, $k_{1,t}$, $k_{2,t}$, etc., (i.e., all age classes in year t) and given the survival rates p_0, p_1, etc., we can use Eq. (8.1) to calculate $k_{1,t+1}$, $k_{2,t+1}$, etc., in the following year.

We need an additional equation to calculate the number of new-born female calves in year $t + 1$. Suppose m_x is the mean number of female offspring produced by a kudu cow that is x years old. We can write

$$k_{0,t+1} = m_1 k_{1,t+1} + m_2 k_{2,t+1} + \ldots + m_{12} k_{12,t+1}$$

or

$$k_{0,t+1} = \sum_{x=1}^{12} m_x k_{x,t+1} \qquad (8.2)$$

Once we have calculated the number of females (other than calves) in each age class at time $t + 1$ from Eq. (8.1), we can use (8.2) to estimate the number of new-born female calves. Note that we are not implying in Eq. (8.2) that one-year-old cows will necessarily produce calves. They do not, so we merely set m_1 equal to 0. Note too that although we have not specifically indicated that the rates p_x and m_x may change with time, there is nothing to prevent us from altering the rates from one time step to the next.

Equations (8.1) and (8.2) describe what is known as a *cohort* model of the population. Cohort analysis is described in depth in Caughley (1977), and we have used his notation and definitions for the survival rates p_x and the fecundity rates m_x. Sometimes it is useful to talk about the survival rates p_x; at other times it is more convenient to talk about the mortality rates q_x. Obviously, $p_x = 1 - q_x$.

An alternative way of writing Eqs. (8.1) and (8.2) is as follows. From (8.1) we know that

$$k_{x,t+1} = p_{x-1}k_{x-1,t}$$

If we substitute this in (8.2) we get

$$k_{0,t+1} = \sum_{x=1}^{12} m_x p_{x-1}k_{x-1,t} \tag{8.3}$$

Equations (8.1) and (8.3) then give us the age structure at time $t + 1$ in terms of the age structure at time t only. We can combine the two equations and write them, using matrix notation, in the form:

$$\begin{bmatrix} k_{0,t+1} \\ k_{1,t+1} \\ k_{2,t+1} \\ \cdot \\ \cdot \\ k_{12,t+1} \end{bmatrix} = \begin{bmatrix} a_{0,0} \, a_{0,1} \, a_{0,2} \ldots\ldots\ldots\ldots\ldots a_{0,12} \\ a_{1,0} \, 0 \ldots\ldots\ldots\ldots\ldots\ldots 0 \\ 0 \quad a_{2,1} \, 0 \ldots\ldots\ldots\ldots\ldots 0 \\ \ldots\ldots\ldots\ldots\ldots\ldots \\ \ldots\ldots\ldots\ldots\ldots\ldots \\ 0 \ldots\ldots\ldots\ldots\ldots a_{12,11} \, 0 \end{bmatrix} \begin{bmatrix} k_{0,t} \\ k_{1,t} \\ k_{2,t} \\ \cdot \\ \cdot \\ k_{12,t} \end{bmatrix} \tag{8.4}$$

The square matrix with coefficients $a_{0,0}$, etc., in Eq. (8.4) is known as a *Leslie matrix*.

By the rules of matrix multiplication, it follows from (8.4) that

$$k_{0,t+1} = a_{0,0}k_{0,t} + a_{0,1}k_{1,t} + \ldots + a_{0,11}k_{11,t} + a_{0,12}k_{12,t}$$
$$k_{1,t+1} = a_{1,0}k_{0,t}$$
$$k_{2,t+1} = a_{2,1}k_{1,t}$$

and so on. Thus in this particular case, where we have a distinct calving season (what Caughley calls the *pulse-birth model*) and where we calculate our population immediately after the calving season, the formulation contained in Eqs. (8.1) and (8.2) is equivalent to (8.4) provided we put

$$a_{0,0} = m_1 p_0, \, a_{0,1} = m_2 p_1, \ldots a_{0,11} = m_{12}p_{11}, \, a_{0,12} = 0$$

and

$$a_{1,0} = p_0, \, a_{2,1} = p_1$$

and so on.

Note that implicit in our mathematics is the idea that no kudu die during the calving season. Points such as this may seem unimportant when we are building a model, but they can take on importance when we try to compare the model with field data.

We thus have two ways of representing population changes from one year to the next. The first way, using a straightforward cohort model, has the advantages that it is easier to interpret the coefficients directly as survival and fecundity rates and it is easier to implement on a computer.

The second way, because it uses matrix notation, lends itself to manipulation using the results of matrix algebra.

For example, we note from (8.4) that all the elements of the Leslie matrix are 0 except for those in the first row and in the subdiagonal starting at the first element of the second row.

Certain mathematical results follow from this special structure. The most important result states that no matter what the initial population might be, after a number of years the population will eventually increase (or decrease) by a fixed proportion each year. That proportion can be calculated directly from the Leslie matrix and is called the *sustained* rate of increase of the population. Also, the *percentage* of animals in each age class will remain the same from one year to the next, and those percentages can also be calculated directly from the Leslie matrix. They define what is known as the *stable age distribution*.

The results quoted in the last paragraph make certain assumptions about the shape of the graph of fecundity versus age. In the case of kudu, these assumptions are satisfied. The results also assume that the fecundity and survival rates m_x and p_x are constants that do not change from one year to the next. However, the whole purpose of the field study was to determine how these rates *do* change as a function of the available browse, for example, so it is not obvious that the concept of a stable age distribution with a constant rate of increase (or decrease) in the total population is pertinent. This simple model can, however, serve as a starting point for more complex models. We have seen in previous chapters that one can often glean useful information from models that are patently too simple. Before looking carefully at the available field data with the idea of modifying this preliminary model, let us therefore see what happens if we insert some numbers for the survival and fecundity rates into the model.

Results from the Preliminary Model

An interesting question is how fast a kudu population can grow under very favorable conditions. We will postulate a calf survival rate (p_0) of 0.80, which is likely to be high, and a yearling survival rate (p_1) of 0.96, which is also likely to be high. Then we will suppose that the prime females have a survival rate (p_2 through p_9) of 0.97, while the very old have a survival rate (p_{10} and p_{11}) of 0.95. Our model assumes that thereafter the survival rate is effectively 0.

Most kudu cows first calve at three years of age, but under good conditions they can produce their first calf at two years of age. We will therefore assume that all cows first calve at two years and thereafter regularly give birth to one calf per year—i.e., we put m_1 equal to 0 and m_2 through m_{12} equal to 0.5. (Remember that we are modeling the female segment of the population only, so if each cow produces one calf per year, each cow will on average produce only 0.5 female calves per year.)

TABLE 8.1 SENSITIVITY STUDIES ON THE SUSTAINED GROWTH
RATE OF A KUDU POPULATION

Parameters that differ from standard run	Sustained growth rate (%)
None (i.e., standard run)	25.7
Survival rate of age classes 10 and 11 reduced from 0.95 to 0.90	25.6
Yearling survival rate reduced from 0.96 to 0.92	24.6
Survival rate of age classes 2 through 9 reduced from 0.97 to 0.94	23.6
Fecundity of 2-year-olds reduced from 0.50 to 0.25	22.6
Fecundity of 2-year-olds reduced from 0.5 to 0	19.8
Calf survival rate reduced from 0.80 to 0.60	18.6

With these assumptions we find that the population is capable of growing at a *sustained* rate of 25.7 percent per annum. There are two ways we can deduce this result. The first is to start with any kudu population and apply Eqs. (8.1) and (8.2) to it, year after year, until the percentage increase in the total population from one year to the next is constant. That percentage increase will be the sustained growth rate.

The second way is to compute the coefficients of the Leslie matrix, then calculate what is known as its largest eigenvalue using a standard computer package. This will return a value of 1.257 (i.e., 25.7 percent).

How sensitive is this growth rate to the assumed values for the survival and fecundity rates? In Table 8.1 we summarize a series of computer experiments in which we varied sets of parameters, one set at a time. First we doubled the *mortality* rates in various age classes. Then we halved the fecundity of two-year-old cows. Finally, we reduced their fecundity to zero. The table shows that the sustained growth rate is only really sensitive to two parameters—the calf survival rate p_0 and the age at first calving. This is extremely useful information because it gives us some indication, even before we go into the field, of what we need to measure most carefully.

Note that yet again we are vindicated in devoting some time to a simple model. Also note that it would be possible to measure a larger rate of increase in the field than the maximum we have deduced here (for instance, if the age distribution happened to be skewed in favor of mature cows), but a larger rate of increase could not be *sustained*.

THE FIELD DATA

The first objective of the field studies was to measure the age-specific survival and fecundity rates of female kudu, and to relate these rates to measurements of the quantity and quality of the vegetation they depended on. It was thought that the best way to estimate this was to actually try and see the vegetation through the eyes of the kudu. This was done by making minute-by-minute observations of how kudu selected their food and what they actually ate. A great deal was learned about the feeding ecology of kudu during one season of observations of this kind but, as mentioned earlier, the study was far too intensive to be repeated every year.

Some other way of assessing how food availability varied from one year to the next had to be found. Changes in the annual production are likely to follow rainfall patterns. Since good data on rainfall were available it was decided, as a first step, to try and compare the data collected on survival and fecundity rates with the annual rainfall.

Figure 8.1 shows the calf mortality ($q_0 = 1 - p_0$) in the two study areas plotted versus time. Also shown in the figure is the annual rainfall for each study area. Looking at the figure we are tempted to compare calf mortality directly with rainfall, as in Fig. 8.2. Here the data from both study areas have been combined. There is a fair amount of scatter in the

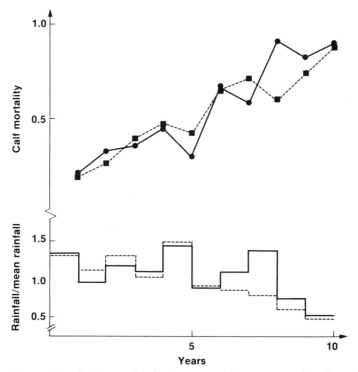

Figure 8.1   Calf mortality in the two study areas as a function of time. The ratio of annual rainfall to mean annual rainfall for each area is also shown. *(From Owen-Smith, in press.)*

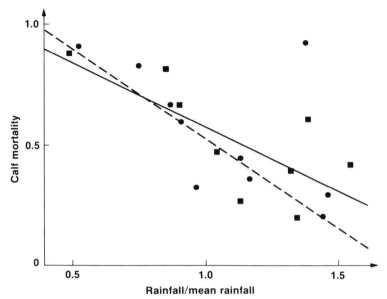

Figure 8.2   Calf mortality plotted against annual rainfall. The dashed line is the best fit to the data points (circles) for the first study area, and the solid line is the best fit for the second study area (squares). *(From Owen-Smith, in press.)*

diagram, but also evidence of a trend. The trend suggests that calf mortality is indeed related to rainfall. The scatter implies that mortality depends on other paramters as well. Three prime candidates are:

1. Population density. Competition for resources could influence the relationship between rainfall and calf survival.
2. Location. The vegetation in the two study areas may differ in composition and hence influence the relationship between rainfall and calf survival in different ways.
3. Predation and/or competition with other browsers.

Figure 8.3 shows the same mortality data as in Fig. 8.2, but this time plotted against the ratio of rainfall to kudu biomass per unit area. This removes a great deal of the scatter. It also makes sense. If rainfall is a measure of the abundance of food, the ratio of rainfall to biomass per unit area is a measure of food available per kudu. The line that best fits the data is called the *regression line* and can be found using standard formulas or computer codes. The regression line has been drawn in Fig. 8.3, and the fit is so good that we feel justified in ignoring location—there are no consistent differences between data from the two study areas—along with predation and competition with other browsers as factors contributing to the scatter.

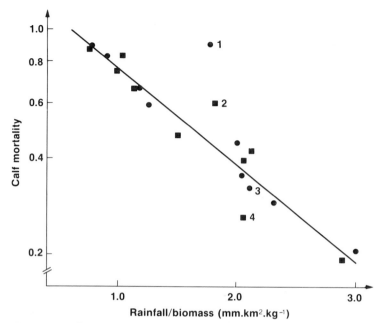

Figure 8.3 Calf mortality plotted against the annual rainfall divided by the kudu biomass for each study area. A single line fits both sets of data. (Data from the first study area are plotted as circles, and from the second as squares.) Note that the calf mortality is plotted on a log scale. *(From Owen-Smith, in press.)*

The straight line fitted to the data in Fig. 8.3 is potentially very useful. In a single equation it combines the two important effects of annual production (represented by rainfall) and kudu density on the most important parameter of the model (calf survival). It helps us see how we can improve our preliminary model. First, we adjust the model to ask, each year, for an estimate of the annual rainfall. Next, we estimate the biomass from the size and age structure of the population. Then we compute the calf mortality rate q_0 from the regression line and hence find the survival rate p_0.

(Recall that q_0 is the mortality rate between birth and one year. In practice it is very difficult to take a census of the population at the end of the calving season—first, because calves are left hidden for two to three months after they are born; second, because vegetation is normally rank at that time. Field measurements were therefore made at the end of the dry season, just before the next rainy season, so the data in Fig. 8.3 actually represent mortality from conception to the age of nine months. To align our model with these data we would have to interpret the first age class as conception to 9 months, the second as 9 to 21 months, and so on, and we would then have to interpret the fecundity rates m_x as conception rates. It is far easier to reinterpret the model in this way than to attempt to deduce survival rates for the zero to one age class, one to two age class, and so on, from the field data.)

Similar regression lines could be found for other age classes but, as Table 8.1 indicates, their significance will not be as great. In fact, if we look at Table 8.1 we realize it is the fecundity of the younger cows that we should concentrate on next. Here the field data are straightforward: No cows aged two years produced calves that survived and almost all cows aged three years and older produced one calf each year.

At this stage we might feel justified in maintaining that 10 years of study had paid handsome dividends and that the new model, based on mortality regression lines (particularly the calf mortality regression), could be used with confidence and without major modifications in the future. There are of course one or two data points that do not lie close to the regression line, and one point in particular that is way off. That point was in fact neglected when we calculated the regression line. From a statistical point of view this might be justifiable, but from the management point of view it would make a great deal of difference if the model predicted a reasonably low calf mortality in a given year and it transpired that calf mortality was unusually high. Are the points that do not lie close to the regression line unfortunate measurements, in which case we can ignore them, or are there good ecological reasons for the discrepancy, in which case we should find out more about them?

If we go back and ask the researcher who collected the data about the point labeled 1 in Fig. 8.3, we discover that he has an explanation of why the calf mortality in that particular year, despite good rainfall, was so high. He hypothesized that there was an unusually severe cold and damp spell toward the end of winter that killed many of the calves. Moreover, the topography of one of the study areas (corresponding to point 1) was such that cold air drained into the plains and stayed there, which is why calf mortality was so high. The other study area was hilly and cold air drained away, which explains why point 2 (representing the same year in the second study area) is closer to the regression line.

An explanation can also be proposed for data points 3 and 4. In this case the previous year had been particularly good, the adult cows had built up their fat reserves, and calf mortality in the following year was therefore lower than the regression line would have predicted.

Statisticians are inclined to reject "bad" data points—those that do not fit the trend of the rest of the data. What we learn from this discussion is that there are often very good explanations for the deviations from the trend, and those explanations often tell us as much about the dynamics of the kudu population as the regression line itself. It is precisely because calf mortality in the year corresponding to data point 1 was so unexpectedly high that anticipating it is particularly important to the game manager. The lesson we learn is that our model, if it is to be useful, must also account for sporadic or episodic events because their impact can often be more important than the normal trends.

MODELING EPISODIC EVENTS

The structure of our preliminary model is very simple:

1. We input the initial population (for each age class) and values for the age-specific fecundity and survival rates.
2. The model uses those rates to project the population forward one year at a time.

The next level of sophistication is a model based entirely on regression lines such as the line shown in Fig. 8.3. The structure is:

1. We input the initial population and age-specific fecundity rates and the *equations* of the regression lines for age-specific survival rates.
2. The program is coded to *ask the user* to estimate the rainfall each year.
3. The model uses that estimate, together with its own calculation of kudu density, to compute the survival rates from the regression equations.
4. The model then projects the population forward one year.

This is a much more realistic model because it *reacts* to changes in rainfall and kudu density.

Our problem now is to incorporate into the model not only the information implicit in the regression lines, but also the information contained in the data points that do *not* lie on the regression line. Suppose, for example, that we wanted to include what we had learned from data points 1 and 2 in Fig. 8.3. The computer program would have to ask for more than just the annual rainfall. It could, for example, ask the user whether there had been a cold spell toward the end of winter and, if so, whether it had been very severe or only moderately severe. The logic of the model would then calculate the calf mortality from the regression line and would use this value if there had been no cold spell, but modify it, depending on severity, if there had been a cold spell.

The structure of the model would then be as follows:

1. We still input the initial population, age-specific fecundity rates, and the equations for the age-specific regression lines.
2. The program is coded to ask the user for an estimate of annual

rainfall as before, but is also coded to ask the user a series of questions that elicit direct or indirect information about the weather, the kudu, their food supply, predators, and so on.

3. The program is coded to make decisions on the basis of the answers given by the user to these questions. The logic incorporated in the program decides whether to compute the survival rates from the regression lines, whether to modify the values so obtained, or whether to replace them by alternative values.

4. The model then projects the population forward one year.

The result is a model that looks much more like a simulation model, but one that interacts with the user, asking for information that would be difficult to simulate from the beginning.

There is a significant difference in approach between this model and the previous model. The simple regression model only asks the user for numbers, then uses the numbers it is given in a very straightforward calculation. The more complex model ask for information in a more general sense, then applies *rules* to that information. These rules can be complicated.

The new model is interactive on a different plane. It asks the user to be more discerning, and the model itself is correspondingly more intelligent. The emphasis in the model has shifted away from the computational details of either cohort analysis or Leslie matrices to the gathering of information via questions and the logical structures that process that information. We will call this a *rule-enhanced* model.

There is another important difference between the two models. As we have seen, the data for the regression model were collected intensively over 10 years. Once sufficient data had been obtained to fit regression lines, the data collection phase was essentialy completed. We might still want to monitor the kudu population to see how well the regression model works, but we would not want to collect data as intensively as before.

However, data collection is *never* completed for the rule-enhanced model. Episodic events, by definition, will occur rarely, and the circumstances under which they do occur will never be quite the same. For example, the field studies showed no instance of a two-year-old cow producing a calf, but we know from studies elsewhere that this can happen. We may suspect that this is a regional phenomenon and that two-year-olds will never drop calves in the two study areas, but it could well be that we have not had the opportunity, during the 10-year study, to observe the circumstances under which two-year-olds will calve. It follows that we must keep this option open in the model.

The rules will *always* be subject to modification in the light of new experience. This has implications for the way in which the model is structured and the way in which it is used. These are discussed in the next two sections.

AN IMPROVED STRUCTURE FOR RULE-ENHANCED MODELS

The rule-enhanced model asks the user a series of questions at each time step, then calculates or modifies the fecundity and survival rates on the basis of the answers supplied. The program code thus contains output statements that ask the questions, input statements that record the answers, and conditional statements (the rules) that compute the various rates. This structure has one major disadvantage—each time a question or rule is added or modified, the code itself has to be modified. As we have seen, the model is likely to be modified fairly frequently. The program is therefore likely to become unwieldy, and the chances of introducing errors or losing control of the structure will multiply.

A far more robust structure is one in which the questions and rules are kept in a separate data file which the computer program is written to read like any other data file. The program itself will thus have a general structure that enables it to ask questions, record the answers, and apply rules based on those answers. However, that capability will be like an empty shell. The program will not know what questions to ask or what rules to apply until it has read the text for the questions and answers and the syntax for the rules from the data file. We are all familiar with the idea of a program that is capable of adding two numbers but does not know which numbers to add until it has read a data file; our model structure is merely an extension of the same idea. It has the following advantages:

1. The program itself, once written, need never be altered.
2. The information in the data file can be stored in an orderly fashion, which makes it easy to update and control.
3. The questions and rules can be written in a form that is easy to understand. This makes the rules readily accessible to all, promotes discussion and argument about them, and facilitates updating.

The questions and rules can be formatted in the following way. First, the questions and answers are all numbered. The format of a typical question with three possible answers would be:

Q5: [text] ; A1 [text] , A2 [text] , A3 [text] .

Some specific examples are:

Q1: Were fruits and creepers during the wet season;
    A1 abundant,
    A2 sparse.

Q2: Were most deciduous trees bare by;
    A1   early winter,
    A2   mid-winter,
    A3   late winter.
Q3: Was there a noticeable browse line on evergreen species by;
    A1   mid-winter,
    A2   late winter.
Q4: Was there a cold spell at the end of winter that was;
    A1   very severe,
    A2   moderately severe,
    A3   not severe at all.

The rules (also numbered) can be written in the general form:

R[number]: IF [condition] THEN [instructions]
                     ELSE [instructions] .

The condition is a logical or Boolean expression consisting of statements connected by the operators *and, or,* and *not.* The statements may refer to previous rules (e.g., "Rule 1 applies") or to specific answers to questions (e.g., "Question 5 Answer 2 is correct"). The instructions are recipes for calculating one or more of the fecundity or survival rates. Typical instructions would be "put p_1 equal to 0.2" or "compute p_1 from the regression line and then multiply it by 0.5". The *else* portion of the rule is optional.

The rules can be written in a compact form. Some examples are:

R1: If Q2A1 AND Q3A1 AND Q4A3 THEN set p_1 equal to 0.3.
R2: If Q2A1 AND Q3A1 AND NOT Q4A3 THEN set p_1 equal to 0.15.
R3: If (R3 OR R4) AND Q1A2 THEN multiply p_1 by 0.7.

These rules all relate to the early onset of dry season conditions (question 2 answer 1) and a relatively high density of browsers (as implied by question 3 answer 1). Rule 1 suggests that under the combination of these conditions the additional stress of even a mild cold spell toward the end of winter will lead to relatively high calf mortality. Rule 2 suggests an even higher calf mortality if the cold spell is not mild. Both these rules override the rainfall regression line for calf survival. The reasoning behind this is that if the conditions defined by the rules prevail, the actual value of the rainfall will be irrelevant. Rule 3 further reduces calf survival if the conditions described by either of the first two rules prevail and if conditions for the growth of the calves during the summer were unfavorable.

How to write the computer program to access the question-and-rule data file and then implement it is beyond the scope of this book. Different ways of doing it can be found in some of the references at the end of the next chapter. What is relevant here is that it can be done, and that in doing it we facilitate new approaches to building and using models. These are highlighted in the next section.

DISCUSSION

This chapter has been refreshingly different from others in this book because it has been based on good and relevant field data. Those data contributed in two ways to the development of a kudu population model. First, they provided a useful relationship between the important survival rates and annual rainfall (divided by the kudu density). Second, they highlighted the importance, over and above this relationship, of episodic events such as unusually severe cold spells.

Detailed studies of animal populations elsewhere have often yielded a similar relationship between survival rates and some important environmental factor or some aspect of the size of the population itself. Bunnell and Tait (1981), for example, show a relationship between litter size and the latitude of the denning area for polar bears, while Eberhardt (1981) demonstrates the relationship between pup survival and the size of the population for the Pribilof fur seal.

These relationships can be useful from both the modeling and management points of view, but they are often tenuous, not only because of the potential impact of episodic events, but also because the causal link that lies beneath the observed correlation may be complex or even coincidental.

For example, the rainfall does not affect the kudu directly, but acts through its influence on the quantity and quality of the food supply. First, it controls the production of high-quality vegetation components such as fruits, creepers, and other leafy forbs during the wet season. This presumably has an effect on the supply of milk for the calves born at this time of the year, and also on the building up of fat reserves by adults.

Second, rainfall influences the period of leaf retention by the deciduous trees and shrubs that form the staple food sources for most of the year. This affects the duration of the period at the end of the dry season when kudus must subsist on poor quality forage.

It follows that the timing of the rains can be as important as the rainfall itself. Moreover, mortality resulting from limitations in food supply is mediated by predators (they find it easier to catch animals in poor condition), by parasites (which build up when an animal's condition is poor), and, as we have seen, by cold weather (which can bring about hypothermia if an animal's fat reserves have been depleted).

Inevitably, therefore, there will be times when the relations break down or are overridden by other factors. When this occurs, the impact on management of the population can be crucial. The approach we have developed uses the established relationships in a conventional type of model, but also modifies or replaces them via rules that can easily be added to the model. These rules can be used to represent the influence of various types and combinations of environmental conditions. They can cater for episodic events and for cases where a certain concatenation of events may lead to precipitous changes in one or more of the survival rates.

We have called this type of model *rule-enhanced*. It provides an approach that recognizes the difficulty of forecasting episodic events and enables us to incorporate their impact when it is experienced. A rule-enhanced model would, for instance, be ideal for modeling seedling survival in a forest.

Rule-Enhanced Models and Adaptive Management

The fact that managers have to make decisions, often in a crisis and irrespective of whether they truly understand the workings of the system they are managing or fully comprehend the consequences of their actions, is a point that has been made frequently in this book. Under these circumstances, one of the first options that managers should consider is referring to or building a model. This is relatively cheap and easy to do and serves a useful purpose if it leads to even a marginally better understanding of the key system processes or the implications of alternative management actions. It is healthy to take this pragmatic viewpoint because on the one hand it prevents us from expecting too much of a model and on the other hand it underscores the fact that even a crude but carefully constructed model is in a very practical sense better than no model at all.

It is even healthier to recognize that under these circumstances managers (and modelers) will inevitably make mistakes, and to ask how one can learn from those mistakes. This is in line with the philosophy of *adaptive management* proposed by Walters and Hilborn (1978) and Holling (1978). They view management actions as experiments that, particularly when they have unexpected results, enable us to learn more about the system being managed. For this process of "doing and learning" to be effective, management action must take place within an intellectual framework that includes:

1. Making use of the best data available
2. Interpreting the data via the most sensible model that can be built at the time
3. Using the data and model to make the best decision under the circumstances
4. Monitoring the consequences of that decision

5. Reviewing the arguments that led to the decision in order to improve the model in the light of those consequences

The rule-enhanced model described in the previous section lends itself to this approach. It provides a model that in the first place incorporates the best available data and the most current knowledge in a usable form. In the second place it can readily be updated in the light of further experience, new data, or a better understanding of the existing data. A set of rules developed during a period of unusually dry years could, for example, be reviewed and modified when observations are made during a period of higher rainfall. The format we have suggested, where the rules are stored in a separate data file, facilitates these changes.

Questions of Detail

The reader should look carefully at the examples given for the questions in the section that describes rule-enhanced models because they introduce concepts and themes that are radically different from those we have built into our models so far.

Consider, for example, the question about the deciduous trees (question 2). The dry season is a period of stress for the kudu, and the question of leaf retention is therefore an important one, so let us look at how we might have tried to model it in a more conventional way. The approach we would have taken would probably have been similar to the way we modeled moribund grass in Chap. 5. First, we would have had to specify the rainfall, every week or every fortnight. From this we would have kept track of the number of continuous weeks without rain. Depending on that number and how heavy the rainfall had been just prior to this dry spell, we would have *invented* a plausible calculation to decide whether leaves still remained on the deciduous trees. We might even have gone so far as to calculate a "leaf retention index"—all of this to try and calculate something that anybody could *see* just by stepping outside and looking around!

Whenever we build a model there is a conflict between the amount of realistic detail we would like to see built into it and our ability to do so in a meaningful way and without losing control of the overall structure and objectives of the model.

This conflict has haunted us throughout this book, particularly in our attempt in Chap. 5 to build a realistic model of a system. So far we have developed two strategies for trying to resolve it. The first is to be parsimonious and use the objectives of the model as criteria for including only the level of detail that is absolutely essential. The second is to cut through the detail whenever it threatens to engulf us. (A good example of the latter is the way we chose to input the number of lions and the number of wildebeest kills per year in Chap. 2 instead of trying to model the dynamics of the lion population and predator-prey interactions.)

Both of these strategies are bold. Even when they are successful we often feel uncomfortable with the resulting model because it ignores much of what we actually see and take note of in the field. The idea of a rule-enhanced model offers us a third and more subtle possibility. Instead of trying to simulate and predict details, it enables us to ask questions that relate directly to what can be observed in the field, then to assimilate the answers into our model. By providing this direct link between the model and what we see, we encourage a situation in which field biologists and managers can relate to the model. They can argue effectively about it because the questions and rules impinge on their experience. Also, because the model is interactive and asks questions about the system, the user is forced to become involved in the simulation and is therefore more likely to think critically about the results.

It should be stressed that in advocating rule-enhanced models, we are not suggesting the indiscriminate inclusion of detail in the model. A cluttered data file of rules would be confusing and virtually impossible to update. The principle of parsimony still applies, and it is as essential as ever to make sure that all the different components of the model are represented at the appropriate level of resolution. That is why it was so useful in the kudu exercise to first test the sensitivity of the simple Leslie matrix model. The results of the sensitivity analysis tell us that the questions and rules in the more complex model will largely be concerned with those things that influence the age at first conception and the calf survival rate. We would, for example, deliberately disregard rules that implied small changes in the survival rate of prime cows.

Qualitative Modeling

One of the objectives of building the kudu model was to help management decide if and when kudu should be cropped. The main reason for cropping would be that the kudu were endangering their food supply. If we look back at the examples we gave of questions we might ask in a rule-enhanced kudu model, we notice that one of them (question 3) asks when a browse line first became apparent on evergreen species. The reason for the question was to help us determine how to modify the survival rates of the kudu —i.e., we were interested in the impact of the state of the vegetation on the kudu, *but the browse line on evergreen trees and bushes is equally an indicator of the impact that the kudu are having on the vegetation.* By noting how early in the dry season a distinct browse line first develops, and taking into account other factors such as leaf retention by the deciduous trees (an indicator of how rainfall has influenced food availability), we could *deduce* whether or not kudu densities were too high.

The process of taking into account other factors and deducing whether or not kudu densities are too high can be formalized. It amounts to asking a series of questions and formulating a set of rules based on the answers to those questions—precisely the format we have introduced into our rule-enhanced model.

If we carry this line of reasoning to its logical conclusion, we realize that just as a conventional model asks for input data (in the form of numbers), then manipulates that data (via equations) to give an output (again in the form of numbers), so we can build a model that asks for input data in the form of answers to questions, then manipulates that data via a set of rules, and gives output in the form of conclusions or decisions.

The question-and-rule format we introduced in the rule-enhanced model could thus be developed on its own to provide a totally different type of model—what we might call a *rule-based* rather than a *rule-enhanced* model. This new form of modeling can be qualitative instead of quantitative, and might lend itself particularly well to the kind of information usually available to managers and to the types of decisions they often have to make. This is an idea we will explore in depth in the next chapter. We need only note here that our attempt to model episodic events has led to a new and potentially exciting form of model building.

FURTHER READING

Further information on the feeding ecology and population dynamics of kudu can be found in Owen-Smith (1979), Owen-Smith and Novellie (1983), Owen-Smith et al. (1983), and Owen-Smith (in press).

Leslie (1945) first suggested using matrices for population projections. Usher (1972) and Emlen (1984) describe various applications and extensions of this idea, and Boyce (1977) develops a stochastic version of the Leslie matrix model. Flipse and Veling (1984) rescale the coefficients of the Leslie matrix to represent the influence of hunting, while DeMaster (1981) explicity introduces both density-dependent effects and harvesting. Eberhardt and Siniff (1977) perform a sensitivity analysis on a small Leslie matrix model and show the importance of survival through the immature stages.

An introduction to matrix algebra and the properties of Leslie matrices can be found in Jeffers (1978) and Legendre and Legendre (1983). Pielou (1977) also discusses the properties of Leslie matrices, but uses the more general terminology of projection matrices. Beddington (1974) analyses the stability of matrix models.

Two examples of models where rules are built directly into the model are Walters et al. (1975) and Starfield et al. (1980). References relating to the way in which one might structure the program for a rule-enhanced model can be found at the end of the next chapter.

Decision Trees,
Tables, and
Expert Systems

All the models developed in this book have been oriented toward questions of management and have been built to help managers understand their problems and so help them make better decisions. In building the models, we have described the relevant processes or interactions with equations that have either been implemented directly on a computer or investigated using analytical mathematical techniques. The models are essentially *quantitative*. We have had to input *numbers* directly into the computer. Even when our mathematical analyses have led to results that can be interpreted in a general sense, they ultimately require numbers before they can be applied to a specific case.

There are two major difficulties with this quantitative approach. First, the numbers are seldom available. Second, there are often important processes that are extremely difficult to model in the conventional way. We saw an example of this in the last chapter when we pointed out the futility of trying to build a model that would predict when the leaves on deciduous trees would fall. However, this is what we notice in the field, and it is the type of information that provides input for intuitive or experience-based decision making. We begin to see that one of the reasons why the numbers are not available for conventional models is because the observers have often concentrated on data of a different kind.

If one thinks about it, those who make decisions on the basis of experience must also use models, although they may not be conscious of doing so. What form could these models take? Obviously they will differ from person to person, but we know that they must have some common features. For instance, we know that the input data must consist of observations, probably in the form of key indications or symptoms that reflect the state of the system. We also know that the output will be in the form of a decision. Presumably the "model" between the input and output consists of a logical sorting based on previous experience, but we cannot be sure. Not only are the details never spelled out, but even the person concerned may not have thought it through in an explicit way.

It is because the model is not explicit that we have to be wary of decisions based on experience. It is like having a computer with a program we are never allowed to see. It may give results, it may even give very good results, but without seeing the program we cannot argue about the way the results are obtained, we cannot be sure whether the program is valid for certain situations but unreliable under different conditions, and nobody except the original programmer can ever modify or improve it.

There is therefore much to be gained by trying to document the thought processes of experienced individuals. At the least, it will provide a solid basis for argument. At best, if the field observations they react to do indeed indicate the state of the system, and if the logic that leads them from those observations to a decision can be *seen* to be systematic and sensible, then experience-based decision making could be a very effective management tool. Can we produce a model that represents these thought processes, one that manipulates information in a qualitative and deductive way rather than a quantitative way?

In this chapter we will look at three different ways of doing this. We will also explore some of the exciting possibilities and applications inherent in qualitative modeling.

DECISION TREES

The simplest way of representing the qualitative arguments that lead to one decision rather than another is in what is called a *decision tree*. An example is shown in Fig. 9.1. The structure is similar to a dichotomous key for classifying plants and looks like a flow chart for a computer program. The questions are underlined, and the arrows, depending on the answers to those questions, control the flow of the logic. To use the tree, we simply

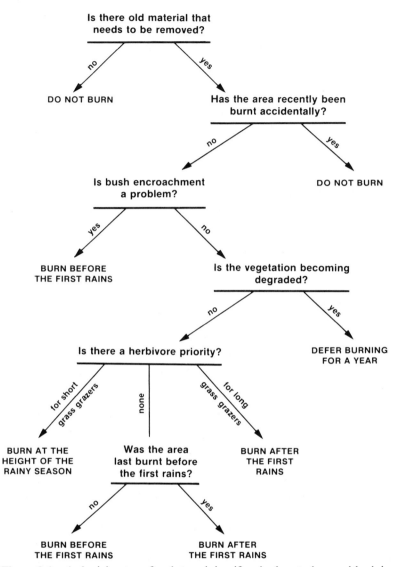

Figure 9.1   A decision tree for determining if and when to burn a block in an area of a park.

start at the top and answer questions, as directed by the arrows, until we are led to a decision.

It is worth looking at the problem addressed in Fig. 9.1 in some detail because we will use it as an example for most of this chapter. The problem relates to the use of fire as a management tool. Fires are a natural feature of African savannas. They play a functional role, controlling the balance between bush and grass, removing accumulated dead material, opening up areas too congested for animals to penetrate, and promoting a flush of short, fresh grass that attracts many of the herbivores. Fires are, however, usually rigidly controlled in a game park and are prevented from spreading by a system of fire breaks. As a result, they occur far less frequently than under natural conditions. To compensate, a deliberate policy of controlled burning is implemented in some parks.

Decisions then have to be made about whether or not to burn different areas of a park, and when (i.e., at what time of the year) a fire is likely to be most effective. These decisions are usually taken on the advice of experts after they have inspected the areas involved. The decision tree in Fig. 9.1 was constructed with the help of one such expert. It is an ordered, systematic representation of how he makes a decision. Just looking at the questions tells us what information the expert requires and what factors he takes into consideration. Some of them are given here:

1. Whether there is sufficient combustible material in the area to sustain a fire. The first two questions at the top of the tree relate to this issue.
2. If the purpose of burning is to thin out shrubs and bushes, the fire should be as intense as possible, so burning before the first rains is indicated.
3. Depending on the soil type and depth, burning too frequently can be deleterious, leading to soil erosion and the proliferation of those grasses and plants that thrive on disturbed soils.
4. Fire can be used to alter the vegetation in such a way as to favor one herbivore species rather than another. Management objectives and priorities with regard to the herbivores can thus be important.

Looking at the structure of the tree gives us insight into the thought processes and priorities of the expert. For instance, the order in which questions are asked is important. It is no coincidence that the questions about the state of the vegetation are asked before the question about the priorities for the management of herbivores. The expert clearly believes that the latter are only relevant if the state of the vegetation is not a problem.

The order of the questions also tells us what the expert would do if faced with a situation in which bush encroachment is a problem but the area has been burned so frequently that the vegetation is becoming degraded. When we built the decision tree shown in Fig. 9.1, the expert on fires pointed out that there were two different regions (based on soil type and topography) in the park. The tree was constructed with only one of these regions in mind; in that region the expert knew that bush encroachment was more of a problem than degradation of the vegetation. This might not be true in other regions. A more general version of the decision tree might thus contain the additional question: Is bush encroachment of greater concern than degradation? with suitable changes to the flow of the logic.

The reader should try to amend the decision tree in Fig. 9.1 to include this question. We found it impossible to make the amendment without repeating either the question about bush encroachment or the question about degradation. This demonstrates the Achilles heel of decision trees: Although they are always easy to use and follow once they have been constructed, unless they are very simple they are not easy to build and can be extremely difficult to modify. Since the problems we need to represent are bound to be complex, and since we will frequently want to amend our model in the light of experience, it follows that we will often need a more pliable representation.

DECISION TABLES

In Table 9.1 we have drawn a decision table that contains exactly the same information as the decision tree of Fig. 9.1. The questions contained in the decision tree are written down the left-hand side of the table (in any order) with only one difference: The questions are all rewritten as statements that can either be true or false. The decisions are written (again in any order) across the top of the table. The entries in the table consist of T (for true), F (for false), or X (for irrelevant).

Note that while there is only one row for each question, there can be more than one column corresponding to each decision. Each column represents a set of conditions that would lead to (or *validate*) that decision; there are often two or more ways of validating a particular decision. Thus

TABLE 9.1 DECISION TABLE FOR DETERMINING IF AND WHEN TO BURN

	Do not burn		Defer for a year	Burn after first rains		Burn at height of season	Burn before first rains	
There is old material that needs to be removed	F	X	T	T	T	T	T	T
The area has recently been burned accidentally	X	T	F	F	F	F	F	F
The vegetation is becoming degraded	X	X	T	F	F	F	X	F
Bush encroachment is a problem	X	X	F	F	F	F	T	F
There is a herbivore priority for long grass grazers	X	X	X	T	F	F	X	F
There is a herbivore priority for short grass grazers	X	X	X	F	F	T	X	F
The area was last burned before the first rains	X	X	X	X	T	X	X	F

the first column in Table 9.1 tells us that the decision "do not burn" is valid if the statement "there is old material that needs to be removed" is false. The second column tells us that this decision is also valid if the statement "the area has recently been burned accidentally" is true. Both of these columns are unusual because the decision in each case depends on only one statement (all other entries in the column are X). Column three contains a more complex set of conditions for validating the decision "defer burning for a year." Here, the first and third statements must both be true and the second and fourth statements must both be false.

Decision tables are much easier to build than decision trees because the order of the questions is no longer important. The table is constructed as follows:

1. First we write all the relevant statements down the left-hand side of the table.
2. Next we write the first decision at the top of the table and, going down the first column, we ask ourselves what combination of T's, F's, and X's will lead unambiguously to that decision. We fill them in.
3. Then we ask whether another combination would lead to the same decision and keep on adding columns until we are satisfied we have included all sensible routes to the first decision.
4. We write the next decision at the top of the table, and so on.

It does not matter if at first our list of statements is incomplete; to introduce a new statement, all we have to do is add one more row to the table. Similarly, if we subsequently think of an additional set of circumstances that would lead to a decision, all we have to do is add a column. It follows that decision tables are easy to modify and update. The reader should confirm this by trying to modify Table 9.1 to include the statement "bush encroachment is more serious than degradation." All that is needed to weave this into the logic is one extra row and one extra column.

Decision tables can easily be implemented on computers. The information contained in the table can be stored as a matrix. A program can be written that asks the user to reply true or false to each of the statements. The program then compares these replies with the stored matrix (one column at a time) to see which decisions are valid.

Decision tables can be very large. In fact, their major disadvantage is that the rows and columns tend to proliferate. Because the questions have to be written as statements that are either true or false, questions with more than two answers have to be broken down into a series with an additional row for each statement. For example, in the decision tree we had the question, "Is there a herbivore priority?" with three possible answers: "for long-grass grazers," "for short-grass grazers," and "none." In the decision table we had to break this up into two statements: "priority for long-grass grazers" and "priority for short-grass grazers" (the answer "none" is implied by replying "false" to both of these statements). Similarly, we would have to introduce four columns in a decision table to represent a situation that could be written down quite simply as "this decision is valid if either A or B is true and either C or D is true."

The last sentence of the previous paragraph should remind us of the concept of a *rule* as introduced in the previous chapter. This suggests yet another way of representing the logic contained in a decision tree or table.

IF-THEN RULES AND EXPERT SYSTEMS

We can state each column in a decision table as a simple rule. For example, the third column in Table 9.1 reads "*If* old material is present *and* the area has *not* recently been burned accidentally *and* there is degradation *and* there is *not* bush encroachment *then* the decision to defer burning for a year is valid." Note that the operational words here are *if, then, and,* and *not,* and that the structure of the rule is similar to the structure we introduced in the previous chapter for rule-enhanced models. In fact the only difference is that in the previous chapter the *then* part of the rule modified survival or fecundity rates in a population model, whereas here the *then* part validates a decision.

The *if* part of the rule is called the *condition,* while the *then* part is called the *action.* A single column of a decision table is thus an *if-then rule,* but one where the condition can contain only two logical operators: *and* and *not.* In general, the condition of an if-then rule can also contain the operator *or.* It follows that one of the advantages of if-then rules over decision tables is that more than one column of a decision table can be combined in a single rule. For example, the fourth and fifth columns in Table 9.1 lead to the rule

> IF   old material is present
> AND   the area has NOT recently been burned accidentally
> AND   there is NOT degradation
> AND   there is NOT bush encroachment
> AND   there is a priority for long grass grazers OR (there is no herbivore priority AND the area was last burned before the first rains)
> THEN the decision to burn after the first rains is valid

Another advantage is that the questions and answers can be numbered, so one question can have more than two possible answers.

In Table 9.2 we show how the information in Fig. 9.1 and Table 9.1 can be written as a list of decision, questions, and if-then rules. Computer programs can be written to read the information contained in Table 9.2

TABLE 9.2 THE KNOWLEDGE BASE FOR THE BURNING PROBLEM

Dec 1   Do not burn
Dec 2   Burn after the first rains
Dec 3   Burn at the height of the rainy season
Dec 4   Burn before the first rains
Dec 5   Defer burning for a year

Q1: Is there old material that needs to be removed?
    Why   old material provides fuel
    Ans   1   yes
           2   no

Q2: Has the area recently been burned accidentally?
    Why   if so, unlikely to be enough fuel for a fire
    Ans   1   yes
           2   no

Q3: Are the shrubs in the area becoming dense or growing high?
    Why   looking for evidence of bush encroachment
    Ans   1   yes
           2   no

Q4: Is the density of *Bothriochloa* higher in recently burnt neighboring areas?
    Why   looking for evidence of degradation in vegetation because of burning
    Ans   1   yes
           2   no

Q5: Is there a herbivore management priority?
    Why   must provide suitable grazing for priority herbivores
    Ans   1   for long grass grazers
           2   for short grass grazers
           3   no priority

Q6: At what time of the year was the area last burned?
    Why   we may want to rotate burning seasons
    Ans   1   before the first rains
           2   after the first rains
           3   at the height of the rainy season

Rule 1
Why   context: cannot sustain a fire with insufficient fuel
      IF Q1A2 OR Q2A1 THEN D1.

Rule 2
Why   context: hot fires are needed to destroy bushes;
      bushes can be a problem in this area
      IF (NOT D1) AND Q3A1 THEN D4.

Rule 3
Why   if there is no urgent reason to burn, we want to avoid degradation
      IF (NOT D1) AND Q3A2 AND Q4A1 THEN D5.

Rule 4
Why   if vegetation is not a problem we can look to herbivore priorities
      IF (NOT D1) AND Q3A2 AND Q4A2 AND Q5A1 THEN D2.

Rule 5
Why   if vegetation is not a problem we can look to herbivore priorities
      IF (NOT D1) AND Q3A2 AND Q4A2 AND Q5A2 THEN D3.

Rule 6
Why   rotate time to burn if there is no reason for doing anything else
      IF (NOT D1) AND Q3A2 AND Q4A2 AND Q5A3 AND Q6A1 THEN D2.

Rule 7
Why   rotate time to burn if there is no reason for doing anything else
      IF (NOT D1) AND Q3A2 AND Q4A2 AND Q5A3 AND (NOT Q6A1) THEN
      D4.

---

provided the questions (and answers) and decisions are numbered and presented in the format shown in the table. Such a program will ask the user to answer the questions and will then deduce (from the rules) which decision is valid.

The program is called a general-purpose *expert system* (or *expert system shell*) and the information in Table 9.2 is called the *knowledge base* for the expert system. An expert system shell is thus a computer program that reads the information contained in a knowledge base in exactly the same way as a conventional program reads the numbers contained in a data file. Whereas the conventional program performs numerical operations on the numbers, the expert system shell uses the knowledge base to operate logically on the answers to the questions. The knowledge base is thus our "qualitative model" and the expert system shell is simply a general-purpose program for exercising that model.

The knowledge base in Table 9.2 has been designed more thoughtfully than the decision tree and decision table of the previous two sections. For example, an expert on site could answer the question, "Is the vegetation becoming degraded?" and different experts would probably agree on the definition of "degraded" within the context of this decision. However, our purpose is to enable a perceptive but not necessarily expert observer to answer the questions, and for such a person the question about degradation is too subjective. We therefore force the expert to think of a test that would determine whether the vegetation is becoming degraded. In this case the abundance of *Bothriochloa* (a grass species that thrives in disturbed areas in this particular park) is the appropriate test. The question, "Is the density of *Bothriochloa* higher in recently burned neighboring areas?" is not subjective and is unambiguous.

An important reason for building a qualitative model is to *demonstrate* how the expert reaches a decision. The question about *Bothriochloa* is unambiguous, but the user of the expert system may well wonder why it was asked. The knowledge base in Table 9.2 has a built-in explanation feature. The reason for asking each question is included after the key word *why*, and similarly a reason is given for every rule.

These explanations serve two very important functions. First, they force those building the knowledge base to think clearly and explicitly about the purpose of every question and rule. Second, the expert system shell can be written to present these explanations on request, in such a way that the user is able to follow the logical pathways by interacting with the computer. This is illustrated in Table 9.3, which records part of a "conversation" between a user and an expert system shell. In this example the data for the shell were provided by the knowledge base of Table 9.2.

Decision tables are also knowledge bases and are in fact easier to implement on a computer than if-then rules. Our purpose, however, is not ease of computation but to explain how a decision is reached. If-then rules

TABLE 9.3   INTERACTION BETWEEN A USER AND THE EXPERT SYSTEM
The user's responses are in boxes.

Question:
Is there old material that needs to be removed?
   1) yes
   2) no
Press the number of the answer, or **W** or ?

W

old material provides fuel

W

context: cannot sustain a fire with insufficient fuel

1

Question:
Has the area recently been burned accidentally?
   1) yes
   2) no
Press the number of the answer, or **W** or ?

W

if so, unlikely to be enough fuel for a fire

2

Question:
Are the shrubs in the area becoming dense or growing high?
   1) yes
   2) no
Press the number of the answer, or **W** or ?

W

looking for evidence of bush encroachment

W

context: hot fires are needed to destroy bushes; bushes can be a problem in this area.

W

I can't explain any further.

do this far better than decision tables. They are both easier to understand and easier to build and are just as easy to update or modify. We will therefore use them throughout the rest of this chapter as our vehicle for qualitative modeling.

BUILDING A KNOWLEDGE BASE

A knowledge base is in some ways easier to build than a conventional model because it has such a well-defined format. As we saw in the previous section, it consists of a decision list (which specifies the problem to be solved), a list of questions with answers (this tells us what information is needed to solve the problem), and a list of rules (which describes how one progresses logically from the answers to the decisions). Both the questions and rules should have explanations that help us understand the reasoning behind the knowledge base.

The Decisions

As in any modeling exercise, the first step is to establish clearly the objectives of the qualitative model. The next step is to ask what alternatives there are for action within the scope of those objectives. These alternatives define the list of decisions. In our example our objectives were to determine whether an area should be burned and, if so, at what time of the year. Three alternatives for the time of year were identified: before, during, and after the rainy season. In addition there was the possibility that burning could be deferred for a year. The list of decisions in Table 9.2 follows directly from these considerations.

The list of decisions thus reflects in a very obvious way the objectives of the model. It therefore defines the resolution of the model. By drawing up the list of decisions before the rest of the knowledge base we make sure that the model addresses the right issues and that we approach the right experts. In our example, if we had been given different objectives we could have built a *less* detailed model by limiting the list to the one decision "the area should be burned." We could also have built a *more* detailed model by expanding the list to include decisions such as "burn on a windy day."

Care must be taken in the wording of the decisions. If a model is unable to validate the decision "the area should be burned," it does not imply that the decision "the area should not be burned" is valid. It only tells us that the model was unable to find a rule that validated the first decision; possibly the model has insufficient rules. If we definitely want to conclude that the area should not be burned, we should have a decision in our list that says precisely that. It is not unusual to find both the positive and negative statements of the same action included in the decision list.

The Questions and Answers

The next step is to establish what information is needed to reach the decisions and to write this information in the form of questions and answers. There are a number of ways of doing this.

Sometimes all the expertise can be obtained from one or two individuals, as in our burning example. The expert should be asked to list all the necessary information. (Experts do not always find this easy to do. It is fascinating to discover the extent to which they make decisions subconsciously, and one often has to be imaginative in looking for ways to "unlock" their thought processes. In fact a whole new science at the borders of computer science and cognitive psychology is concerned with this problem of knowledge acquisition.)

One useful device is for the expert to imagine being away on vacation. A less experienced colleague phones for help in making a decision about, say, when and how to burn the grass in a certain area. What questions would the expert ask over the telephone? These are the questions that should go into the knowledge base.

Another device is to ask the expert to think aloud while making a real or hypothetical decision or perhaps reconstructing a case history. A transcript of every spoken word is called a *protocol*. It is often far easier to extract the information the expert has used from protocols than to ask the expert directly. With help from the expert, this information can then be reformulated as a series of questions with answers.

Techniques such as these are useful when only one or two experts are involved, but decisions in wildlife or resource management often call for information and expertise from a number of different people. For example, a decision on whether or not to crop part of a herbivore population in a game park could depend on:

1. The purpose of the game park and management objectives
2. The state of the vegetation
3. The size and physiological condition of the herbivore population
4. Competition between the target population and other rare or protected species.
5. Weather or rainfall patterns
6. Economic and logistical considerations

An interdisciplinary workshop provides an ideal environment for building the knowledge base under these circumstances. Individual experts understandably tend to concentrate on what they know, often with little regard for where their expertise fits into a more general problem. The give and take in a workshop encourages them to contribute selectively. The common purpose of building the knowledge base also encourages participants with conflicting interests to draft questions that help determine the circumstances under which one set of interests has priority over another. Questions such as these are what distinguishes a strong knowledge base from a weak one.

Whether they are drafted by an individual or a committee, the questions and answers should be phrased carefully. Wherever possible the questions should be objective rather than subjective. (The question about *Bothriochloa* in Table 9.2 is an example of an objective question.) The resolution of the questions and answers should match the resolution of the decisions to be made.

In some instances "we do not know" could be an appropriate answer to a question. We then have two options: (1) to ask questions that will elicit the required information in an indirect manner or (2) to decide (and build into the logic) how we would still reach a decision without that information. Both of these options demand clear and careful thinking from those building the knowledge base. Care should also be taken with the explanation attached to each question. This should be concise but must clearly convey the reason for asking the question.

The Rules

The final and usually most difficult step in the construction of a knowledge base is the formulation of the rules. Here we have to ask ourselves (or the experts) questions such as "Under what circumstances would you burn before the first rains?" or "What distinguishes burning before the rains from burning after the rains?" The rules should flow from the answers to these questions. The advantage of the if-then structure is that the rule base can be built up slowly, one rule at a time; we do not need to grasp the nature of the whole decision-making process. We do have to make sure every rule is correct and appropriate.

When the source of expertise is a single person, an outsider can often help with the construction of the rule base. The outsider should try to formulate rules from protocols of the expert at work. The expert then usually finds it easy to correct or modify those rules. In the workshop environment a useful strategy is to ask each participant to construct two or three rules. These can then be modified or rejected in subsequent discussion. Often, bottlenecks in constructing the rules can be overcome by proposing a rule that is blatantly too simple. The indignation it generates eventually gives way to constructive amendments.

It is always advantageous to have a number of shorter rules (each with an apposite explanation) rather than a few long and complicated rules. A closer look at rule 2 in Table 9.2 reveals that the conditional part of a rule can refer to other decisions as well as the answers to questions. This can simplify the rules considerably, and it often pays to add intermediate decisions to the decision list so they can be used in this way. For example, if we were to add a rule to the list in Table 9.2 that said

IF (NOT D1) AND Q3A2 and Q4A2 THEN D6 ,

we could rewrite rule 4 as

IF D6 AND Q5A1 THEN D2 ,

with similar abbreviations for rules 5, 6, and 7. These intermediate decisions may be of interest in themselves. But more importantly, because they can be used to make the rules more succinct, they also make them easier to understand.

One of the disadvantages of the if-then structure is that it is sometimes difficult to decide whether the set of rules is adequate or complete. The only way to test this is to actually implement and exercise the knowledge base via an expert system. If the system frequently fails to find a valid decision, the rule base is probably too slim. The process of exercising and interacting with the knowledge base helps to identify those situations that need to be addressed by additional rules.

A knowledge base, like any other model, will grow wildly unless it is built purposefully and with restraint. Just as we have to be wary of putting too much detail into simulation models, so we have to avoid providing too many alternative answers for the questions in a knowledge base. Rewriting question 1 in Table 9.2 as

Q1: 'How much old material is there?'
Ans 1 'none at all'
2 'a little'
3 'a fair amount'
4 'a lot'

might give the impression of providing the model with more information, but in fact we are only making it more difficult to develop suitable rules.

We also have to guard against the tendency to address too many questions in each rule. In Table 9.2 it may be possible, if we think about it long enough, to find a reason for incorporating question 6 in rule 3. To do so would be counterproductive. The cost of adding marginal information to rules is that each rule becomes too specific and so we have to add many more rules to produce a useful system.

The actual process of building a knowledge base seldom proceeds in an orderly way from the objectives to the decisions, to the questions and answers, and finally to the rules. Additional decisions or distinctions are sometimes suggested at a later stage, and the need to modify or add questions often arises during the rule construction phase. If the model is large or difficult to build, it may be useful to restrict its scope (the knowledge base depicted in Table 9.2 is restricted to one of the two soil types in that park) or break it down into a series of smaller models that can ultimately be combined. The structure of a knowledge base makes it particularly easy to do this. The structure also encourages one to take an adaptive approach: First build a modest knowledge base, then refine it with use and experience.

APPLICATIONS OF QUALITATIVE MODELS

The size of a knowledge base is usually measured by the number of rules it contains. The large knowledge bases that have been built in recent years for such applications as medical diagnosis or mineral exploration contain hundreds of rules and required many work-years of effort to build. The qualitative models described in this chapter are meant to be much more modest; they will probably contain only tens of rules and require work-days rather than work-years to build. They nevertheless have some exciting applications.

Decision-Support Systems

In any organization or department concerned with ecological management there are decisions that need to be made routinely. In wildlife management, these decisions might relate to hunting or fishing quotas, disease control, cropping or harvesting, burning, and so on. A *decision-support system* is a pretentious but apt title for an expert system shell that exercises a knowledge base containing the rationale behind any of these routine decisions.

In this section we will outline a recent attempt to build a decision-support system and will discuss what was learned from it. We will then speculate on the way in which the system is likely to be implemented, and the benefits we envisage. As with most modeling techniques, these benefits do not depend on the power of the technique itself as much as on how the technique is implemented and the spirit in which it is used. Our discussion will attempt to convey that spirit.

The example relates to the park described in Chap. 5—i.e., an area of about 25,000 ha containing a number of different herbivore species but no major herbivore predators. Previously we tried to simulate the interactions between the herbivores and the vegetation. Our objective was to predict how the cropping of one or more herbivore species would affect the other herbivores in the park. Here, our objectives are concerned more with the reasons for cropping and the type of cropping policy that should be implemented.

The motivation to look at the whole question of cropping more broadly came from those responsible for the control of this and similar parks. They convened a week-long meeting that included representatives from all levels of the organization: park wardens, regional scientists, administrators, and managers. The first four days were devoted to discussions of problems that had arisen, the issues involved, and the principles to be used when making decisions about cropping. The final day was devoted to a workshop to summarize the work of the previous four days in a knowledge base to be used as a decision-support system.

The list of decisions reflects the broad objectives of this exercise. Some of the decisions were:

1. Do not crop at all.
2. Maintain a fixed stocking rate (i.e., crop to maintain the population at a predetermined level).
3. Crop to keep densities low in certain target areas of the park.
4. Crop to simulate predation.
5. Crop on the borders of the park to simulate dispersal.

A list of questions and answers (with explanations) was then compiled. Some of the issues addressed by the questions were:

1. The size of the reserve in relation to the size of the herbivore's home range
2. The accuracy of population (and recruitment rate) estimates
3. The distribution of water in the park
4. Whether dispersal was an important population regulation mechanism for the species
5. Management objectives
6. The importance of tourism and game-viewing
7. Whether the herbivore was endangering important plant species or habitat types

About 60 rules were then compiled and the knowledge base implemented via an expert system shell.

The exercise ended with a critical review of the day's activities. There was general agreement that, irrespective of whether the knowledge base that had been produced could be used, the workshop itself and the task of constructing the knowledge base had been very useful indeed. In particular:

1. The participants had been forced to think carefully about what to put into the knowledge base and what to leave out. This left them with a far better feel for priorities than the previous four days of discussion. Deciding what information was really needed to make the appropriate decisions also had implications for routine measurements and monitoring in the park.
2. The process of building the model helped to raise issues and focus policies more effectively than the general discussion of the previous four days. As a result, the workshop raised several new and important questions and led to the reevaluation of ideas that

previously appeared sensible but were now seen to be somewhat naive.

3. Providing explanations for the questions and rules was unexpectedly difficult to do, but perhaps more than anything else disciplined the thinking of the participants.

It was also agreed that the decision-support system produced at the end of the workshop was far from a finished product. However, it was felt that there was little to be gained by continuing to work on it for a few more days or even weeks. A far more sensible approach was to ask how to implement it in such a way that it could be tested and improved over the years. It was decided that the only way to do this was to make the system an integral *formal* part of the decision-making process.

Finally, the benefits to be gained from even an incomplete decision-support system were identified:

1. At the simplest level the decision-support system provides a safety net for inexperienced staff and an intelligent checklist for more experienced staff.
2. It helps to ensure continuity despite changes in staff.
3. It helps to differentiate between situations that are routine and those where more careful analysis or data collection (or the opinion of an expert) are needed.
4. It could provide a stable reference when emotions run high. Those who disagreed with its recommendations would be forced to give explicit reasons for their disagreement.
5. It is an effective communication device, either for explaining the reasoning behind a recommendation to those who have to authorize the decision, or to present the same reasoning (if the subject is a controversial one) to the public.

The explanation feature was felt to be a vital component of most, if not all, of these benefits.

In summary, here are the ingredients for a successful decision-support system:

1. It should be built by a small group that contains representation from all levels of the organization and all interested parties.
2. A great deal of attention should be devoted to the explanations for both the questions and rules.
3. Maintenance of the system should be the responsibility of a designated individual or individuals.
4. The system should be consulted regularly as part of the formal procedures for making decisions.

5. The performance of the system should be reviewed regularly and the knowledge base updated in the light of that performance.

Emphasis here should be placed on the word *consult*. The decision-support system is meant to be precisely that —a *support* system and not a mechanical decision maker. Like all other models, its primary purpose should be to help the user *think* about his problem.

Applications in the Classroom

If building a decision-support system in a workshop environment helps the participants to think about their problem in a structured way, we might well ask whether a similar exercise would be useful in the classroom. It is difficult to teach students how to synthesize information, yet it is essential for them to learn how to link concepts and principles to the solution of practical problems. Experience in engineering classes indicates that synthesis is learned by doing, not by watching, and that the process of building a small knowledge base can be a very effective learning experience.

The following is based on the approach we developed for building decision-support systems, suitably modified for use in the classroom:

1. Introduce the idea of an expert system in the classroom, explain the structure of a knowledge base and if-then rules, and demonstrate a small system.
2. Divide the class into groups of two or three and ask each group to suggest a few suitable topics where small expert systems could be useful. Discussing these suggestions can help to highlight the difference between problems that need conventional models and those that lend themselves to a more qualitative approach.
3. Ask each group to build a knowledge base as an assignment (over a period of one to two weeks). Care should be taken to ensure that the scope of each assignment is not too broad. The groups should be told to pay particular attention to their explanations for the questions and rules.
4. Demonstrate the systems, perhaps invite experts to critique them, and encourage groups to use and comment on the systems produced by their peers.

Apart from learning how to build expert systems, students gain from an exercise such as this in two important ways. First, they learn how to synthesize and apply their knowledge purposefully; second, they discover that they cannot do this without improving their understanding of the subject itself.

Applications in Extension-Type Activities

In our description of decision-support systems we did not draw a clear distinction between the builders and the users of the system. This was deliberate. We view a decision-support system more as a device for communication between peers and for mutual reinforcement than as a one-way channel for transmitting advice from the expert to the novice. There are, however, situations where the latter is needed. We might, for example, want to present the latest research information in pest or disease control in a form that can be put to use by a manager. This is akin to the extension activities of agricultural research organizations.

The format of an expert system lends itself to this type of application and can be far more effective than, for example, pamphlets or slideshows that try to convey the same information. The users of the expert system *interact* with it, and so feel they are a part of the solution to the problem (again, the explanation facility plays a vital role). The process of answering questions also induces the feeling that it is the users' particular problem, not some abstraction, that is being addressed, and this is precisely what a well-designed expert system can do—provide the logic that applies sophisticated concepts in specific circumstances.

Predictive Qualitative Models

Most numerical models predict changes in a system or a population over time. Some changes, however, are better described in a qualitative rather than a quantitative way. Can we build a model to predict these qualitative changes?

The qualitative models we have described so far have all been built according to the structure of if-then rules, where the *if* part relates to a set of conditions and the *then* part to a decision of some sort. Suppose, however, that we use the *then* part of the rule to specify an outcome or specific state of the system. This would allow us to formulate rules of the form

IF   the state of the system is P,
   AND   B is true,
   AND   C OR D is true,
THEN   the state of the system will change to Q.

Rules such as this would form the backbone of a predictive qualitative model. Just as the expert system shell searches through the rules in a decision-oriented model until it finds a decision that is valid, so the shell can be used to search through the rules in this type of model to determine the next stage in the state of the system.

There are two ways of modeling how time progresses. The most common way is equivalent to the ticking of a clock —i.e., we measure time in a sequence of similarly sized intervals (this is the method we have used throughout this book). The second way is to measure time from one specific event to another; the intervals that elapse between events will not, in general, be the same. If we use the second method, then (as mentioned in Chap. 1) we call the model an *event-driven model*. Qualitative models are likely to be event-driven. The actual time scales are built into the rules: Either the *if* part contains a condition that specifies the time (example, "*If* so many years have elapsed since such-and-such an event") or the *then* part specifies it (e.g., "the state of the system will change to Q after so many years").

It is not difficult to find situations where this kind of model could be useful. For example, the species composition in a vegetation community that is subject to recurrent disturbance will always be in a state of flux. (Think of a forest community subject to forest fires.) We would like to be able to describe the changes in composition that are likely to occur, not in definite terms but in general terms such as "if the interfire period is greater than 20 years but less than 100 years, then immediately after the fires species A will dominate, to be replaced by a mix of species B, C, and D, while species E will become inconspicuous in the community."

Noble and Slatyer (1980) describe a methodology for predicting replacement sequences on the basis of what they call the "vital attributes" of the species involved. These attributes include the method of arrival or persistence of the species at the site either during or after a disturbance, the time taken for the species to reach certain critical life stages, and so on. Their methodology is in fact a predictive, qualitative model, even though it is not structured formally in the way we have suggested. However, their approach lends itself to that kind of formal structure.

RECAPITULATION AND DISCUSSION

Building models for ecological management is not an easy task, and we began this chapter by reminding ourselves of some of the difficulties that have recurred in virtually every example used in this book. One of these is that while there is often a plethora of data that are peripheral to our problem, there tends to be a conspicuous lack of data we really need. Another is our inability to model, in a meaningful way, details that can be crucial; our example was the futility of trying to model when the leaves will drop off deciduous trees.

Just as our models have been shaped by management objectives, so our philosophy and approach to modeling has been shaped by these difficulties. We have learned to circumvent questions of detail and to build models with very little data. We have also learned to use these models to improve our understanding of the problem or our appreciation of the management alternatives, even though we may not always have been successful in answering the original management questions directly. In a sense we have learned to think in a qualitative way using a medium that is essentially quantitative.

On the whole, we have been remarkably successful in this endeavor, but it is a subtle process and we should not be too surprised when people with scant experience of modeling and a great deal of field experience are skeptical. One reason for their skepticism is that they tend to concentrate on the assumptions we have made. Their field experience tells them that the assumptions are inadequate, but they do not have the experience of modeling to tell them how to live with those inadequacies. Another, and perhaps more important, reason for skepticism is that the substance of our models (our concern with processes and numbers) is alien to the substance of their field experience, which they would describe in terms of observations and the consequences they deduce from those observations.

In this chapter we have tried to extend our toolkit of modeling techniques by asking whether it is possible to actually build models directly from field experience. How, we have asked ourselves, can we build a model that will draw conclusions without calculations? We know that people do this all the time and that the basis on which they do it is one of experience. We therefore set out to find an organized, explicit format for representing experience, and in fact found three different ways of doing it: decision trees, decision tables, and expert systems based on if-then rules.

All three of these representations use information to draw a conclusion or reach a decision in nonnumerate ways. All three have advantages and disadvantages. Decision trees are easy to use but difficult to build and amend. Decision tables are easy for the computer to use but can become too large and clumsy for the people who build them. Expert systems divide the information in a decision table into self-contained rules that are easily built and modified, but the computer then needs an expert system shell to read and manipulate the knowledge base.

Which method should we use? For problems that are relatively small and uncomplicated, a decision tree is the obvious choice; it so easily communicates the logic. What is less obvious is that the construction of the decision tree can often be simplified considerably, first by drawing up a decision table (where one does not have to be concerned with the order of the questions), then building the decision tree from it. For larger or more complex problems it makes sense to build a knowledge base using a set of if-then rules, then to exercise the knowledge base via an expert system shell.

The flow of the logic is patently obvious in decision trees but is less obvious in decision tables and if-then rules. We can compensate for this by providing an explanation feature in our expert system. This enhances our understanding at two levels: while building the system (providing the explanations helps to ensure the builders have thought carefully about both the questions and the rules), and while using the system (the explanation feature helps the user to keep track of the logic).

Although very large expert systems have been successfully built and used in other fields, the idea of using a smaller knowledge base (with tens rather than hundreds of rules) as a qualitative model is novel and relatively untested. Where it has been tested it has elicited a favorable response from field biologists (including those who had previously been wary of conventional models). It offers a mechanism that captures and organizes the type of information they are accustomed to using. The advantages of structuring that information in a qualitative model are soon evident:

1. The structure forces the expert to be explicit and consistent in his reasoning.
2. If the personal biases of the expert are built into the model, they are explicit and hence open to criticism and discussion.
3. The discipline of modeling forces the expert to identify the information that really is essential for reaching a decision. (In one workshop an expert began by explaining how he could not possibly build a model because he took so many factors into account when he made a decision. In the process of building the model he realized that only six factors were important.)

It is also evident that qualitative models can be useful in situations where conventional modeling is inadequate. Earlier in this chapter we used the example of deciding if and when to burn a specific area of a park to illustrate the differences between decision trees, tables, and if-then rules. It is instructive to compare these qualitative models with the way in which we tried to simulate the effects of fire in Chap. 5.

The first consideration in the qualitative models is whether there is sufficient material in the area to sustain a fire. The same question was addressed in the simulation model by the *fuel load factor*, a device we introduced to estimate the amount of combustible material in the area.

The next question addressed by the qualitative models is one of bush encroachment, and this too we could estimate in the simulation model by looking at the amount of woody material in the region relative to the basal area of the grass. Moreover, if we do decide to burn the area, the simulation model attempts to predict how the fire will affect the bushes in the region. But this is as far as the simulation model goes. The level of detail in the simulation model, as far as the effects of fire are concerned, is too primitive to ever envisage using the model to actually decide if and when to burn a section of the park.

Moreover, and this is the crucial point, it is not at all obvious that going into finer detail would make the model any more useful in making the decision about burning. In contrast, there is obviously a lot that could be gained from refining the qualitative model. Our example was thus well chosen.

This is not always true. The reader need only look back at the wildebeest model of Chap. 2 to find an example where conventional modeling is far superior to qualitative modeling. We could indeed build an expert system to help decide, on a year-to-year basis, whether to crop the wildebeest or the lions, but since that decision is so patently a question of numbers, the expert system would at best be an inefficient way of looking at those numbers. It would be a parody, a case of using a qualitative model to help us think quantitatively!

Obviously, different approaches are appropriate to different problems. This lesson is apparent also in the cropping example we used to illustrate a decision-support system. Here the problem is very similar to the problem that generated the system model of Chap. 5, but by addressing it in a philosophical rather than a predictive way, we find the qualitative model to be more useful than the simulation model. (The reader might like to ponder on the design of an expert system that guides the user toward the appropriate modeling technique.)

One application where the use of relatively small qualitative models has at least been partially tested is in the development of decision-support systems. Insufficient time has elapsed to prove the benefits to be gained from using decision-support systems, but there is sufficient evidence to demonstrate that the process of *building* a decision-support system is *always* stimulating and effective. There seems to be a kind of magic in the combination of a number of effects: the psychological effect of working toward a well-defined goal (especially if the workshop begins with a demonstration of a working expert system); the simple, clear structure of the knowledge base; the discipline imposed by the need to explain the questions and rules.

The result of all this is that the following points tend to be covered particularly well during workshops convened to build decision support systems:

1. Different types and levels of information can be pooled, compared, weighed and interpreted.
2. Different viewpoints can be balanced and taken into account.
3. Arguments and discussion tend to be focused in a logical, goal-oriented fashion.
4. The expertise of participants is drawn on and used very specifically and selectively.
5. It soon becomes apparent where information is missing, where there is a need for research or monitoring programs, and where more conventional models could be useful.

We can speculate on the benefits to be gained from developing and using decision-support systems in the longer term. We have frequently commented on the time scales needed to gain insight into the workings of even a part of a savanna ecosystem. For instance, in Chap. 6 we built a model of indirect competition between zebra and buffalo and noticed how easily fluctuations in rainfall could mask the effects of that competition for periods as long as 20 or 30 years. In the previous chapter we noticed the importance of episodic events and pointed out the need to make observations for many tens of years to appreciate the impact of such events. We also pointed out the necessity, in the interim, of making management decisions. This led us to the idea of adaptive management.

The way in which we have suggested that decision-support systems be implemented (first build a prototype model, consult it regularly, compare its performance with what actually happens, and update it on a regular basis) is in line with the concepts of adaptive management. In fact, *decision-support systems provide a vehicle for implementing the concepts of adaptive management.* A properly designed and implemented decision-support system can capture long-term management experience in the same way as data banks capture long-term information.

Experts or people with field experience do not always agree with each other. They are seldom able to pinpoint where they disagree. Experience is not a commodity that is easy to communicate, and how and why a person reaches a decision is something that tends to be distorted with hindsight. Ultimately there can be no real progress in any subject unless those working in it have a common and unambiguous form of communication. Perhaps the most important quality of models, be they quantitative or qualitative, is that they provide a disciplined basis for discussion and argument. To quote Benjamin Whorf:

> We dissect nature along lines laid down by our native language . . . . Language is not simply a reporting device for experience but a defining framework for it.

He might have been writing about models!

FURTHER READING

Information on the role of fires in African savannas can be found in Afolayan (1978) and Eltringham (1976). The burning example used in this chapter is described in more detail in Starfield and Bleloch (1983b). Davis and Nanninga describe an expert system that predicts fire behavior in a heterogeneous environment. An example of a small decision tree in the context of wildlife management can be found in Harris and Kochel (1981). A decision-support system in pest management is described by Rykiel et. al. (1984).

Duda (1981) and Hayes-Roth (1984) have written good general overview articles on expert systems and their uses. Shortcliffe (1976) describes one of the more successful large expert systems (in medical diagnosis) and Gaschnig (1982) describes another (for mineral exploration). Applications in agriculture are discussed by Tou and Cheng (1983) and Michalski et al. (1983). Applications in the classroom are discussed by Starfield et al. (1983).

The structure of expert systems as described in this chapter may be thought of as deterministic in the sense that questions have clear-cut answers (even if the answer is "I do not know") and lead to unambiguous decisions. An alternative approach is one where, instead of answering questions, the user rates the truth or otherwise of statements on a scale of, say, one to five. The expert system then deduces the degree of certainty it is justified in attaching to various decisions. This, and other approaches, are described in books by Naylor (1983), Hayes-Roth, Waterman, and Lenat (1983), and Waterman (1986). Starfield et al. (1985) discuss an expert system shell for the sort of knowledge base introduced in this chapter, while a shell for the more probabilistic approach is described in Cendrowska and Bramer (1984).

Hunt (1982) has written a popular book on recent advances in cognitive psychology in which he discusses the problem of extracting expertise from the expert, and Ericsson and Simon (1984) have written a more technical book on the use of protocols.

References

Afolayan, T. A. 1978. Savanna burning in Kainji Lake National Park, Nigeria, *E. Afr. Wildl. J.* 16:245–255.

Anderson, D. R. 1974. Optimal exploitation strategies for an animal population in a Markovian environment: a theory and an example, *Ecology* 56:1281–1298.

Anderson, J. 1980. The re-establishment and management of a lion *Panthera leo* population in Zululand, *Biol. Conservation* 19:107–117.

Bartlett, M. S. 1960. *Stochastic Population Models in Ecology and Epidemiology.* Wiley, New York.

Bartlett, M. S., and Hiorns, R. W. (eds.) 1973. *The Mathematical Theory of the Dynamics of Biological Populations.* Academic Press, London.

Beddington, J. R. 1974. Age distribution and stability of simple discrete time population models, *J. Theor. Biol.* 47:65–74.

Beddington, J. R., Free, C. A., and Lawton, J. H. 1976. Concepts of stability and resilience in predator-prey models, *J. Anim. Ecol.* 45:791–816.

Beddington, J. R., and May, R. M. 1977. Harvesting natural populations in a randomly fluctuating environment, *Science* 197:463–465.

Bell, E. F. 1977. Mathematical programming in forest, *J. For.* 75:313–319.

Beneke, R. B., and Winterboer, R. 1973. *Linear Programming Applications to Agriculture.* Iowa State University Press, Ames, Iowa.

Berry, H. H. 1981. Population structure, mortality patterns and a predictive model for estimating future trends in wildebeest numbers in the Etosha National Park, *Madoqua* 12:255–266.

Bertram, B. C. R. 1973. Lion population regulations, *E. Afr. Wildl. J.* 11:215–225.

———.1975. Social factors influencing reproduction in wild lions. *J. Zool. Lond.* 177:463–482.

———.1978. *Pride of Lions.* J. M. Dent and Sons, London.

239

Botkin, D. B., Janak, J. F., and Wallis, J. R. 1972. Some ecological consequences of a computer model of forest growth, *J. Ecol.* 60:849–872.

Bottoms, K. E., and Bartlett, E. T. 1975. Resource allocation through goal programming, *J. Range Mgmnt.* 28(6):442–447.

Boyce, M. S. 1977. Population growth with stochastic fluctuations in the life table, *Theor. Popn. Biol.* 12:366–373.

Bunnell, F. L., and Tait, D. E. N. 1981. Population dynamics of bears—implications, in *Dynamics of Large Mammal Populations* (C. W. Fowler and T. D. Smith, eds.). Wiley, New York.

Caughley, G. 1976. Wildlife management and the dynamics of ungulate populations, in *Applied Biology*, vol. 1 (T. H. Coaker, ed.). Academic Press, New York, 183–246.

———.1977. *Analysis of Vertebrate Populations.* Wiley, London.

———.1981. What do we know about the dynamics of large mammals, in *Dynamics of Large Mammal Populations* (C. W. Fowler and T. D. Smith, eds.). Wiley, New York.

Cendrowska, J., and Bramer, M. A. 1984. A rational reconstruction of the MYCIN consultation system, *Int. J. Man-Mach. Stud.* 20(3):229–317.

Charnes, A., Haynes, K. E., Hazleton, J. E., and Ryan, M. J. 1975. A hierarchical goal-programming approach to environmental land use management, *Geographical Analysis* 7:121–130.

Clark, C. W. 1976. *Mathematical Bioeconomics: The Optimal Management of Renewable Resources.* Wiley, New York.

Clark, C. W. and Tait, D. E. 1982. Sex-selective harvesting of wildlife populations, *Ecol. Model.* 14:251–260.

Comins, H. N., and Hassell, M. P. 1976. Predation in multi-prey communities, *J. Theor. Biol.* 62:93–114.

Connolly, G. E. 1978. Predator control and coyote populations: a review of simulation models, in *Coyotes: Biology, Behavior and Management* (M. Bekoff, ed.). Academic Press, New York, 327–345.

Conte, S. D., and de Boor, C. 1972. *Elementary Numerical Analysis: An Algorithmic Approach,* 2nd ed. McGraw-Hill, Kogakusha.

Davis, J. R., and Nanninga, P. M. GEOMYCIN: towards a geographic expert system for resource management, submitted to *J. Environ. Mgmt.*

DeAngelis, D. L., Adams S. M., Breck, J. E., and Gross, L. J. 1984. A stochastic predation model: application to largemouth bass observations, *Ecol. Model.* 24:25–41.

DeMaster, D. P. 1981. Incorporation of density-dependence and harvest into a general population model for seals, in *Dynamics of Large Mammal Populations* (C. W. Fowler and T. D. Smith, eds.). Wiley, New York.

Duda, R. O. 1981. Knowledge-based expert systems come of age, *Byte* 6(9):238–281.

Eberhardt, L. L. 1981. Population dynamics of the Pribilof fur seals, in *Dynamics of Large Mammal Populations* (C. W. Fowler and T. D. Smith, eds.). Wiley, New York.

Eberhardt, L. L., and Siniff, D. B. 1977. Population dynamics and marine mammal management policies, *J. Fish Res. Board. Can.* 34:183–190.

Eltringham, S. K. 1976. The frequency and extent of uncontrolled grass fires in the Rwenzori National Park, Uganda, *E. Afr. Wildl.* J. 14:215–222.

Emlen, J. M. 1984. *Population Biology: The Coevolution of Population Dynamics and Behavior.* Macmillan, New York.

Ericsson, K. A., and Simon, H. A. 1984. *Protocol Analysis: Verbal Reports as Data,* MIT Press, Cambridge, Massachussets.

Estes, R. D. 1976. The significance of breeding synchrony in the wildebeest, *E. Afr. Wildl. J.* 14:135–152.

Euler, D., and Morris, M. M. J. 1984. Simulated population dynamics of the white-tailed deer in an any-deer hunting system, *Ecol. Model.* 24:281–292.

Everitt, R. R., Putterman, M. L., Sonntag, N., and Whalen, P. 1978. A mathematical programming model for the management of a renewable resource system: the Kemano II development project, *J. Fish Res. Board Can.* 35(2):235–246.

Flipse, E., and Veling, E. J. M. 1984. An application of the Leslie matrix model to the population dynamics of the hooded seal, *cystophora cristata erxleben, Ecol. Model.* 24:43–59.

Gardner, R. H., O'Neill, R. V., Mankin, J. B., and Kumar, D. 1980. Comparative error analysis of six predator-prey models, *Ecology* 61:323–332.

Gaschnig, J. 1982. PROSPECTOR: an expert system for mineral exploration, in *Introductory Readings in Expert Systems* (D. Michie, ed.). Gordon and Breach, New York, pp.47–64.

George, L. C., and Grant, W. E. 1983. A stochastic model of brown shrimp (*penaeus aztecus ives*) growth, movement and survival in Galveston Bay, Texas, *Ecol. Model.* 19:41–70.

Goel, N. S., and Richter-Dyn, N. 1974. *Stochastic Models in Biology.* Academic Press, New York.

Goel, N. S., Maitra, S. C., and Montroll, E. W. 1971. *Nonlinear Models of Interacting Populations.* Academic Press, New York.

Goicoechea, A., Duckstein, L., and Fogel, M. M. 1976. Multiobjective programming in watershed management: a study of the Charleston watershed, *Water Resources Research* 12(6):1085–1092.

Goicoechea, A., Hansen, D. R., and Duckstein, L. 1982. *Multiobjective Decision Analysis with Engineering and Business Applications.* Wiley, New York.

Goodall, D. W. 1972. Building and testing ecosystem models, in *Mathematical Models in Ecology* (J. N. R. Jeffers, ed.). Blackwell, Oxford.

Hall, C. A. S., and Day, J. W. (eds.). 1977. *Ecosystem Modelling in Theory and Practice.* Wiley, New York.

Hanby, J. P., and Bygott, J. D. 1979. Population changes in lions and other predators, in *Serengeti: Dynamics of an Ecosystem* (A. R. E. Sinclair and M. Norton-Griffiths, eds.). University of Chicago Press, Chicago.

Harris, L. D., and Kochel, I. H. 1981. A decision-making framework for population management, in *Dynamics of Large Mammal Populations* (C. W. Fowler and T. D. Smith, eds.). Wiley, New York.

Hayes-Roth, F. 1984. The knowledge-based expert system: a tutorial, *Computer* 17(9):11–28.

Hayes-Roth, F., Waterman, D. A., and Lenat, D. B. (eds.) 1983. *Building Expert Systems,* Addison-Wesley, Reading, Mass.

Hilborn, R. 1975. The effect of spatial heterogeneity on the persistence of predator-prey interactions, *Theor. Popn. Biol.* 8:346–355.

Holling, C. S. 1965. The functional response of predators to prey density and its role in mimicry and population regulation, *Mem. Entomol. Soc. Can.* 45:1–60.

———.(ed.). 1978. *Adaptive Environmental Assessment and Management.* Wiley, Chichester.

Hunt, M. 1982. *The Universe Within.* Harvester Press, New York.

Hunter, D. H., Bartlett, E. T., and Jameson, D. A. 1976. Optimum forage allocation through chance-constrained programming, *Ecol. Model.* 2:91–99.

Huntley, B. J. 1982. Southern African savannas, in *Ecology of Tropical Savannas* (B. J. Huntley and B. H. Walker, eds.). *Ecological Studies* 42. Springer-Verlag, Berlin, 101–119.

Innis, G. L. (ed.) 1978. *Grassland Simulation Model, Ecological Studies, Analysis and Synthesis* 26. Springer-Verlag, New York.

Jeffers, J. N. R. 1978. *An Introduction to Systems Analysis: With Ecological Applications.* Edward Arnold, London.

Jewell, P. A., and Holt, S. (eds.). 1981. *Problems in Management of Locally Abundant Wild Mammals.* Academic Press, New York.

Jones, D. D. 1977. The application of catastrophe theory to ecological systems, *Simulation* 29(1):1–15.

Joubert, S. C. J. 1974. The social organization of the roan antelope *Hippotragus equinus* and its influence on the spatial distribution of herds in the Kruger National Park, in *The Behaviour of Ungulates and its relation to Management.* IUCN, Morges, Switzerland.

Karlin, S., and Taylor, H. M. 1975. *A First Course in Stochastic Processes.* Academic Press, New York.

Legendre, L., and Legendre, P. 1983. *Numerical Ecology.* Elsevier, Amsterdam.

Leslie, P. H. 1945. On the use of matrices in certain population mathematics, *Biometrika* 33:183–187.

Lett, P. F., and Benjaminsen, T. 1977. A stochastic model for the management of the northwestern Atlantic harpseal (*pagophilus groenlandicus*) population, *J. Fish Res. Board Can.* 34:1155–1187.

Ludwig, D., Jones, D. D., and Holling, C. S. 1978. Qualitative analysis of an insect outbreak system: the spruce budworm and forest, *J. Anim. Ecol.* 47:315–332.

Mann, K. H. 1982. *Ecology of Coastal Waters: A Systems Approach.* Blackwell, Oxford.

May, R. M. 1973. *Stability and Complexity in Model Ecosystems.* Princeton University Press, Princeton, New Jersey.

———.1977. Thresholds and breakpoints: ecosystems with a mutiplicity of stable states. *Nature (London)* 269:471–477.

———.(ed.). 1981. *Theoretical Ecology: Principles and Applications,* 2nd ed. Blackwell, Oxford.

Maynard Smith, J. 1974. *Models in Ecology.* Cambridge University Press, Cambridge.

Meissner, H. H. 1982. Theory and application of a method to calculate forage intake of wild southern African ungulates for purposes of estimating carrying capacity, *S. Afr. J. Wildl. Res.* 12(2):41–47.

Michalski, R. S., Davis, J. H., Bisht, V. S., and Sinclair, J. B. 1983. A computer-based advisory system for diagnosing soybean diseases in Illinois, *Plant Disease* 67(4):459–463.

Miller, D. R. 1974. Sensitivity analysis and validation of simulation models, *J. Theor. Biol.* 48:345–360.

Miller, W. C., Brinks, J. S., and Sutherland, T. M. 1978. Computer assisted management decisions for production systems, *Agric. Systems* 3(2):147–158.

Milner, C. 1972. The use of computer simulation in conservation management, in *Mathematical Models in Ecology* (J. N. R. Jeffers, ed.). Blackwell, Oxford.

Mohn, R. K. 1979. Sensitivity analysis of two harp seal (*Pagophilus groenlandicus*) population models, *J. Fish Res. Board Can.* 36:404–410.

Murdoch, W. W. 1978. Stabilizing effects of spatial heterogeneity in predator-prey systems, *Theor. Popn. Biol.* 11:252–273.

Naylor, C. 1983. *Build Your Own Expert System.* Sigma Technical Press, Wilmslow, Cheshire, U.K.

Nelson, J. R. 1978. Maximizing mixed animal species stocking rates under proper-use management, *J. Wildl. Mgmt.* 42(1):172–174.

Nisbett, R. M., and Gurney, W. S. C. 1982. *Modelling Fluctuating Populations.* Wiley, Chichester.

Noble, I. R., and Slatyer, R. O. 1980. The use of vital attributes to predict successional changes in plant communities subject to recurrent disturbances, *Vegetatio* 43:5–21.

Noy-Meir, I. 1975. Stability of grazing systems: an application of predator-prey graphs, *J. Ecol.* 63:459–481.

———.1978. Stability in simple grazing models: effects of explicit functions, *J. Theor. Biol.* 71:347–380.

———.1981. Theoretical dynamics of competitors under predation, *Oecologia (Berl)* 50:277–284.

O'Neill, R. V., Gardner, R. H., and Mankin, J. B. 1980. Analysis of parameter error in a non-linear model, *Ecol. Model.* 8:297–311.

Overton, W. S. 1975. The ecosystem modelling approach in the coniferous forest biome, in *Systems Analysis and Simulation in Ecology,* Vol III (B. C. Patten, ed.). Academic Press, New York, 117–138.

———.1977. A strategy of model construction, in *Ecosystem Modelling in Theory and Practice* (C. A. S. Hall and J. W. Day, eds.). Wiley, New York.

Owen-Smith, N. 1979. Assessing the foraging efficiency of a large herbivore, the Kudu, *S. Afr. J. Wildl. Res.* 9:102–110.

———.(ed.). 1983. *Management of Large Mammals in African Conservation Areas.* Haum, Pretoria.

———.(in press). Demography of greater kudu in relation to rainfall, *Acta Zoologica Fennica.*

Owen-Smith, N., and Novellie, P. 1983. What should a clever ungulate eat? *Am. Nat.* 119:151–178.

Owen-Smith, N., Cooper, S. M., and Novellie, P. 1983. Aspects of the feeding ecology of a browsing ruminant, the Kudu, *S. Afr. J. Anim. Sci.* 13:35–38.

Packer, C., and Pusey, A. E. 1982. Cooperation and competition within coalitions of male lions: kin selection or game theory? *Nature* 269:740–742.

———.1983a. Adaptation of female lions to infanticide by incoming males, *Am. Nat.* 121:716–728.

———.1983b. Male takeovers and female reproductive parameters: a simulation of oestrous synchrony in lions (*Panthera leo*), *Anim. Behav.* 31:334–340.

Pellew, R. A. P. 1983. The impacts of elephant, giraffe and fire on the Acacia tortilis woodlands of the Serengeti, *Afr. J. Ecol.* 21:41–74.

Phipps, R. L. 1979. Simulation of wetlands forest vegetation dynamics, *Ecol. Model* 7:257–288.

Pielou, E. C. 1977. *Mathematical Ecology*. Wiley, New York.

Pojar, T. M. 1981. A management perspective of population modelling, in *Dynamics of Large Mammal Populations* (C. W. Fowler and T. D. Smith, eds.). Wiley, New York.

Porterfield, R. L. 1974. A goal programming model to guide and evaluate tree improvement programs, *Forest Science* 22(4):417–430.

Preston, E. M. 1973. Computer simulated dynamics of a rabies-controlled fox population, *J. Wildl. Mgmt.* 37(4):501–512.

Reed, K. L., Rose, K. A., and Whitmore, R. C. 1984. Latin hypercube analysis of parameter sensitivity in a large model of outdoor recreation demand, *Ecol. Model* 24:159–169.

Rudnai, J. 1973a. Reproductive biology of lions (*Panthera leo massaica Neumann*) in Nairobi National Park, *E. Afr. Wildl. J.* 11:241–253.

———.1973b. *The Social Life of the Lion*. Garden City Press, Hertfordshire, England.

Rykiel, E. J., Saunders, M. C., Wagner, T. L., Loh, D. K., Turnbow, R. H., Hu, L. C., Pulley, P. E., and Coulson, R. N. 1984. Computer-aided decision making and information accessing in pest management systems, with emphasis on the Southern Pine Beetle (*Coleoptera: scolytidae*), *FORUM: J. Economic Entomology* 77:1073–1082.

Schaller G. B. 1972. *The Serengeti Lion*. University of Chicago Press, Chicago.

Schenkel, R. 1966. Play, exploration and territory in the wild lion, *Symp. Zool. Soc. London* 18:11–22.

Schuler, A. T., Webster, H. H., and Meadows, J. C. 1977. Goal programming in forest management, *J. For.* 75:320–324.

Shoemaker, C. A. 1977. Pest management models of crop ecosystems, in *Ecosystem Modelling in Theory and Practice* (C. A. S. Hall and J. W. Day, eds.). Wiley, New York.

Shortcliffe, E. H. 1976. *Computer-based Medical Consultation: Mycin*, American Elsevier, New York.

Shugart, H. H., and West, D. C. 1977. Development of an Appalachian deciduous forest succession model and its application to assessment of the impact of the chestnut blight, *J. Environ. Mgmt.* 5:161–179.

Silvert, W. L. 1978. The price of knowledge: fisheries management as a research tool, *J. Fish Res. Board Can.* 35:208–212.

————.1981. Principles of ecosystem modelling, in *Analysis of Marine Ecosystems* (A. R. Longhurst, ed.). Academic Press, New York.

Simon, H. A. 1982. *The Sciences of the Artificial* (2nd ed.). MIT Press, Cambridge, Massachussets.

Sinclair, A. R. E. 1975. The resource limitation of trophic levels in tropical grassland ecosystems, *J. Anim. Ecol.* 4:497–520.

Sinclair, A. R. E., and Hilborn, R. 1979. A simulation of the wildebeest population, other ungulates, and their predators, in *Serengeti, Dynamics of an Ecosystem* (A. R. E. Sinclair and M. Norton-Griffiths, eds.). University of Chicago Press, Chicago.

Smuts, G. L. 1976a. Population characteristics of Burchell's zebra (*Equus burchelli antiquorum*, H. Smith, 1841) in the Kruger National Park, *S. Afr. J. Wildl. Res.* 6:99–112.

————.1976b. Population characteristics and recent history of lions in two parts of Kruger National Park, *Koedoe* 19:153–164.

————.1978a. Interrelations between predators, prey and their environment, *Bio. Sci.* 28:316–320.

————.1978b. Effects of population reduction on the travels and reproduction of lions (*Panthera leo*) in Kruger National Park, *Carnivore* 1:61–72.

————.1982. *Lion*. Macmillan South Africa, Johannesburg.

Smuts, G. L., Hanks, J., and Whyte, I. J. 1978. Reproduction and social organization of lions from the Kruger National Park, *Carnivore* 1:17–28.

Sposito, V. A. 1975. *Linear and Non-Linear Programming*. Iowa State University Press, Ames, Iowa.

Spriet, J. A., and Vansteenkiste, G. C. 1982. *Computer-Aided Modelling and Simulation*. Academic Press, London.

Spronk, J. 1981. *Interactive Multiple Goal Programming*. Martinus Nijhoff Publishing, The Hague.

Starfield, A. M., Adams, S. R., and Bleloch, A. L. 1985. A small expert system shell and its applications, in *Proc. Fourth International Phoenix Conference on Computers and Communications*. IEEE Computer Society Press, Silver Spring, Maryland, pp. 262–267.

Starfield, A. M., and Bleloch, A. L. 1983a. An initial assessment of possible lion population indicators, *S. Afr. J. Wildl. Res.* 13:9–11.

————.1983b. Expert systems: an approach to problems in ecological management that are difficult to quantify, *J. Environ. Mgmt.* 16:261–268.

Starfield, A. M., Butala, K. L., England, M. M., and Smith, K. A. 1983. Mastering engineering concepts by building an expert system, *Eng. Education* 74(2):104–107.

Starfield, A. M., Furniss, P. R., and Smuts, G. L. 1981a. A model of lion population dynamics as a function of social behaviour, in *Dynamics of Large Mammal Populations* (C. W. Fowler and T. D. Smith, eds.). Wiley, New York.

Starfield, A. M., Joubert, S. C. J., Cohen, B. H., Hague, E. K., and Stein, D. J. 1980. An exploratory model of impala population dynamics, in *Lecture notes in Biomathemtics,* Springer-Verlag 33:338–355.

Starfield, A. M., Shiell, J. D., and Smuts, G. L. 1981b. Simulation of lion control strategies in a large game reserve, *Ecol. Model.* 13:17–28.

Starfield, A. M., Smuts, G. L., and Shiell, J. D. 1976. A simple wildebeest model and its applications, *S. Afr. J. Wildl. Res.* 6:95–98.

Stocker, M., and Walters, C. J. 1984. Dynamics of a vegetation-ungulate system and its optimal exploitation. *Ecol. Model.* 25:151–165.

Swartzman, G. L. 1979. Simulation modelling of material and energy flow through an ecosystem: methods and documentation, *Ecol. Model.* 7:55–81.

Swartzman, G. L., and Singh, J. S. 1974. A dynamic approach to optimal grazing strategies using a succession model for a tropical grassland, *J. Appl. Ecol.* 11:537–548.

Talbot, L. M., and Talbot, H. 1963. The wildebeest in Western Massailand, East Africa, *Wildl. Monogr.* 120:1–88.

Tomovic, R. 1963. *Sensitivity Analysis of Dynamic Systems,* McGraw-Hill, New York.

Tou, J. T., and Cheng, J. M. 1983. Design of a knowledge-based expert system for applications in agriculture, *Proc. Trends and Applications IEEE:* 181–189.

Tukey, J. W. 1977. *Exploratory Data Analysis.* Addison-Wesley, Reading, Mass.

Usher, M. B. 1972. Developments in the Leslie matrix model, in *Mathematical Models in Ecology* (J. N. R. Jeffers, ed.). Blackwell, Oxford.

Vandermeer, J. 1981. *Elementary Mathematical Ecology.* Wiley, New York.

Walters, C. J. 1975. Optimal harvest strategies for salmon in relation to environmental variability and uncertain production parameters, *J. Fish Res. Board Can.* 32:1777–1784.

———.(in press). *Adaptive Management of Renewable Resources.* Macmillan, New York.

Walters, C. J., and Bunnell, F. 1971. A computer management game of land use in British Columbia, *J. Wildl. Mgmt.* 35:644–457.

Walters, C. J., and Gross, J. E. 1972. Development of big game management plans through simulation modelling, *J. Wildl. Mgmt.* 36(1):119–128.

Walters, C. J., and Hilborn, R. 1976. Adaptive control of fishing systems, *J. Fish Res. Board Can.* 33:145–159.

———.1978. Ecological optimization and adaptive management. *Ann. Rev. Ecol. Syst.* 9:157–188.

Walters, C. J., Hilborn, R., and Peterman, R. M. 1975. Computer simulation of barren-ground caribou dynamics, *Ecol. Model.* 1:303–315.

Walters, C. J., Stocker, M., and Haber, G. C. 1981. Simulation and optimization models for a wolf-ungulate system, in *Dynamics of Large Mammal Populations* (C. W. Fowler and T. D. Smith, eds.). Wiley, New York.

Waterman, D. A. 1986. *A Guide to Expert Systems,* Addison-Wesley, Reading, Massachusetts.

Watt, K. E. F. 1963. Dynamic programming, 'look-ahead programming' and the strategy of insect control, *Can. Entomol.* 95:525–536.

Williams, H. P. 1978. *Model Building in Mathematical Programming.* Wiley, New York.

Wu, L. S., and Botkin, D. B. 1980. Of elephants and men: a discrete, stochastic model for long-lived species with complex life histories, *Am. Nat.* 116:831–849.

INDEX

INDEX